THE
TCHAIKOVSKY
PAPERS

Pyotr Ilyich Tchaikovsky in 1893

THE TCHAIKOVSKY PAPERS

UNLOCKING THE FAMILY ARCHIVE

EDITED BY
MARINA KOSTALEVSKY

Translated by Stephen Pearl
Adapted from the Russian edition
compiled and edited by Polina E. Vaidman

Yale UNIVERSITY PRESS
New Haven and London

Published with assistance from the foundation established in memory of Calvin Chapin of
the Class of 1788, Yale College.

Yale University Press books may be purchased in quantity for educational, business, or
promotional use. For information, please e-mail sales.press@yale.edu (U.S. office) or
sales@yaleup.co.uk (U.K. office).

Set in Sabon type by Newgen North America.
Printed in the United States of America.

ISBN 978-0-300-19136-3 (hardcover : alk. paper)
Library of Congress Control Number: 2017953038
A catalogue record for this book is available from the British Library.

This paper meets the requirements of ANSI/NISO Z39.48-1992 (Permanence of Paper).

10 9 8 7 6 5 4 3 2

Contents

Preface

This book is a translation of previously unreleased letters and other archival documents from the Tchaikovsky State House-Museum that appeared in the original Russian volume titled *Neizvestnyi Chaikov-skii,* edited and compiled by Polina Vaidman and published in Moscow in 2009. The letters here were translated by Stephen Pearl. The editor of this volume, Marina Kostalevsky, translated the notes (which were provided by the Russian contributors Polina Vaidman, Ada Ainbinder, and Valery Sokolov) and wrote an Introduction for the book, along with introductory notes for each section that follows. She also made some alterations to the notes to adapt the material for English readers.

A note on the Russian calendar: dates here are often given in both the Julian (old style) and Gregorian (new style) calendars. Russia adopted the Gregorian calendar only after the Revolution of 1917.

A general note on Russian names. Russian names consist of a given name, a patronymic, and a surname. The male patronymics end in *-ovich* or *-evich,* and female patronymics in *-ovna* or *-evna.* These endings mean "son of" or "daughter of" the father whose first name is converted into a patronymic. For example, Ilya Petrovich means Ilya, son of Pyotr; Aleksandra Andreevna means Aleksandra, daughter of Andrey. The male surnames end in *-ov, -in, -oy,* or *-y* (sometimes transliterated as -*ii*). For example, Goncharov, Pushkin, Tolstoy, Tchai-kovsky. The female surnames end in -*a,* or -*aya*. For example, Goncha-rova, Pushkina, Tolstaya, Tchaikovskaya.

The editor of this publication is above all indebted to a leading Tchai-kovsky scholar, the senior curator at the Tchaikovsky State House-Museum in Klin and editor of the original Russian edition *Neizvestnyi Chaikovskii,* Polina Vaidman, who sadly passed away during the prep-aration of the American edition of the book.

I am also grateful to Frances Brent, Elizabeth Frank, and Olga Voronina for their comments and suggestions. Finally, I would like to thank the anonymous readers for making my quest for accuracy even more meaningful.

Introduction

It is hard to imagine how such a large—indeed impressive—number of letters, official papers, and notes related to someone as beloved, famous, and familiar as Tchaikovsky could have remained, until recently, unknown. Moreover, it's not as if these documents have been sitting, for more than a century, in an abandoned attic waiting for some lucky person to come along and discover them. On the contrary, they have been faithfully preserved at one of Russia's most esteemed cultural institutions: the archive of the Pyotr Ilyich Tchaikovsky State House-Museum in Klin. Why then did these important documents remain either unpublished for many years or published only in part, with deliberate distortions and omissions? The reasons are simultaneously public and private, cultural and political, specifically Russian and more or less general. Tchaikovsky's monarchism, his adherence to the Russian Orthodox tradition, and his homosexuality have presented, at different times, different but similarly uncomfortable topics for the composer's biographers. Some taboos were implemented over the course of Tchaikovsky's lifetime, others after his death in 1893, and most of them under the Soviet regime.

The Soviet historians usually dismissed out of hand Tchaikovsky's ardent patriotism toward Imperial Russia and his sincere loyalty to Alexander III, whose patronage the composer enjoyed in his later years.[1]

Needless to say, during the Soviet period, this kind of ideological "makeover" was methodically applied to all famous Russian figures of the past. In order to enter the Soviet pantheon, the Russian greats had to be purified of their ideological and moral "errors." In Tchaikovsky's case, his respectful references to the Russian monarchy and its policies were deliberately erased from any public discussion of the composer's life. As a result, the notification letters of awards and gifts sent to Tchaikovsky from the office of Alexander III were not published until recently.[2]

The same ideologically motivated approach was applied to his musical heritage. It is telling that in the Soviet Union, Tchaikovsky's *1812 Overture* (from 1880) was performed without its climactic section, the old Russian national anthem "God Save the Tsar" [*Bozhe, Tsarya khrani*]. The new and "improved" version of the famed overture was reworked with the help of a Soviet composer, Vissarion Shebalin, who replaced the "God Save the Tsar" section with the chorus "Glory" [*Slav'sya*] from Mikhail Glinka's opera *Ivan Susanin*. In all likelihood, the irony of such a rearrangement would not have escaped the well-educated and intelligent Shebalin: the original title of Glinka's opera had been *A Life for the Tsar,* and the original opening line of his chorus used to be "Glory to Our Tsar."[3] In similar fashion, Tchaikovsky's sacred works, such as the *Liturgy of St. John Chrysostom* (1878) and the *All-Night Vigil* (1882), were excluded from performance in the atheist Soviet Union, and his contribution to the art of Russian Orthodox music was consciously ignored.[4]

The central prohibition concerning Tchaikovsky's life has been his homosexuality—public discussion of the topic has been taboo in his home country for almost a century. Ironically, in early Soviet publications from the archive of the Tchaikovsky House-Museum in Klin, the editors regarded the composer's homosexuality as a matter that should not be excluded from scholarly study of his life.[5] But aside from a few such exceptions, Tchaikovsky's intimate life was zealously concealed by his family members, by *au courant* music scholars, and by the officials of such opposing regimes as the Romanov empire and Stalin's Soviet Union. In the eyes of the authorities, it would have been unthinkable to accept the idea that Pyotr Ilyich Tchaikovsky, Russia's national treasure, was a homosexual. Therefore, he wasn't. Outside of Russia, also, the issue was not properly addressed for a long time.

Though the fact of Tchaikovsky's homosexuality was fairly known in the West and often mentioned in studies of the composer, his biographers did not elaborate on it any further.[6] In general, even apart from this point, an interval between the fiftieth anniversary (in 1943) of Tchaikovsky's death and the last decades of the twentieth century cannot be considered particularly fruitful for research on Tchaikovsky in the West.[7] A significant exception during this period of calm seas is David Brown's monumental four-volume study of the composer's life and music from his early to his final years.[8]

The discourse on Tchaikovsky started to pick up steam in the late twentieth century, when homosexuality and related issues had finally become a legitimate part of scholarly inquiry. It has notably benefited from the most recent historical and sociological methods in biographical studies and put the issue of Tchaikovsky's sexuality in the relevant sociocultural context. As it happened, the new direction in Tchaikovsky scholarship has been additionally energized by a whiff of sensationalism resulting from the publication of articles by an émigré musicologist from the Soviet Union, Aleksandra Orlova.[9] According to her interpretation of the circumstances surrounding Tchaikovsky's death, he committed suicide in order to avoid a public homosexual scandal that was about to break. Orlova's version has provoked "the great suicide debate," which has involved energetic participants from opposite camps.[10] Years later, Richard Taruskin, who refuted the idea of the suicide plot in favor of the official "death in the time of cholera" scenario, expertly provided analysis of the debate within its broader setting.[11] Yet another expert in Tchaikovsky studies, Roland John Wiley, has also summed up the pros and cons of the theories about Tchaikovsky's death and come to a more cautious conclusion: "the singular failing of the cholera theory is that it cannot disprove that Tchaikovsky poisoned himself with something similar in its effect."[12]

The most comprehensive study of Tchaikovsky, his homosexuality, and the question of his death has been produced by Alexander Poznansky, who had the chance to examine, back in the 1980s, the originals of Tchaikovsky's intimate letters, kept in the Tchaikovsky House-Museum Archive. Poznansky efficiently used his findings to shape the biographical narrative in his book, *Tchaikovsky: The Quest for the Inner Man.*[13] He followed this influential volume with a number of publications focused on discrediting the suicide theory.

Meanwhile, the Tchaikovsky archive began more and more actively to publish previously unknown materials, including some concealed or censored letters of the composer. These commendable, though arguably belated, efforts led to the publication of *Neizvestnyi Chaikovskii*—the original for our translation.[14] Unquestionably, this edition of the archival documents accompanied by precise references to primary sources filled in conspicuous gaps in both public knowledge and research.

Both the Russian and English versions are composed of correspondence between Tchaikovsky's parents; letters from his governess, Fanny Dürbach; Tchaikovsky's letters to his brothers, friends, and associates; and some official papers. Taken together, they remind us that Tchaikovsky was a product of a cultural environment that encompassed not only important characteristics of his own time but also sensibilities of the preceding century.[15]

The first part of the book, the letters of the composer's parents, offers an intimate glimpse into the everyday life of a family from the Russian gentry in the first half of the nineteenth century. More importantly, it brings us closer to understanding Pyotr Tchaikovsky as a man born into this milieu. Regarding the first point, these letters, written between April 1833 and September 1851, clearly demonstrate an established social practice of privileged classes everywhere in Europe, including the vast Russian Empire, where travel and letter writing came—literally—with the territory. For the members of the Russian nobility, frequent travel, either in government service or for personal reasons, shaped in many ways the dynamics of relations with family and friends.

Letters, of course, were the common form of communication during periods of absence. At the same time, the practice of correspondence became the best answer not only to the difficulties of separation but also to the aesthetic challenge of writing a text and went hand in hand with the sentimental style in literature. Similar to its visual model of the family portrait eulogizing emotional ties between husbands and wives, and parents and children, an epistolary adaptation of the sentimentalist trend also relied on an image of the family as emotional unit.[16] Metaphorically speaking, within the domestic universe of Sentimentalism, the familiar letters acted as a reassuring representation of the gravitational force that held all family members together.

For families that were well off, writing letters didn't require a special occasion, but was part of daily activities and as customary as a cup of tea in the morning and a shot of stronger drink in the evening. Often, because of irregular mail collection, people would stretch the writing of a letter over a number of days, thereby blurring the distinction between letter and diary. One historian has described letter-writing practices of the period this way: "Letters, between parents and children, siblings and spouses, use emotional declarations, nicknames, conversational language, and occasional vulgarity to express and create intimacy between writer and audience. Family news, gossip and business are interspersed with descriptions of emotional and physical health and queries about that of others. Although the letters encompass a number of distinct relationships, a common concern with domestic harmony and emotional intimacy marks the correspondence as a whole."[17]

Though it would be a stretch to claim that the correspondence of Tchaikovsky's parents belongs to the literary genre of familiar letters,[18] the literariness of these texts (especially those penned by Pyotr Ilyich's father) is rooted in the same tradition of epistolary writing that flourished among all distinguished Russian writers, such as Nikolay Karamzin, Vasily Zhukovsky, Pyotr Vyazemsky, and many others. Like his renowned contemporaries, Ilya Petrovich Tchaikovsky used various narrative devices to create a lively picture for the enjoyment of his reader, who happened to be his wife, Aleksandra Andreevna Tchaikovskaya.

> Today I can picture you, my Angel, if not in St. Petersburg itself, at least very near there. I can feel your heart beating when you think how far it is to the last way-station and how slowly your coachman is driving. Kolya is showering you with questions: "Isn't this St. Petersburg? Mommy, over there I can see a lot of churches, it must be St. Petersburg, mommy." "No, darling, it's Tsarskoye Selo." [...] There you all are, stopping for a rest, shaking the dust from your clothes, hurrying to get washed. [...] You are being offered food, but you're not hungry. Finally you're seated again in the carriage, moving fast, although it seems slow to you.

It is not difficult to notice that the language and tone employed with considerable grace by Pyotr Tchaikovsky's parents echoes a literary model popular among educated Russians through the late eighteenth and early nineteenth centuries, and represented foremost by the doyen of Russian Sentimentalism, Nikolay Karamzin. In accordance with the culture of sensibility, their letters are permeated with expressions of love, tender reproaches, and descriptions of feelings, as in the following example written by Aleksandra Andreevna to her husband-to-be.

> May is almost over, and you will be back in August, I hope. So there will still be those two cruel months to wait; June and July! Oh dear! If they would only fly by! I have so much to tell you that I can't possibly write it!! It's so dull and dreary without you. I just can't wait for the moment when I will see you and convince you of the sincerity of my devotion to you! How happy I will be then! In your letter from Voronezh you really hurt me—you wrote that you were even sure that I don't love you, and that I couldn't love you—but who then could force me to give you my hand and my heart as long as I live?

Letters from the age of Sentimentalism are embellished with emotional exclamations, characteristic diction, and distinct stylistic devices, which were employed to convey the sensitivity of the author, whether it was a novelist or an epistolarian. This kind of emotional refinement is expressed, in the words of a scholar of Russian literature, by "means of a highly stylized language and specific lexical markers, such as selected epithets to describe a person's psychological traits, the physical repercussion of certain mental conditions (such as sighs, tears, paleness, faintness), and culminating in highly emotional utterances."[19] Many passages in Ilya Tchaikovsky's letters reveal his predilection for these figures of speech and verbal gestures, such as this one written to his wife:[20]

> My Angel! When I said goodbye to you yesterday evening, I had to hold back my tears, because I didn't want to seem weak in the eyes of the people around me, but no matter how hard I tried, the tears welled up—and I had to keep my eyes closed while I was trying to comfort Petya who was crying inconsolably because his mommy didn't take him to St. Petersburg. While I was seeing you off, as well as the whole procession following you, I felt so keenly the pain of separation that I could hardly contain myself.

While "mommy" visits St. Petersburg, her son Pyotr (Petya) does what anyone of his time would do: he writes letters. The very first epistolary example of Pyotr Ilyich Tchaikovsky's handwriting, included in his parents' correspondence, looks like a zigzagging outline of non-verbal exclamation. His sensitive father helpfully "translates" the boy's scribble: "Dear Mommy, I'm well, don't forget to bring me toys and candy." Another following message from the future composer is, as might be expected, musical in nature: "Sasha and Petya," their father reports, "have composed a song, 'Our Mother is in St. Petersburg.'" When Aleksandra Tchaikovskaya returned home, she brought her children not only toys and candy but also a governess, Fanny Dürbach, who would remain part of the Tchaikovskys' "emotional unit" until the family left Votkinsk in September of 1848.

Although "Fanny's reign" lasted less than five years, Tchaikovsky scholars agree that the composer's first mentor had significant influence on the formation of his personality and his general development. What kind of influence, we may ask?

The second section of this volume, which contains Fanny Dürbach's letters, gives us some answers. Especially telling is the information about the reading materials she used in her classes with the Tchaikovsky children:

> Apart from "L'Education Maternelle" by Mlle. Amable Tastu, I also had "Family Education" by Mrs. Edgeworth in several volumes. In natural history, I also had a small illustrated copy of Buffon. For reading: the "Tales of Guizot" and also Schmidt's "Canon," and my class books, which I also used. One of our favorite volumes was "Celebrated Children" by Michel Masson; we read it and recounted it in the evenings and on Saturdays.[21]

Just like Tchaikovsky's parents' letters, the reading list of the future composer belongs to a particular cultural paradigm ushered in by the age of Sensibility. The first author in Fanny Dürbach's pedagogical library is Amable Tastu.[22] During her long life, Tastu proved herself a prolific writer, working in many genres and fields such as children's literature, the pedagogical treatise, historical writings, short fiction, literary criticism, travelogue, and translation. However, Tastu's early reputation as a French woman of letters was established in 1826 when she published her first collection of poetry; this was praised by the foremost literary critic of the time, Charles-Augustin Sainte-Beuve, who characterized one of her poems as a model of the "domestic elegy." In one of her later pieces of literary criticism, Tastu eloquently elaborated on the poetic virtues of sensibility, claiming that "sentimental poetry expresses more than domestic affection or resignation," but also awakens our sympathies for the sorrows of others.[23]

The "Tales of Guizot" read by the children in Tchaikovsky's home could have been one of the French editions of *Moral Tales* or *Popular Tales* written by Pauline Guizot (née Pauline de Meulan),[24] the first wife of the celebrated French historian, political thinker, and statesman François Guizot.[25] Before her marriage in 1812, Pauline de Meulan was already known as a respectable woman of letters, contributor to the periodical press, and an author of sentimental novels. But her union with Guizot created a husband-and-wife team that had a great impact on the intellectual and political climate of early nineteenth-century France. Together, they published the six-volume collection *Les Annales de l'éducation*, which included many of Pauline Guizot's stories and articles on morality and education. By all accounts, she had an enormous influence on her husband and, according to his biographer, Gabriel de Broglie, taught him to value emotions and sentimental intimacy.[26]

Another author on Fanny's list for the Tchaikovsky children is Maria Edgeworth.[27] She wrote one of the most famous sentimental novels, *Castle Rackrent*, which stands in the same row as Samuel Richardson's *Pamela*, Laurence Sterne's *Sentimental Journey*, Henry Mackenzie's *The Man of Feeling*, and Rousseau's *Julie, or the New Heloise*. We don't know exactly which of Mrs. Edgeworth's works Fanny included in her pedagogical practice, but most likely she used collections of children's stories as well as Edgeworth's *Practical Education*, a theory of education in which she made sensible use of the ideas introduced by John Locke and Jean-Jacques Rousseau.

The information provided by Fanny Dürbach further illuminates the cultural landscape of Tchaikovsky's upbringing, which served as an aesthetic background for him throughout his entire creative life.

For many reasons, Tchaikovsky's reunion with his "old teacher and friend" on the eve of 1893 held a special meaning for both of them. We can also say that it was symbolic, as this turned out to be the composer's final year. Their first and last meetings, separated by almost fifty years, served as emotional bookends to Tchaikovsky's sentimental education. After seeing Fanny Dürbach in Montbéliard, Tchaikovsky wrote to his younger brother and future biographer Modest:

> Upon her return to Montbéliard, she spent the next 42 years living quietly and uneventfully. And her younger years, so different from the rest of her life in Montbéliard, remained completely undisturbed in her memory. At times, I have been so vividly transported to that distant past that it felt somewhat eerie but also sweet; we both were holding back tears all the time.[28]

During his visit, Tchaikovsky learned that all these years Fanny Dürbach had safeguarded his childhood notebooks, which contained compositions, writing assignments, and drawings as well as letters from his family members. In Fanny's own words, "those precious letters" and notebooks possessed great sentimental value for her. As she later expressed herself to Modest Tchaikovsky, "if time destroys everything, [. . .] it has no power over those sincere affections which, like our most treasured possessions, we will carry with us beyond the grave."[29] After Pyotr Ilyich Tchaikovsky's death, Fanny Dürbach kept up an active correspondence with Modest Ilyich. She provided him with a substantial portion of her archive and promised to bequeath the remaining documents to the Tchaikovsky House-Museum in Klin, then just established.[30]

Pyotr Ilyich Tchaikovsky's own letters reproduced in the third section of this volume are an especially valuable and engaging addition to the corpus of previously published correspondence between the composer and his numerous addressees. They represent only a fraction of Tchaikovsky's correspondence, and naturally should be read in the context of the entire body of his letters and diaries. Considering that Tchaikovsky left more than five thousand presently known letters and presumably a few hundred missing ones, the term "man of letters" characterizes him quite literally. As numerous examples from the composer's epistolary output testify, he possessed natural gifts of verbal expression. After all, his childhood teacher, Fanny Dürbach, had reason to call him "my dear little poet" and even believed that his main talents lay in literature. A particular set of Tchaikovsky's letters goes as far as to echo a literary genre—the epistolary novel—which was very popular in the eighteenth century but had fallen out of favor by his time.[31] I am referring here to the composer's remarkable correspondence with Nadezhda von Meck, which mirrors the literary convention of a long-distance love affair unfolding through writing. Their relationship developed exclusively through letters, and they never actually met in person.[32] Furthermore, in his letters to von Meck, his "best friend" and patroness, Tchaikovsky often uses the rhetorical devices favored by Sentimentalists, as in this instance:

> You ask whether I can call you my friend. Could you truly doubt this; is it possible that you did not see within the lines of my letters how deeply I value your friendship, how sincere and most warm are my friendly feelings towards you. How pleased I would be at some time to show you, not in words but in deeds, the full measure of my gratitude and my love for you![33]

In later years, such stylistic features as emotional declarations, dramatic questions, and expressions of feeling appear less and less in Tchaikovsky's writing. However, the overall "rhetorical orchestration" of his letters underlines their affinity with the epistolary practice of late eighteenth and early nineteenth-century Russia. In the spirit of that tradition, the composer's letters speak of intimacy and the atmosphere of trust conveyed by both sensibility in subject matter and style. Similar to Karamzin and his younger contemporaries, such as Konstantin Batyushkov, Vyazemsky, and Alexander Pushkin, Tchaikovsky, over time, moved in his letters from lofty observation and emotional outpourings to daily reports casually peppered with a different kind of emotional release—obscenities and self-deprecating vulgarities. In a letter to his publisher, Pyotr Jurgenson, for example, Tchaikovsky refers to his music as excrement:

> Well, my dear fellow, for some time now I have been feeling that this miniature march is just a miniature piece of shit. To be frank, I would like to discard this garbage altogether.
> [. . .]
> *Yours P. Tchaikovsky*
> (Begetter of the little piece of shit)

Modest Tchaikovsky provides a valuable commentary on the reasons behind the changes in his brother's writing style:

He [Tchaikovsky] preferred the system of brief and imperfect notes, because in reading through the diaries of his childhood and youth, in which he had gone more fully into his thoughts and emotions, he had felt somewhat ashamed. The sentiments and ideas which he found so interesting, and which once seemed to him so great and important, now appeared empty, meaningless and ridiculous, and he resolved in the future only to commit facts to paper without any commentary. Disillusioned by their contents, he destroyed all his early diaries.[34]

Needless to say, however, Tchaikovsky's desire to convey his sentiments to the world was not undermined by his embarrassment over his youthful attempts to do it verbally. He had long been aware that the language best suited for him to express human feelings was music. "Where words leave off, music begins," he asserted, quoting Heinrich Heine. Comparing the process of composing to writing a poem, he elaborated further: "the difference is just that music has incomparably more powerful resources and a more subtle language at its disposal for expressing a thousand different nuances of inner feeling."[35]

Tchaikovsky's explicit attention to "nuances of inner feeling" should be seen not only as an indicator of his personal emotional traits but also as the artistic attitude that corresponds to the fundamental idea of Sentimentalism: an intrinsic ability of all people to feel and to love is the key to higher truth and harmonious society. The ideas of Sentimentalism certainly did not vanish with the end of the eighteenth century and even with the related period of early Romanticism. A number of celebrated artists and writers of the nineteenth century, such as Charles Dickens and Fyodor Dostoevsky, inherited the rich culture of feeling that had been instigated by the "cult of sentiment."[36] Tchaikovsky's emotional sensibilities as an artist, as well as his appeal to the emotional sensibilities of his listeners, were also shaped by the cultural paradigm of Sentimentalism. The collection of letters published in this volume provides a new ground for understanding the composer's connection to that European movement. They also allow us to take a new look at Tchaikovsky's rather infamous sentimentality. For it is important to see this not just as the reflection of his psychological and sexual makeup but as the manifestation of his loyalty to Sentimentalism—a positive culture of feeling. Arguably, such an approach can offer yet another perspective in our search for new insights into Tchaikovsky's life and music.

THE
TCHAIKOVSKY
PAPERS

The Tchaikovsky family. From left to right: Pyotr Tchaikovsky, his mother
Aleksandra, sister Aleksandra, half-sister Zinaida, older brother Nikolay,
younger brother Ippolit, father Ilya; St. Petersburg, 1848. (All photographs
are reprinted courtesy of the P. I. Tchaikovsky State Museum-Reserve)

1 Correspondence Between Pyotr Ilyich Tchaikovsky's Parents

PYOTR ILYICH TCHAIKOVSKY was born into the family of a mining engineer and manager of the Kamsko-Votkinsk iron factories in the Ural Mountains, Major General Ilya Petrovich Tchaikovsky (1795–1880).

The composer's father was the youngest child in a large family belonging to the gentry. Ilya did not follow in the footsteps of his older brothers, who were sent to military schools. Instead, in 1817 he entered Russia's first higher technical college, established by Catherine the Great, the Mining Cadets' Corps in St. Petersburg.[1] Six years later he graduated from the school with a silver medal.[2] His career lasted more than forty years and was marked by many contributions to the Russian mining industry, including its management and education.

At the time when Ilya Petrovich Tchaikovsky began courting the future composer's mother, Aleksandra Andreevna Assier (1812–1854), he was a widower with a very young daughter from his first marriage, to Maria Karlovna Keiser.

Aleksandra Assier was born to a French émigré, Andrey Mikhailovich Assier, and a Russian mother, Ekaterina Mikhailovna Popova. The composer's grandfather arrived in Russia in 1795 to teach German and French at the Artillery and Engineering Gentry Cadet Corps in St. Petersburg.[3] There he met his future wife, a daughter of an Orthodox deacon. The couple became parents of five children, the youngest being Aleksandra, but Ekaterina Assier (née Popova) died when the girl was only four years old. At that tender age, Aleksandra was placed in the Patriotic Institute for Girls in Moscow, where she eventually received her education.

Ilya Petrovich Tchaikovsky and Aleksandra Andreevna Assier married in October 1833. The bride was seventeen years younger than the groom.

◆ ◆ ◆

1. ILYA PETROVICH TCHAIKOVSKY TO ALEKSANDRA ANDREEVNA ASSIER

St. Petersburg, April–May 1833[4]

What was the meaning of those tears? Please tell me frankly. I didn't expect to see them, but having seen them, I had to assume that I was the reason for them. My darling whom I adore! I have long been seeking an opportunity to declare my feelings, but there have always been other people around, and to tell you the truth, it is hard to bring myself to speak of something so important, something on which my whole fate depends. From the very moment when you pronounced that fateful word, "yes," when fire raced through my veins, when I felt I was on the very summit of heavenly bliss, when everything went dark before my eyes except the vision of you—one thought has been tormenting me more and more: are you not regretting the haste with which you uttered that word which bespoke my happiness. It's difficult to read your eyes, but those tears . . . why oh why didn't you hide them from me? Better to be deluded for a time than forever. I haven't closed my eyes for three nights. Now your tears have condemned me to a fourth sleepless night—don't think I'm complaining, no, all that time I have been with you in spirit—I have been cheerful, joyful, right up to this moment when that very first thought came back to me. I knew—it was something impossible to miss—the passion—or more simply—the love for you of a certain young man. You didn't know me at that time—but tell me, did you have the same feelings for him? If you did, then on the strength of my passionate love for you, let me build a sincere friendship, and in the way a friend would tell you, that you were indeed too quick to utter that word which made me so happy, before you had searched your heart. You should know, my dear Conqueror of hearts, that my love for you is not news to you. Do you believe in predestination and the notion of soul mates? If you do, then by the same token, do not reject premonition either! But we'll leave that subject for another time. As it is, by that single word you have given me leave to love you, and it inflamed me, and I love you more than life itself. I know of nothing I would not sacrifice for you. But I have reached that stage of life when, for all this noble passion, my reason has not deserted me, and the wound is perhaps not too deep for it to heal, and I will have the strength to rip my desolate heart away from yours, if you tell me frankly and confess that you acted in haste. Don't torment me. You were born with a good heart, so try to understand how hard it will be for me to bear this confession in four months' time. At that time, I can't be certain how I will feel, but right now there is still time, I'll forget—I'll convince myself that it was all just a lovely dream, a mirage; I'll go away and you'll never see me again, and I'll devote myself to raising my motherless daughter,[5] and in fifteen years' time, I'll come back and witness your happiness. My dear one, I adore you, and fall to your feet to beg you to decide my fate—the sooner the better. It would be foolish of me to condemn you, and even worse to despise my rival, when in fact I respect and admire that young man precisely because he shares my tastes. He is my superior in every respect and I won't be surprised in the slightest if he prevails . . . As for my passion, I can only repeat that there is still time—make the best use of it, and don't forget that for me it has to be all or nothing. Marriage is life's most important step. A man and his bride to be must put themselves to the test over a long period. Perhaps you have been told that I am a kindly man—don't believe it, I am capricious and short tempered, and can flare up at any time. You've heard that I am rich; well you have simply been misled, I have nothing, nor do I want to marry into wealth. In this regard, my philosophy could not be more different from that of society at large; I want to be happy without wealth, and happy in the same way I was before—that is in my family; I don't want to be made happy because of wealth, but I want to make as happy as is within my power the one with whom fate has ordained that I be united. I am someone who is happy when my love is pure, unreserved, and sincere. In a word, it has to be all or nothing. What people think and what they say means nothing to me; I don't give a fig for their opinions. You perhaps respect those opinions, and I won't argue with you or judge you, and you will act as you see fit. Finally, I must tell you that if you sacrifice yourself on the altar of my complete happiness, you run the risk of forfeiting the pleasures of society, for it has been my fate to spend my life far removed from society and, I have to confess, I prefer the quiet life away from the hustle and bustle, and have grown accustomed to living within a small circle of good people, and am a great believer in Caesar's dictum: "It's better to be number one in your village, than the last man in Rome."

Anyway, it's high time I finished. It's beginning to get light, and you, angel of my heart, are asleep—please don't take offense, don't follow my example!

May the King of heaven take you under His protection. Whether you are mine, I do not know, but no one can stop me loving you! No it's not that I love you, that's not the right word, I adore you—and you are worthy of it. God give me the strength to endure what I expect—and must expect!

Don't make me wait for an answer. If you can't tell me, then write, and destroy what I have written.

◆ ◆ ◆

2. ILYA PETROVICH TCHAIKOVSKY TO ALEKSANDRA ANDREEVNA ASSIER

Moscow, 10 May 1833

Feeling and writing are two completely different things. There are people who can combine the two, but I am not one of them. My soul mate! I am just not capable of expressing what I was feeling as I took leave of you, nor what I am feeling now—not to see you, not to feel you near me for four months is really hard on me! You can imagine what an ordeal it is. But God is merciful, and with His help I will withstand this ordeal. Moscow has nothing of interest to offer me, so, housebound by necessity, it is the thought of you that keeps up my spirits. I have my nice nephew Pyotr I[vanovich][6] to talk to—after all what is there for me to do in Moscow, I've seen the city several times, I've lived here—the sooner I get to the Caucasus and back to you the better, so that I can fall at your feet, my darling whom I adore.

I can't describe our journey as romantic, as people are wont to do—that's been frightfully overdone. To put it simply and frankly, I just

went along, kept silent, and did more thinking and musing than talking. There were various topics of conversation, but there was just one,
and only one, subject of my thoughts and reveries. You and Zina,[7] Zina
and you occupied my entire being. Do you know, my darling, do you
recall how that innocent being, even before it might have happened,
betrothed us with rings. It must have been something she sensed, or
else the Almighty was prompting her. You should find out if she had
been coached; if she hadn't, then it must have been the work of the Almighty, who, not for the first time, was revealing to me my destiny. My
darling! When you gave me your hand, you took on the job of being a
mother to that child—love her my dear, for my sake, and protect her!
By so doing, you will be expressing your love for me doubly, just as I
will be striving twice as hard to deserve it.

You promised to write to me; for the love of God, please do! I will
find your precious letter everywhere. That is my only joy. Even now I
am feeling the need for your letters—write, but don't make it a burden; just a line, or even a word will do! I would like to write more,
but people keep interrupting. I smother your hand with letter-borne
kisses—I kiss all of you. Your first timid kiss when we parted kept my
lips aflame long afterwards, and even now I feel its sweet caress, and
with it I shall remain faithful to you to the grave.

I[lya] T[chaikovsky].

P.S. I'll write from Voronezh.

✦ ✦ ✦

3. ILYA PETROVICH TCHAIKOVSKY TO
ALEKSANDRA ANDREEVNA ASSIER

Voronezh, 15 May 1833

My soul mate! Can you imagine that you are with me everywhere
and always, and don't think I am just paying idle compliments, because
up to now there hasn't been a minute, even a second when I haven't
been thinking of you; you actually and truly inhabit my imagination,
my thoughts, my head. I am even astonished at myself, a man of my
years with graying temples, a wrinkled forehead, a man of so much
experience of life, who can still be moved by his feelings as strongly
as a young lad. For some time now I have been feeling as if I've taken
on a new lease of life, and my past now seems like a dream. I know

and remember that six years ago I was loved and was in love myself,[8] but you shouldn't be jealous, my dear, my love then was just as pure and unblemished as it is now, but fate has rewarded me generously for my loss; and you know what fills me with delight, and why that same noble, unsullied passion has been born again within me. It's the fact that you, my dear, have freely, spontaneously and without hesitation yielded your hand and heart to a man of my advanced years. I am sure, and it is only natural, that you have not yet had time to grow to love me truly, well, so be it, I will earn it and convince you of my own love in time.

In Voronezh, I have made it my first duty to kneel in worship at the tomb of the saint,[9] and to have a prayer said for your and Zina's health. Since the fourth of the month you have been included in my daily prayers, and I'll be bringing you back an icon and other sacred objects of St. Mitrofan.

What is my Zina doing? I'm sure she hasn't been left without her "mommy's"[10] guidance. Oh, if only I had found a letter, or at least could look forward to finding your first one soon on my arrival. Only, when you write it, please don't use such sweet ink as this, otherwise I might very well eat it. I kiss both your hands and their dear fingers, and even take the liberty of grazing your tender cheek. This is the last letter from me while I'm on the road. On from Novocherkassk there stretch sparsely settled regions which even the mountain people frequent on occasion. What if I'm captured? Although, of course, that can't happen since I'm already captive. Goodbye, my soul mate.

Yours until the grave
I[lya] T[chaikovsky]
P.S. Please give Zina my blessing.

◆ ◆ ◆

4. ALEKSANDRA ANDREEVNA ASSIER TO ILYA PETROVICH TCHAIKOVSKY

[St. Petersburg,] 29 May [1833]

My dear incomparable friend!

How long you've made us suffer from your silence. Precisely two weeks after you left, on Thursday the 18th, Pyotr Ivanovich[11] arrived bringing your letters. For a whole two weeks we didn't know what to think. Every day Daddy[12] grew more and more worried and kept on repeating: "It must mean something!" Zina's nanny[13] and I both suspected Panov, who went with you, and were really sorry that you didn't take your own manservant with you, but finally Pyotr Ivanovich was able to set our minds at rest! You won't believe how happy I was to see him! I was sitting in my room looking anxiously out of the window for the postman, sure that he would be bringing us a letter from you, when suddenly I heard a familiar voice. I ran into the living room and saw Pyotr Ivanovich, and even then had to wait impatiently for a good hour before I was handed the letter addressed to me, because Mommy[14] didn't want to give it to me in his presence.

He comes to visit us quite often, and talks to me about your life in Moscow, and by the way, he told me that you very often sing the romance "The Ring of the Fair Maiden . . ."[15] I also sing it very often, and think of my own ring, which you wear on your hand! Pyotr Ivanovich has noticed it. I would like to know if he knows something, I imagine that you've been open with him!

In your first letter, you write that you are going to be away for another four months, so, as I see, it, that means that there's much less time to wait now. May is almost over, and you will be back in August, I hope. So there will still be those two cruel months to wait; June and July! Oh dear! If they would only fly by! I have so much to tell you that I can't possibly write it!! It's so dull and dreary without you. I just can't wait for the moment when I will see you and convince you of the sincerity of my devotion to you! How happy I will be then!

In your letter from Voronezh you really hurt me—you wrote that you were even sure that I don't love you, and that I couldn't love you—but who then could force me to give you my hand and my heart as long as I live? I would like to know the reason why you suppose I made that decision! Surely you don't think that I did it out of some kind of desperation—not at all, I was free, happy, and carefree living in my parents' home; or perhaps you think I did it to please Daddy, absolutely not! I love you, it would be impossible to love you more than I do!

Zininka, thank God, is healthy, happy and in good spirits, and up to her tricks all day long; and every day she grows to love her grandma and grandpa[16] more and more. She talks about you often. She has also become really attached to me, and I love it when she cuddles up to me. She's such a dear and so obedient that you can't help loving her, and what's more she's the living image of her daddy. You also happen to mention my duties towards her—I understand them very well, and I am sure the time will never come when you have to remind me of them again! After yourself, of course, there is no one else I will ever care for more.

Mommy, of course, will be writing to you herself about Katerina Grigorievna's misfortune. I won't describe to you how upset everyone is over it, Fyodor Vasilievich most of all. You know this from your own experience!

For the love of God, please write more often, and tell me about your health. For me that's the most important thing. Nanny and Zina send you their best, and Zina kisses your hands; and hugs from both of us.

Yours until the grave
A. Assier

✦ ✦ ✦

5. ALEKSANDRA ANDREEVNA ASSIER TO ILYA PETROVICH TCHAIKOVSKY

[St. Petersburg,] 18 July [1833]

I'm sorry, I'm totally at fault for missing the last post. I hadn't written to you, but I somehow just couldn't get round to it—I can't remember why. So I'm relying on your kind heart, and am sure that you will forgive me, especially now that I've confessed my guilt! I don't have much good news for you! In her last letter I know Mommy has told you that Daddy has had another one of his attacks; and two weeks later on the 12th of July, Mommy's birthday, and Daddy's name day, the same thing happened again. It was on the day we were planning to go to Pargolovo[17] and spend the whole day there. I got up at four o'clock to see what the weather was like. Well, it was glorious, and I could hardly wait until it was time to go, but I went back to bed. Half an hour later, Mommy comes into my room and says that Daddy is not feeling good again. I was really taken by surprise because it was so totally unexpected, and so we had to stay home! Oh dear, what a disappointment! But there was nothing to be done; it seems that there is some truth to that proverb: "man proposes, God disposes"! Yes, it's really too bad that Daddy is having these attacks so often now,[18] and no wonder since he spends days on end not saying a word to anyone, and doing nothing but dwell on those things which can only have the effect of damaging his health!

Let me send you my best wishes for the forthcoming day of Your Angel,[19] and hope you have a really nice time, it's just a pity that my good wishes will arrive so late in the day. I would have wanted to be the first of all to congratulate you! Nadenka has already been to see us three times since you left. She is in good health, thank God! And is spending most of her time with the Sobolevskys.[20] They are very busy preparing for the weddings. Their oldest girl is getting married on the 21st of this month, so she is helping out there! P. I. Evreinov is a regular visitor. You certainly found the right word to describe him, he is an out and out crook!

Zina is becoming more and more lovable every day, and she'll be writing to you soon!

So, until the next post.

Yours until the grave

A. Assier

✦ ✦ ✦

6. ALEKSANDRA ANDREEVNA TCHAIKOVSKAYA TO ILYA PETROVICH TCHAIKOVSKY

Nizhny Novgorod, 26 March 1837[21]

Ilyichka, my dear, incomparable, divine friend!

When I said goodbye to you, I couldn't immediately grasp how long it would be before I saw you again, but as time goes on I miss you more and more, and am more keenly aware that my Angel, my dear, precious husband is not here by my side! I reproach myself so often now for not being able to persuade you to take me with you, the road, I am told, especially as far as Kazan is still in great condition. Several times now, I have been on the point of packing everything up and following you—but couldn't do it against your wishes; when I'm separated from you, I feel ever more strongly that I can't live without you. The habit of kissing you or your hand every day has become so powerful that, when I wake up in the morning I immediately find myself imagining you or your angelic hand are beside me, and I pick up the first thing that comes to hand, my night-cap or whatever, kiss it passionately. What can I tell you about how I've been spending my time? Since you left, we've visited the Stremoukhovs again. Katenka[22] has made a big hit with everyone here—we've become very popular, but just because of her—but no matter where I am, I miss you, my Angel, my darling! Yesterday I sent for Evenius,[23] but he couldn't come because he was going back to his village. Since I don't know any of the doctors here, I had made up my mind not to use any of them, but two days after you left, the plaster fell off my chest. The next day I put the ointment on a new one and put it back on. But yesterday, when I arrived back from the Stremoukhovs, I felt my chest itching terribly and started to scratch it, and noticed that it was damp under the plaster. I immediately lifted off the plaster and saw that there was a milky substance oozing from me, but not from the nipple, and what looked like white blisters had broken out. Today I made up my mind to send for another doctor, Dr. Lindegrein,[24] who is the leading doctor here and an obstetrician. He came and after asking me a lot of questions, told me that I was suffering from a hidden rash and that there was a sickly bluish look about me. When I told him about the ailment I had been suffering from before my pregnancy, he told me that it had appeared during my pregnancy in the form of a rash, and regretted that it had been cooled and had moved into the breast. When I told him that I had an open hemorrhoid, he said that was from taking sulphur powder, exposed to the cold, but felt that that was all to the good. He wants to treat me with homeopathic medicine, and advised me to take off the plaster and wash it thoroughly, but when I did, I found that some kind of pus was starting to ooze, and it's still going on. Not only that, but now I have a bad headache. He is coming to see me again tomorrow to start the treatment. We had a long conversation and he asked me if my baby was alive. I showed him Katya[25]—she happened to be sleeping—and he found her very weak and sickly, examined her briefly and repeated that she was very weak, and said that she too was suffering from a hidden rash, and that was the reason why she was screaming, and said she should be given some *chamomile* when she screamed, and then gave sulphur both to her and to the wet nurse whom he had also examined. He is obviously very fond of children, and spent a long time with Katya, and examined her again when she woke up. Right now she is indeed extremely pale and just as restless as before, but is becoming more lovable every day, and beginning to clutch with her little hands, and is burbling so endearingly that I simply can't keep back the tears when I look at her. Now I'm telling her: "What message shall I give Daddy from you?" And she replies: "agu, o, ay" etc., and smiles so winningly that you would want to smother her with kisses. Oh, and I forgot to tell you that Lindegrein is set on bringing my rash to the surface. God knows what will be the result of this treatment. Ilyichka, my dear friend! Your prayers for me to the Lord God are my only hope. Zinochka, thank God, is well and smart. Every morning she studies a little, and has learned the prayer Lord and Master of My Life. I bought her material for a dress which I'm making for her for the holiday.

Yesterday, I met Messing[26] in a shop. He deeply resents the fact that you didn't stop by to see him, and says that if he ever happens to pass by the Votkinsk Factory, he will never come to see us. Our servants here are having a very dreary time here, they can't wait for spring. Artemy[27] has several times tried to get me to spring a surprise on you and turn up unannounced. It seems his wife is now pregnant. I've just been brought your letter from the Sherchins,[28] as well as your parcel; the eggs and dolls for Zina I haven't received, but I did get the tablecloths and the pictures. Don't get annoyed with me, my Angel, if I scold you and make fun of you about the tablecloths—to pay 33 rubles for each one is a little extravagant, they're just headscarves that nobody wears anymore, and they were sold to you as tablecloths. I have to confess we all had a good laugh at your expense, it was a complete waste of money. I have to leave you now for a day or two.

✦

28 March. Sunday.
Sherchin[29] has just been here, he told me that he had seen you in Kazan. He is preparing only two of those long carriages—hardly enough for our purposes. I'm thinking of taking an extra vehicle, particularly since we are going to have another person travelling with us, a mining engineer[30] to work as your assistant whom he is sending at your request. Anyway, it's still a long time until that happy event. Viktor Timofeevich says that we won't be able to set off before the twenty something of May, so I won't reach you before June. Now, although my heart is in my mouth, and with tears in my eyes, I'm going to have to tell you, my friend, that I have a bone to pick with you. A wrong cannot be hidden for long. Sooner or later the Lord God will find it out. Yesterday after dinner I went into that small, dark room by the bedroom, and overheard Arisha[31] talking to the landlady upstairs. In the course of the conversation she told her that Zinochka, out of my hearing, had asked you for money which she gave to her for a dress. Yesterday, I didn't pay much attention to those words, since I hadn't

heard them too clearly and was just ticking Arisha off for going upstairs without my permission, especially since the landlady's young son lives up there. But today, to my surprise, I discovered that all this had been done with your approval. Arisha comes into the bedroom to see me, looking none too clean, and I asked her why she hadn't changed her dress for Sunday. She replied that it's all she has with her, and that the day before she had bought some calico with her own money, whereupon Aleksandr,[32] who was here at the time, tells her that she must have money if she was able to buy cloth for a dress. Arisha replied that she only has the money given to her by the young lady.

Zinochka, who was present, went all red in the face and ran over to me, and stammering, confessed to me that you had given her five rubles to give to Arisha and gave her strict orders not to tell me. I didn't say anything to her, and forced myself not to say how upset I was by such behavior, especially since Aleksandr had witnessed the whole thing. You can judge for yourself what he must think of me knowing that you and Zina have secrets from me. I'm not going to reproach you, but you must see for yourself, my friend, that this was not a nice way to treat me, and understand what a difficult position you have put me in vis-à-vis Zina. If it had been Katya, I would have come down hard on her, especially if she had dared to hide something from me, especially in league with you, but all I said to Zina was that you had told me about it.

Right now, I just don't know what to think about your opinion of me, if you think that I'm stingy, I don't understand what could have given you that idea, up to now I've done my best to protect you from your own endlessly inappropriate generosity, and if you think that it's only with Zina that I'm stingy, then I must tell you that not just with her, but with anyone at all, I've never tried to stop you or even dissuade you, as long as it has been in accordance with your wishes. The hundred rubles you gave to Fyodor, which I wasn't supposed to know about, only confirms my feeling that you must have a very poor opinion of me. From now on I must ask you no longer to make me spend your money, I don't want to put you in the ridiculous position of doing things behind my back, particularly when it all belongs to you anyway. Please forgive me, my dear friend, for writing to you about such petty matters, but I can't conceal from you what's on my mind and in my heart, and how it troubles me when all our servants know that you did this behind my back. I won't write any more about this, nor will I mention it again, I only ask you to understand me better. You can be sure, my Angel, that you have no need to hide anything from me, because *your wish is my command,* it always has been, and always will be, and that not only in these trivial matters, but in all things, I am ready to follow your wishes. If sometimes my advice may seem to be more like a refusal, or you feel it is inappropriate and out of place, then you only have to say so openly, and you'll never hear advice from me again!

I started the treatment yesterday, i.e. I've started taking the medicine, and so have Katya and the wet nurse. Yesterday, the doctor spent a long time feeling my pulse and breast, and found that I still have a lot of hardening. He applied a poultice and gave me some medicine. Today we were all invited to General Rebinder's,[33] but I didn't go—Katenka and Aleksandr[34] are not at home, they went there to eat. But once again, don't think that it was just a caprice; not at all, as I'm sure you know, homeopathic treatment doesn't permit any vegetable roots or perfume. I am staying home alone with the children. Zina is sitting by my side busy with her sewing, she thanks you for those little pictures which she finds very interesting, and I've just fed Katya some porridge, and then she fell asleep. Lindegrein said not to give her any porridge, but just breast-feed her, but she had gotten so used to porridge that at those times when she was usually fed it, she would just start to scream, and there's no way you can suddenly break her of the habit. Without telling the doctor, I feed her porridge once a day and she eats it with relish. Since I am at home alone, there is no one to prevent me chatting with you, and that's what gives me the greatest pleasure these days, I just hope I'm not boring you, my delight, my lovely angel! In your letters, you say you are afraid of boring me. How can you of all people think that, when you know how I adore you, and the only thing that makes me happy is being with you, or thinking about you? Katenka[35] has just come back from Rebinder's. Goodbye for now.

✦

31 March
Even though I'm not at all keen on visiting people, there is no way I can refuse an invitation from Rebinder. His concert for Katenka was scheduled for yesterday. When he discovered I wasn't feeling well, he came round in person to try to persuade me, but I replied that the doctor hadn't been to see me the day before, so I couldn't possibly go without his permission. On that very same day, he persuaded the

doctor to allow me to go, and sent the doctor himself to see me the very next day and Lindegrein gave me permission to go, so *bon gre, mal gre* [French: like it or not] I had to force myself to go out and meet people. Yesterday morning, he sent a servant round again to ask about my health, and to invite us again to his house. So I decided to go. He had told us that no one else would be there, and that he wasn't going to invite anyone. It was true, he didn't invite anyone, but as soon as word got out that we were going, people decided to go to his house supposedly in order to hear Katenka.[36] Pyotr Mikhailovich[37] found out that people were planning to come and warned us, and Katenka decided that on no account would she agree to sing. When we arrived there, we found the rooms full of guests, ladies and gentlemen, the former dressed to the nines, all arrayed in fine lace and flowers, while we, not expecting to see such a crowd, were dressed very simply. I felt so embarrassed that I had to keep my eyes lowered. It became apparent that everyone had been waiting for us, even though such personages as Mme. Zubova, the wife of the deputy governor, Baroness Shlipenbach, and others were present. The concert began the moment we appeared. The first item was called "Ouverture" from some opera or other. Then Pelagini[38] sang a rather long and difficult aria, but was terribly intimidated by the sight of Katenka. This was followed by a string quartet, very nice! Then Pelagini sang another, again rather difficult aria; and finally there was some other "Ouverture," and that was it. After the concert, there was a game of whist for two rubles. I joined in and won 1 r[uble] 80 kop[ecks] from Pyotr Mikhailovich. No matter how hard people tried to get Katenka to sing something, it didn't work, and she was just playing *une difficile* [French: hard to get]. *A propos* [French: Incidentally], Messing did most of the persuading.

I advise you, my darling Ilyichka, to send for me soon. Since you've long since stopped noticing my good looks, I never hear any compliments from you about them, while here I hear nothing *but* compliments. As for Katenka, my sister of course, what can I say, she goes round telling everyone what a beauty I am, and she's not the only one. Yesterday, for example, at the party, a lot of people found me not at all unattractive. Messing, for one, told me three times that I had pretty eyes; even old Pyotr Mikhailovich Stremoukhov told me that I had beautiful eyes. As for me, I'm finding a lot of pretty eyes, noses, lips, and intelligent company, so that if you don't make an effort to send for me, I won't want to leave here, and I'll even start forgetting you, my little old man; as it is I'm now even finding it a great effort to write to you, my divine Angel. I'm even surprised to find that for all my reluctance, here I am filling a third page. Our Katisha is very restless. In the town, there's smallpox going around, and it scares me a little, and that's why I want to get her vaccinated against it as soon as possible. Karl Maksimovich Rebinder even promised to get me a sample from a healthy child. At first, Lindegrein himself agreed to vaccinate her against the smallpox, but after giving her a physical examination, pronounced her too weak and thin; on top of everything, the weather here is not too good. So I really don't know what will happen; will the Lord God spare her this disease? Zinochka, thank God, is healthy and happy. I've bought all the servants[39] new clothes for the holiday, but so far I haven't bought anything for myself. I'm still pleased with all of them, especially Lukeria, who is constantly nauseated and throwing up; she won't eat this, she won't drink that, and can't stand the smell of tobacco. Katenka and Aleksandr,[40] thank God, are in good health. They're so affectionate and unbelievably loving towards me. I miss you, my only treasure in the whole wide world, my Angel and dearest friend, and I can't find pleasure in anything. Every day, from the moment I wake up, I can't wait for it to be evening. In short, I have never found myself in a more painful position than I am now, my only delight is—writing to you, my pet. Zina and Katya kiss your hands and ask for your blessing. Although I hate to part with you, there's no help for it, I have to prepare this letter for the post. I kiss your dear hands, your bright blue eyes, your forehead, your hair, your nose, your cheeks, all of you, and especially your lovely Angelic lips.

I close with your blessing.

Your faithful, adoring friend and wife Sasha.

✦ ✦ ✦

7. ILYA PETROVICH TCHAIKOVSKY TO ALEKSANDRA ANDREEVNA TCHAIKOVSKAYA

Votkinsk Factory, 27 March 1837, Saturday, 11 p.m.

My Angel, my incomparable dear wife! Finally, after a long journey, I arrived this morning, or should I say, dragged myself here. I was advised to take the shortest route from Kazan, but God help us, what a terrible road! It's full of ruts and potholes, and the carriage is always in danger of keeling over and falling into a pit, and it would take four horses to pull it upright. That was bad enough, but the worst was that the sides of the carriage were scraping the trees, and sometimes it took us an hour or more to struggle along for one verst.[41] Just imagine my predicament. Of course, all this would have to happen at night. The horses were no problem, but the coachmen, damn them to hell, they're all Tatars, Ostyaks, Chuvashes, and Cheremises, and not a word of Russian among the lot of them. So I spent three whole days of constant hardship, unable to wash or shave, or even drink a drop of tea. When I reached the main road, which you will be using, I gave up the idea of taking the country road to the Votkinsk factory, and went straight to the Izhevsk factory, and got there early yesterday morning. The police chief (Kun's brother-in-law) found me a nice apartment, and immediately came to see me. I put on my full dress uniform and went with him to call on General Neratov.[42] He gave me the warmest of welcomes, and arranged for me to visit the factory and the arsenal. He offered to show me around himself, but couldn't spare the time from his duties, so I went round the factory with the police chief.

The general invited me to dinner, and so warmly that I couldn't refuse. After our tour of inspection, the police chief asked me round for a snack. His wife (Kun's sister, Susanna Ivanovna),[43] a delightful woman, was really upset because I didn't want to stay with them, so she made me promise to insist on your stopping by, if only for a moment, so I do urge you, my dear friend, to do as she wishes. They have a large family, and they're both really wonderful people.

By two o'clock I was already at the general's, and he introduced me to his wife.[44] What a wonderful woman! I'm sure you will like her. She told me to ask you not on any account to deprive her of the pleasure of your acquaintance, and would even like you to stay with them. They have so many children that I even lost count. I don't know whether it was because of me or not, but there were a lot of officers there; very nice people whom I got to know. On Fridays during Lent people are not usually asked to dinner, so that's what made me think that those guests were invited to mark my arrival. Before dinner I joined them at whist[45] and came out ahead of all of them, even the general's good lady herself, who had been so nice to me. After dinner, we finished off the last hand of whist and I left. Susanna Ivanovna insisted that I visit her for a cup of tea and then go for a ride in her carriage. Meanwhile we had sent a courier to the Votka to tell them that His Honor was on his way. At the way stations (it's seventy versts between the Izh and the Votka [rivers]), fresh horses were supplied promptly, and everywhere we were met and seen off. This morning at six o'clock, I saw the Votkinsk factory and mounted Cossacks in the distance. At the checkpoint I was met by the police chief on horseback who reported to me. The Cossacks were riding ahead; it was just like the cavalcade for Abbas-Mirza.[46] Everyone half asleep, watching me from their windows and gateways as if I were some kind of marvel. Finally, we came to a halt at full gallop at the entrance. Sleepy officials, some with plumes in their hats and some without, rode up. One reported that all was well at the factory, another that all was well in the district, and a third that all was well at the workshops. A young lieutenant of a line battalion paraded his squad and orderlies and yelled: "All is well in my squad." Well, you clear out, I want to sleep. Luisa had gone to Zlatoust and Yekaterinburg and had already returned. I was going to see her in the annex, but she was still sound asleep. Today at twelve noon all the officials reported to me. Father Vasily[47] and his retinue of priests offered me communion. Von Ziegel (our former mayor's son)[48] was waiting to meet me as instructed. He is married to Silina, who was at school with you. She is here with him and is very much looking forward to seeing you. Tomorrow they are going back to Zlatoust.

I saw Luisa last of all. Just imagine, she can only sleep in the morning; she spends all night coughing. The poor thing appears to be suffering from consumption, and she's dreadfully thin, but it cheered her up a lot to see me. I couldn't stay with her for long, and left for the factory just to take a quick look round, and stayed until three o'clock. I dined at Luisa's because she keeps a cook. The house, where we'll be living, is nice and spacious. After dinner I went to the bathhouse, as is the Russian custom, and I'm still lying in my bathrobe in a cubicle. In the meantime, I've been getting down to business, and have had a lot of people coming to see me about various matters. Would you believe, neither our baggage nor our servants have arrived yet. Tomorrow, I'll be sending a courier to Vyatka to find them and bring them back. Yesterday I was kept busy until eleven o'clock. As it happens, I'm keeping the post waiting just for this letter. I'm dying of hunger, and even more anxious to go to bed. I can hardly sit and keep my eyes open. Petya Grenov has spent the whole evening hovering around me and playing with the dogs. I send a thousand kisses to my dear friends, my brother

Aleksandr and dear Katechka, my sister. To you, my precious treasure, a million kisses; I hug you tight to my heart. Tomorrow, I'll be attending church for the service, and then the swearing in, followed by a bite with Father Vasily. My blessing to Zinochka and Katechka,[49] and I'll be praying for you all. I'll write to you every evening. Until tomorrow, light of my life.

Yours with all my heart, body, and soul, Ilya.

✦ ✦ ✦

8. ILYA PETROVICH TCHAIKOVSKY TO ALEKSANDRA ANDREEVNA TCHAIKOVSKAYA

Votk[insk] Fac[tory,] 7 April 1837, Wednesday, Midnight

4, 5, 6 April.

My Sashenka, the most wonderful, beautiful wife in the world! I've been neglecting my journal since Sunday, partly because of so many claims on my attention throughout the day, and partly because I can't think of subjects to interest you. However that may be, I should give you a brief account of what's been happening in the last few days. On Sunday, I had hardly opened my eyes when practically every single official turned up and gathered in the hall—it's the usual practice in factories in these parts. So I had to get dressed in a hurry to go out so that people could greet me and report. Talking business with so many people took up so much of my time that I was almost late for church. Anyway, I hurried there in time to hear a very good concert and the sermon by Father Vasily who came out to see me after the service with the news that he was inviting himself to my place in the evening. After church I made some visits: to the doctor,[50] and was introduced to his wife, nee Meyer (daughter of the former manager of the Gornobl[agodatsk] factory. She has known me since she was a girl in Perm.[51] They have quite a few children and live well. Then there was the first member, Vilegzhenin—his wife is Swedish, and, judging by her accent, probably even Finnish. She is a very simple woman, but judging by her face, good hearted and quiet. Then it was the manager, Major Romanov;[52] his wife is nice looking, but has thick lips—otherwise she might be pretty. However, being pregnant, she was not her usual self physically. They have two or three children, lively kids, who get their good looks from their father. Next it was Penn,[53] the

Englishman—didn't meet his wife, but her picture showed her with a red nose, he says she's a very good woman. I saw the daughters the first day after my arrival at Luisa's, but I've forgotten what they look like—apparently not beauties—but people say they are very nice girls; I think there are more than one of them.[54] I like Mr. Penn, pleasant and intelligent fellow. Finally, I went to see Luisa, drank coffee and had a bite to eat, and spent some time at home looking at my notes—a lot have been accumulating on my desk—and then went to a dinner party at Vilegzhenin's. By way of entertainment I mangled my orchestrina[55] piece. Everyone listened and wept. Conversation and discussion about this and that went on until midnight. Luisa served some snacks, we ate everything, and then everyone went home.

Monday was a normal working day, and began in the usual way. I did some work at home until noon, and then set off for the office. I went from there to the factory, and stayed there until four o'clock. I had dinner at Luisa's, went home to rest and then worked until past midnight, and many officials called on me. Yesterday, i.e. Tuesday, I waited impatiently for the post, hoping for a letter from you, my Angel, but didn't get one. Why did you wait so long after I left before writing—it was quite a few days? It was a bit dispiriting not to have heard from you for three weeks, so I'm feeling a little down in the dumps right now. Yesterday, I had to deal with a lot of paperwork, among other things, which, since I'm still new here, is taking a little more time and effort than I would like. I need some more time to learn how to negotiate all the ins and outs. But I'm confident that I will master all of this. Thank God, I'm in good health, and activity is not only necessary, but is also very good for me. I got a letter from Mommy,[56] which I am attaching. Today I prepared the mail, and not long ago sent it to Siberia or Yekaterinburg.

My rooms are being painted. Goodbye, my treasure. May God bless you with peaceful sleep.

✦

8 April.
I don't know if you will like the way I have arranged the apartment. The corner room I've turned into our bedroom, and the bedroom into the nursery where we'll put in two simple partitions. On one side we'll put Katya with the wet nurse and the nanny, and on the other side

Zina with Glafira Timofeevna.[57] Of course, if you don't like what I've done, then I'm in trouble. Although, of course, you can always re-arrange things the way you want. The walls are finished: the reception room is yellow, and the billiard room is in lilac, the drawing room is light blue, the recess in the round living room with a divan in the shape of a bench is in blue and yellow stripes. The bedroom is also painted lilac, and the nursery pale yellow, the maids' room remains its original pink, and hasn't been repainted, the dining room remains yellow, and the study is still the original green.

The maids' storeroom under the staircase is very small, I'm not sure where to put the new one, but we can deal with that when you come. There is no cold pantry at all, but there is a big iron cupboard. The basement is in good condition and divided into two compartments. The hothouses and greenhouses are not in good shape, but now they're putting in compost for heating. In any case, the cucumbers won't be ready by the time you arrive. Katerina was not very well, but the doctor has been treating her, and she's feeling better. Akulina[58] is putting on weight and is looking as round as a barrel. Mitka has grown up, and does nothing but sleep, the rascal. The dogs are in good health. In any case, you'll be given a full report on all these household matters by F. V. Mironova, my housekeeper, when you arrive, and the floors, doors, and window frames will be painted in time for the holiday.

It's past midnight now. I took a nap after dinner, that's why I'm not sleepy yet. So, how are things with you, my incomparable one? Are you in good health? What are the children doing? And my dear brother Aleksandr and sister Katechka, are they in good health? All this keeps passing through my mind even when I'm busy in the office, in the factory, or at home in my study. Pretty soon you'll have to start preparing to leave. For a long time now I've been using a droshky. At the moment I only have two black horses and a capable coachman, he'll be yours. When you want to drive somewhere we have a trap here, as for a carriage, we'll have to send away for one.

Goodbye. Hugs and blessings for you and the children.

✦

9 April
I usually write to you in the evening, when I've finished working—a substitute for a real live conversation with you. How vividly I can

imagine I'm with you—it's as if you were in this very room with me, my adored friend! My thoughts are mingling with our last conversation about your journey out here. You should already be thinking about the preparations for it. Twenty-one days from now, I'll be waiting for you. It's dry here, but there's still snow in the woods, and the water's not rising in the pond, it's infuriating. Ask my brother Aleksandr if he wouldn't mind inspecting the carriages ahead of time; Vic[tor] Tim[ofeevich] Sherchin will be preparing them, let him decide who is going to sit where.

If two kachalka carriages[59] aren't enough, then take three, but the main thing is your comfort and convenience. I urge you, my Angel, to spare no expense, just so you arrive safe and sound. Make Katechka a basket, as Aleksandr suggested. From Kazan go to Elabuga, there's a good highway, only make sure to get a samovar and cups in Kazan and take them with you; you know how fastidious you are, and you won't want to drink from their dirty samovars and teapots when you are among the Tatars, the Cheremises, and the Votyaki. As far as Kazan you will find excellent way stations where you can rest and sit down for a while, but after Kazan it gets worse and worse, although not everywhere. I think there will be two places where you will have to cross the Volga, the ferries are excellent and safe. There will also be the Vyatka, but nothing after that. If you are travelling at the beginning of May, then in the town of Sviazhsk or just before it, you will have to travel four versts by water. But don't worry, it's quite safe and easy. You'll be going by ship, and I hear that those ships can carry a whole regiment.

Today they finished painting the walls, and washed the floors, and tomorrow they'll be painting just the floors in the drawing room, the bedroom, the other places don't need it. I'm doing everything in my power to please my lovely wife, and I know even now that she will be pleased. I have ordered beds and a cradle. I have given orders that the Lutheran church upstairs[60] is not to be demolished before you arrive, when you'll be able to see for yourself whether you want it removed, in which case it will be done in a few hours. You must be sure to write and let me know the date and even the time of your departure, so that I can work out what time to meet you at the Izhevsk factory or at Sarapul. It's better to come via Izhevsk, but in any case do whatever suits you. If you don't want to meet General Neratov's wife, then come via Sarapul, and let me know so that I can send horses and the various carriages you will need. In springtime the road is very pleasant, there are wonderful views, meadows and woods.

However, please remember that at the beginning of May the Volga area is still cold.

Goodbye, my Angel, my blessings for you and the children, and a kiss for my brother Aleksandr and my sister, that Angel Katechka.

✦

10 April.

The mail just got here, and I hasten to send these scribblings to my adored friend. They will tell her that not just every day, but every minute I long to be with her. My most precious friend! I am reluctant to tell you how much I miss you for fear that it will encourage you to feel the same way. I really don't want you to pine, but want you to be in good spirits in Nizhny;[61] it's so important for your health. You just can't imagine how joyful and delighted I will be to set eyes on your pretty—or rather rosy—plump and cheerful self. I'll be beside myself, I'll shout, shriek, and jump up and down with excitement, and squeeze the breath out of you with my embrace. A good mood and disposition promotes health; it's rare to have one without the other. If you romp and gambol, then I will too, and my working day will seem like a vacation, and everything will become easy for me. But if you start to get bored, then I will too, and my head will grow heavy, and I'll turn into a grumpy old man. So my beautiful, sparkling star, shine for me and gladden my heart. I've just come back from the bathhouse, and I'm not yet fully rested, but supper is ready now. I'm grateful to good-hearted Luisa Karlovna who has taken me under her wing, and makes it her business to see that I am well fed. I have a good dinner, supper, and breakfast with coffee; all this is mostly sent up to my room, but I go to her quarters for dinner.

This morning I spent a long time working, right up to four o'clock. I'm getting used to the St. Petersburg way of life, i.e. having dinner at four o'clock. It looks as if I'll have to make a habit of dining at that time, otherwise it's a problem. Of course, when you come, we'll have to agree about that. Bring some vegetable seeds with you for the garden. Luisa has given me a lot, but they all appear to be too old, and also there don't seem to be any watermelon, melon, cauliflower, or winter radishes among them.

Goodbye, my Angel. Stay healthy and in good spirits. I kiss your dear little hands, fingers, feet, knees, cheeks, lips, forehead, eyes, and all of you. Devoted to you heart and soul, your Ilya.

A thousand kisses to my dear brother Aleksandr and sister Katechka. Oh, if only Aleksandr could unbend enough to allow Katechka[62] to come here to us, I would kneel at his feet, and smother him with kisses, I would consider such a sacrifice a real boon.

✦ ✦ ✦

9. ILYA PETROVICH TCHAIKOVSKY TO ALEKSANDRA ANDREEVNA TCHAIKOVSKAYA

St. Petersburg, 20 January 1841

Now I'm on my way to Kolpino. The problems with Zina are continuing. I have been received by the Heir to the Throne,[63] and was given a very warm reception. Yesterday I asked Mommy[64] to go to see Kavelin[65] to make a request for Zina, and that bastard gave her a very cold reception and pretty well flatly refused.[66] I'm extremely busy today, but tomorrow I'm going to make another attempt; I'll ask the chief of staff, and if he's not willing to help, that's it, I'll enroll Zina at my own expense, and if possible at the Patriotic Institute,[67] where you went to school, my incomparable Angel, a school of the highest moral standards.

I'm thinking of traveling with General Anosov,[68] otherwise expect me in a week.

My blessing for the children, Kolya and Petya.[69] Zina is well.

Your faithful, I. Tchaikovsky.

✦ ✦ ✦

10. ILYA PETROVICH TCHAIKOVSKY TO ALEKSANDRA ANDREEVNA TCHAIKOVSKAYA

6 August 1844, Votk[insk] Fa[ctory]

Sunday

My Angel! When I said goodbye to you yesterday evening, I had to hold back my tears, because I didn't want to seem weak in the eyes of the people around me, but no matter how hard I tried, the tears welled up—and I had to keep my eyes closed while I was trying to comfort

Petya who was crying inconsolably because his mommy didn't take him to St. Petersburg. While I was seeing you off, as well as the whole procession following you, I felt so keenly the pain of separation that I could hardly contain myself. I felt strange, distracted, in a total daze. The horses were ready to go, and Petya had started to calm down. They put him in a carriage with Nad[ezhda] Tim[ofeevna][70] and Pal[ageya?] Petr[ovna]. Six horses and the postillion were there to keep him entertained, but he kept on bursting into sobs, and insisting on catching you up and being put in your carriage. At that moment we rode up. Petya had fallen asleep. Kar[tashev] and Bad[aev][71] were playing pitch and toss out of boredom. I have spent every minute accompanying you in my mind, my incomparable friend! At that time you were probably crying yourself. I consoled myself with the thought that you were not alone, and that [R]omanov was doing his best to supply you with everything you need for a quiet and comfortable journey. As we were traveling, the way stations flew by as if they were only a kilometer apart. At the third one, while we were changing the horses, I drank a glass of porter, and I took Petya and we walked on ahead. We had covered over two kilometers on foot when we were caught up by the carriages and rode on. At Toykino,[72] where I had been advised to go by Vas[ily] Sem[yonovich], we drank tea so as not to use up our travel allowance. The night was dark; I gave Fishka a dressing down for losing the candlestick from your lantern. You didn't have as much light as on the first night, but I'm sure you slept well. By seven o'clock this morning we were already home. We found everything in order. Sasha[73] and Polya[74] shrieked when they saw us. The day before Polinka had been washed in the bath, and slept well that night. It seems that he's over the diarrhea, and at least for now, is doing well. The children went with Nast[enka] and Nad[ezhda] Tim[ofeevna] to the cemetery church for the holiday service, and I was kept busy with the guests and the officials. I'm extremely grateful to Pal. Petrovna for holding Petya in her arms and looking after him for the whole journey. Apart from Kartashev and Badaev no one came to dinner. They left right after dinner, and I went to bed, but I didn't sleep for long. The mail arrived. There was a letter from Vanya Evreinov.[75] He writes that Petinka[76] stayed with them for a short time, and that on my name day[77] Emilia L[illegible] decorated my portrait with flowers and they had a celebration. There was no important news. The children have gone out for a ride. I've been reading the papers. Life is dreary, so dreary without you, my dear good Angel! You're on your way now, may God bless you! Sleep peacefully, my cherub—I'm going to bed. Bless Kolya for me. It's striking midnight.

✦ ✦ ✦

11. ILYA PETROVICH TCHAIKOVSKY TO ALEKSANDRA ANDREEVNA TCHAIKOVSKAYA

8 August 1844, V[otkinsk] F[actory], *Tuesday morning*

I'm very grateful to Nad[ezhda] Tim[ofeevna][78] and Nastenka[79] for taking such good care of me, the children, and the whole house. Each of them has been outdoing the other in trying to please, and so far everything is going perfectly. Nastenka is sleeping in the nursery on Kolya's bed. The children are sleeping soundly, thank God, so I too have been sleeping well. Polya went three times early this morning, but is in good health and good spirits, thank God. However, they've still been feeding him egg white, and rubbing ointment on his tummy. Sasha is in good health and in high spirits, like an Angel. Since he was punished yesterday, Petya has been sensible and obedient. Everything here is going fine.

Please kiss dear Mommy's hand for me, and a proper kiss for Liza and brother Vasinka.[80]

May the Lord God bless you! We'll continue this conversation this evening.

Your true friend, I[lya] T[chaikovsky]

✦ ✦ ✦

12. ILYA PETROVICH TCHAIKOVSKY TO ALEKSANDRA ANDREEVNA TCHAIKOVSKAYA

[Votkinsk Factory,] 15 August [1844,] Tuesday evening

The picture is of Polenka sitting on my desk, using a feather to sweep up the sand he spilled, and Nastenka is sitting in front of him. After sending you a second letter, or rather a complete account of our domestic events, I went to church with everyone except Polenka. Soon after returning from church I got the sacred icons from Vyatka, that is: St. Nikolai Velikoretsky (Yavlennyi), St. Mikhail, and the Tikvinsk Blessed Virgin.

The Father Verger, archpriest of the cathedral,[81] took the service. We all prayed for our most precious mama, and for dear Kolya, and for the Lord God to bless your journey.

I left the Father Archpriest at home to sample my pies. From my place, he went to our neighbor M. S., and then to Olyshev.[82] We dined early. It was a windy day, so the children didn't go out for a ride after dinner, but agreed among themselves to go and see A[leksandr] Pav[lovich] Alekseev.[83] After seven o'clock Nad[ezhda] Tim[ofeevna] together with Lida,[84] Petya, and Sasha set off, and Nastenka and I stayed at home with Polya. This time Polya was nice and very amusing. He is beginning to stand up and babble. He's particularly good at saying: "Give me, take me, go go, here" and an approximation of "pipe" etc. After dinner I was starting to feel bored, but the children entertained me. Then soon after the doctor[85] appeared, and we talked with him for rather a long time, and then Olyshev, followed by the police chief,[86] and that's how we whiled away the time until eight o'clock. After Polya had settled down to sleep, we went to fetch the children. We found them playing happily, stayed no longer than three quarters of an hour, and went home.

✦

16 August. Wednesday Evening.
The arrival of the Kartashevs prevented me from chatting with you this morning. They arrived yesterday evening after I had gone to bed, and was obviously sleeping so soundly that I didn't hear any noise— Pal. Petr. had gone to bed upstairs, and Vas. Sem. in my study. In the morning we talked over tea and coffee. I'm very grateful to him for his help with that business of mine with Izhb.[87] By appealing to that old scoundrel's better self, he managed to talk him round, but it should be said that it was under the influence of his dissolute son that he had behaved so badly. Izhb. willingly agreed to pay 1,800 rubles in September, and gave an IOU to V.S., acknowledging that he had borrowed that sum from him. Now I won't be dealing with Izhb., but with Kartashev. Although I didn't receive any money from him, nevertheless the matter is settled, and I intend to pay that official debt also. That's why I am in a good mood today. Let me know as soon as possible: you didn't give some money to Florovsky, did you? Now you don't need to. I'm going to send him the necessary amount officially

from the office. Accounts will be settled, and I'll be relieved. I think you're due to leave Nizhny today. I hope you managed to cope with the shopping, my dear. I can't wait to get your letter from Nizhny. Did you buy me a couple of mirrors, some chamber pot covers, and some rugs? Kartashev volunteered to order me some good furniture for the living room; it's cheap there, so I need to know in detail what exactly you bought there. You will have done very well, if you didn't forget to buy one or two pieces of that *drap de dames*[88] for the furniture at the fair.

The children are well, and have gone to sleep; we played cards.

✦

17 August. Thursday morning.

I can just see you, my true friend, on your way to Moscow. My heart leaps to think that your days and nights are blessed with fine weather. God grant that there be no interruptions in your journey. That's precisely why it's so tedious travelling in a caravan, willy-nilly, you have to stop for repairs, or for the horses. The time of your return from St. Petersburg will depend entirely on you. Stay there as long as is necessary to achieve *the purpose of the journey,* and when you've had enough, come home. Try to leave when the sky is light at night, and make a point of letting me know the day you are setting out, the route you'll be taking, where you intend to spend the night, whether you would think of going to your sister, Katerina Andreevna, or to Ledengsk,[89] and the precise day when you expect to arrive. Work it all out carefully. Yesterday, Kartashev and I arranged to meet you if you come via Kazan, or if you come by way of Vyatka, then we'll meet you there. In either case, apart from the Kazak, Belokrylov, who you'll find if you place an order, I think maybe in Moscow, or in Yaroslavl, or in Vologda, or in Ledengsk. Anywhere in the Vyatsk province you will be able to place an order through Al. Dm[itrievich] Ignatiev to get an escort and obtain horses immediately. If you feel like going to Ledengsk, which is perfectly possible, then write beforehand to Vanya, or to I[van] Yak[ovlevich], asking to be met in Vologda and escorted to Vyatka. In that case, you'll need to get a voucher for the horses you need only from St. Petersburg to Vologda. Here am I, prattling on about your return journey, before you're even ready to leave. So, I hope that before that time comes, you will enjoy yourself in St. Petersburg . . . They have begun painting the nurseries and they've put cots in the living room. We went to church, and after dinner went out to accompany the icons, and have just come back.

✦

18 August. Friday morning.

Everything was fine yesterday, we thought Polenka had recovered, but tonight his diarrhea started up again, and he's already been four times. He probably caught cold when we were out for a ride. It's really annoying, especially since we've been so careful with him, and just to make things worse we've been giving him kvass and everything just like the others. The doctor has prescribed some medicine, which we'll be giving him. God willing, it will pass; but we'll be continuing him on his diet at much as possible. The doctor says the epidemic had all but ended, when the hot weather started, and it is still with us, it brought the diarrhea back with it. To a degree that exonerates me, because perhaps we are not to blame for the relapse, but I think it's a bit of both, and most of all I blame myself, because yesterday, when I was escorting the icons to Mishkino,[90] at Beryozovka,[91] I sat him on the sand, which I thought was quite warm, when I shouldn't have done. But apart from that I blame myself for giving him some pancake at dinner made from rice gruel, which is, of course, not fatty. But whatever the reason, the fact remains that it's bad, and for that I'm punishing myself by becoming morose, and I won't be myself again until the thing is over, and the worst of it is I can't overcome this tedium which is beginning to really get me down. No, my cherub, don't linger in St. Petersburg out of cowardice, just do what you have to do there, have a good time, and then God speed you home, to me and the children. Ah! how sweet it will be to hug you to my breast! Polenka is constantly in my arms; that's why my writing is so jerky. He has just been playing with the sand on my desk, but he got tired of it. Petya and Sasha are playing outdoors. Sashechka, thank God, is much better now and has filled out, and is her playful self again. Petya is as sweet as ever. He hardly ever cries.

✦

6 o'clock. During tea.

At the factory, I have a lot to take care of. Olyshev manages things quite well, but he lacks experience, and often forgets things and makes mistakes. S[ofia] I[vanovna][92] is getting treatment and never goes out.

At Sashechka's request, the doctor sent his children round today, and they've been kicking up a din upstairs—he himself spent almost the whole evening with me.

✦

19 August. Saturday morning.
Polenka slept well last night, but had to go twice early in the morning. The doctor said that we should continue with yesterday's medicine, but he'll probably change it today.

Augusta is constantly rubbing Polenka the wrong way; if he sees me, then he always rejects her, "Go away, go away!" That's why she was crying so much yesterday, and got mad at Nad[ezhda] Tim[ofeevna] for taking Polya away from her when she was holding him. Today, my Angel, I'm picturing you in Moscow, or near there. How is the journey? Are you and dear Kolya well? I'm with you in spirit every step of the way, and never even for a moment do I part company with you. You and Kolya are my most precious treasures—how could you ever be far from my thoughts? Thinking about you is sheer joy and a balm to my soul. There is no moment of the day or night when I do not picture you on your journey, or at the way station, and seeing you sitting, resting your dear heads on a pink pillow, seeing you casually watching from your carriage a wood, or a village as it flashes past, something of no interest to you, and which you hardly notice, since your imagination is busy picturing your arrival in St. Petersburg, and relishing the prospect of soon reaching the next station, of quickly changing horses and—but suddenly Fishka[93] is reporting that the seventh carriage has a broken wheel, and that V. I. [Romanov] has sent for a carpenter and a blacksmith, and has sent someone to find a comfortable lodging for you. God knows how long you're going to have to wait while they repair that damned wheel. It's annoying, but you console yourself with the thought that, although all these delays are a bore, you are perfectly safe. And that's when you think of me, and say to yourself: "Oh, if only he were here with me! I wonder what they're doing at home now, Petya, Sasha, Polya. I'm never going anywhere again without my friend." And I'm never going to let you go anywhere except to take the waters at Sergiev[94] together with me and the whole family. It's only been two weeks since you left, but already I'm going crazy from boredom.

✦

6 o'clock in the evening.

Polenka is better, but we're still giving him the medicine, and don't take him out of the room. He's lost weight, poor thing, and practically never lets me out of his sight, and I can't bring myself to refuse. I almost forgot to tell you the dream I had today: it seemed that you were married to some handsome, blond young man, and, poor me, I had to be content with trailing after you—and, my God, how galling it was not to be able to see you often. I humbly implore you not to let this happen in real life.

✦

20 August 1844, Sunday morning.

Bonjour, mon ange! [Good morning, my angel!] Polenka slept well last night, but we are continuing with the medicine. He was in good spirits this morning. He almost gave up going to sleep during the day, but now he's getting used to it again, and is sleeping longer. So much for him for the time being. For the last few days, there has been no going out for rides. N[adezhda] T[imofeevna] has been going to church with Petya and Sasha. It's unbearably hot today, the temperature is 21 degrees in the shade, and more than 30 in the sun, so we haven't let the children go out during the day. Sashenka fell asleep before dinner, and suddenly woke up sobbing from a dream, and Nastenka and I rushed in to see her, and what does she tell us? "Mommy came back from St. Petersburg and didn't bring me any candy. She gave some to Petya, but not to me." And that's why she was so upset. A minute later, she had calmed down, and even laughed at herself. Shultz, the forest warden, came to call. I began to think he might be staying to dinner, but the doctor had already got in first with his dinner invitation. In the course of our conversation I alluded to the trouble in the forestry sector in the presence of Vasiliev.

✦

7 o'clock in the evening.

After dinner I slept for a long time, and that's why I am so late in writing to you, my incomparable, precious golden-diamond friend, my soul mate, my heart's delight! God knows what I wouldn't give just to be allowed a look at you, to touch your little hands and lips. Without you even the brightest days are dark, and my only pleasure is thinking about you and writing these words. You will be holding these sheets of paper in your dear hands, and seeing these words before you see me. I would never have imagined that I could miss you so much, and you haven't even reached Moscow yet. Of course, you have nearly completed your business, but you should have a chance to stay a while in St. Petersburg, so I still have a long wait before you return. Well, there's no help for it, I'll just have to wait it out. The post came early today, but brought nothing. It was delivered by mistake to Izh., and was sent on today. I sent a special courier to fetch it.

I'm not expecting a letter from you; it seems that the only place you could write from is Nizhny, and I'll be getting that letter next week. It's really hard to take, hearing nothing from you for two whole weeks. If you decide to return via Vologda, then please write first to Vanya and I[van] Yak[ovlevich] in Ledengsk so that they can come to meet you at Vologda, or even better, at Ustyuzh, Zheleznopolskaya, where you can turn off the Yaroslavsk road in the direction of Vologda. If Vanya or Iv. Yak. are willing to do this for you, I will smother them in kisses and show my appreciation. Of course, you could also return by way of Somina to sister Kat[erina] Andr[eevna]'s village, and from there you will be escorted to Vologda or Priluk. So work out the best route, and stick to it, and please don't spare the expense.

The children are well. Polenka is not being allowed to "giddy up," and Petya and Sasha spend the whole day in the garden. We're all careful not to let them out in the sun. Polya has lost weight, it's true, but I'm told that Lydia was once so thin that it was painful to look at her, but now even she is looking better.

Guests have arrived, Al. Pav. with Af. Iv. and the children,[95] and we're still expecting the archpriest and others.

✦

21 August. Monday morning.

The post arrived at 10 o'clock last night when I had the Doctor,[96] Olyshev, Romanov, and a few others here with me. There are no letters. The newspapers report the death of the Gr[and] Pr[incess] Aleks[andra] Nikolaevna. Someone wrote a splendid article on the subject. So St. Petersburg, where you are, is in mourning. It would be a pity if you didn't get a chance to enjoy the theatre. So, for that alone I'm prepared to let you take two weeks' vacation. So, although I'll miss you terribly, the best thing is for you to stay a little longer, it can't be helped, and later, you won't be able to reproach yourself or me, but I want you to go and see the whole of *The Thieving Magpie*[97] every day until you're sick of it. Today has been just as hot as yesterday, and the last three weeks in a row. I'm afraid that the carriage wheels may crack—which is not so terrible, but it means that it will take time to secure and tighten the metal rims.

When you arrive in St. Petersburg, tell the Kazak and Fishka to make sure everything is in order, and to fix whatever needs fixing so that there's nothing to delay your departure whenever you decide to leave.

I really need to make the rounds of the forest dachas with Schultz, but I'm not sure how to. I don't want to leave home for several days, and still less do I want to stop writing this diary, which, although it contains a lot of trivia, is still interesting to you. I'll think about it.

✦

22 August. Tuesday morning.

Yesterday, I had to stop chatting with you, my angel! In particular, I have become the target of the doctor's attentions. He calls on me every evening with or without a reason and stays until 9 o'clock or even later. I don't find his conversation boring, but it does take up time which I would rather be devoting to you. After he left, I spent a long time preparing things for the post, and then it was time for supper.

Polenka is much better, he's no longer taking the medicine and is in pretty good spirits and I'm caring for him like the apple of my eye. Sashenka couldn't be nicer, but is jealous of my attentions to Polya. As you know, he doesn't like sharing us, and when I am holding him, he shoos everyone away. Petya is still just as well as ever, in good spirits and up to mischief. Tell Arisha that her Vaska never goes anywhere without his balalaika which a kind uncle made for him, and is glowing with health. Today is a holiday. Everyone turned up in their uniforms, and I was just about to set off for church, but there was a shower, so I put it off so that I could continue our conversation. Everyone is telling me off for writing to you so frankly about how dull things are without you, and they say that this will only upset you. But, my dear friend, do be sensible, and don't start your journey before you've taken care of all your business. Be sure to remember everything you were supposed to do, and don't leave without doing it. What can I do? Yes, I may be pining for you, but then I'll be all the happier to see you when I do. Only you don't have permission to stay until the winter and wait for the Romanovs.

Now I'm sealing the letter. Bless you my incomparable friend, and please bless Zina and Kolya for me. Kiss Mommy's hands and say hello to Liza and Vasenka.

A big kiss for my friend Nikolay Ivanovich, and a hug for Pyotr Ivanovich.[98]

Your faithful friend
I[lya] Tch[aikovsky].

P.S. There's no news. Yesterday, the sisters and their governess arrived together with S[ofia] I[vanovna].[99]

Nadezhda Timofeevna and Nastechka send you their warm greetings, and will be sending you a letter by the next post.

Petya, Sasha, and Polya ask for your parental blessing.

✦ ✦ ✦

13. ILYA PETROVICH TCHAIKOVSKY TO ALEKSANDRA ANDREEVNA TCHAIKOVSKAYA

[Votkinsk Factory,] 23 August 1844, Wednesday morning

Today I can picture you, my Angel, if not in St. Petersburg itself, at least very near there. I can feel your heart beating when you think how far it is to the last way station and how slowly your coachman is driving. Kolya is showering you with questions, "Isn't this St. Petersburg? Mommy, over there I can see a lot of churches, it must be St. Petersburg, mommy." "No, darling, it's Tsarskoe Selo." "What does Tsarskoe Selo mean etc.?" Well St. Petersburg really is visible, it can be seen before the last way station at Four Hands. There you all are, stopping for a rest, shaking the dust from your clothes, hurrying to get washed. And you yourself are ordering the baggage to be unlocked. You are being offered food, but you're not hungry. Finally you're seated again in the carriage, moving fast, although it seems slow to you.

Now you've arrived. There's the checkpoint, the dacha, and houses upon houses. There's the Obukhov bridge, the Pavel Military School, the Technological Institute, such familiar places, few changes here. "Which way, lady?" asks the coachman, and Fishka answers: "to the Ap-Aplegran-zous." "I don't understand your babble, I'd better ask the lady again. Which way, lady." "To the Ordonansgauz." "Which one? There's two of them." "The new one." "Oh yes, now I've got it." Then comes Sennaya Street, the Gostinny Dvor. Nevsky Prospekt and turn off into Sadovaya Street. Vas[ily] Ipatovich[100] turned with all the carriages at the Barbazak house, or even before that at the Obuk-hov bridge, or into Meshchanskaya Street at the Varvarin house. Now you're at the entrance where the guard stands. "Where does El. And. Shobert live?" "Ask at the gate behind me." Now you're at the gate. The Kazak has run up. A minute later your sister Lizochka[101] runs out, followed by Mommy,[102] Darya, Fedosya, and so on and so forth. "Oh, Sasha, Sasha, Lizochka, Mommy," and everyone is overjoyed, kissing and hugging on their way up the stairs.

Vas[ily] Andr[eevich][103] was out; he was on duty. He soon appears, shuffling, introducing himself, hopping about, kissing and being kissed.

✦

Evening

I don't know if my imaginings coincide with the reality, but I, in any case, envisage a joyous reunion. The Lord God has kept you in good health throughout your journey, if not because of the prayers of this sinner, then because of the prayers of the pure soul that you are. Prayers for your health are still being said in church, and may God grant that Father Vasily, who has the task of praying for us every Sunday, said the prayers with wholehearted zeal and the conviction that God was listening. The children are in good health and are out for a ride, except for Polya who is still in quarantine, although he too would like to be going for a ride. My companions of the evening, the Doctor and Olyshev, are not here right now. Olyshev is seeing his sisters off to Izhevsky; they had been allowed out for a while. Forgive me, my friend, I feel like drinking a glass of vodka with a snack. I wish you good night in St. Petersburg.

S. I. Olysheva is still sick. The doctor says the illness is not serious, but could become so. Margarita is the intermediary in this, and is now at their place.

✦

24 August. Thursday morning

Yes, you must definitely be in St. Petersburg. I can't imagine that your stopovers, except for the fairs, will be so long that two weeks won't be enough for you to get from Nizhny to St. Petersburg. On Saturday or Sunday, of course, you were in Moscow and went to see your nieces at the Institute. That was nice. Today, and perhaps yesterday too you met Zina. I can imagine how pleased she must have been. That good child must have welcomed you like an emissary from heaven, like a guardian angel, like a mother, a friend—and I'm sure she couldn't hold back her tears of happiness, especially since there were not many people around.

Evening. Because I was busy in the office, the factory, and then at home, I couldn't begin chatting with you, whom I adore, before now at 7:30 in the evening. First it was the police chief, and then the doctor who interfered with my work, but look how quickly I managed to dispose of it all. I had ordered Polenka to be given more oat gruel, but that little rascal doesn't take kindly to it at all, nothing will do for him but "pollidge." It was cold all day today, barely 5 degrees, while two days ago, it was 20, and yesterday 15. Such a drop in temperature makes people sick, and the hospital is full. As a precaution before leaving the house, I've begun to take a glass of vodka with a pinch of pepper. In a couple of days, I intend to get down to painting the rooms, but not the floors because the smell lasts for so long—so don't blame me for that—and as soon as I've painted the walls, I'll have the windows caulked immediately. I can hear someone knocking outside. It's that devil Olyshev; he's going to sit around for ages and there are still some papers I have to finish working on. The bathroom is being renovated, and Polenka will need bathing. The doctor told us to put some heating in the nursery. What's more, he wants to bring in there the big samovar to bathe the child—and all this has been done by my dear Nadezhda Timofeevna and Nastenka.

✦

25 August. Friday morning.

Today, it's overcast and I'm having the windows put back in somehow or other. Vaska has come down with diarrhea, but grandmother doesn't want to treat him, so he's having to cope with it as best he can by himself. Now I'm building an icon case. I want it to be a good one, but not cumbersome and in good taste. There's a lot to be done, but it won't be finished before you return. I've put off painting the big rooms until the weather improves. I'm sleeping in the bedroom, and the children in their usual places. Nastenka, as I've already written, is sleeping in Olya's bed, and Nadezhda Timofeevna in the other nursery. The best possible care has been taken to ensure that they can sleep undisturbed. There are no bedbugs, or very few. All the children have been bandaged to prevent diarrhea, which has begun to spread fast. Petya and Sasha are in perfectly good health, while Polenka, although also well, demands more attention than the others. As you know, Polenka came down intermittently with bouts of diarrhea throughout the summer. And we were only able to treat it successfully when it was diagnosed. The doctor has given us detailed instructions about how to look after him. Now I'm trying not to spend so much time in his company, although he seems to be growing even more attached to me, he wants me to hold him all the time; and he's always in tears when I put him down.

◆

26 August. Saturday morning

Vaska is better now. I've given strict orders that he is not to be allowed outdoors, or to sleep in the hallway. The bout of diarrhea hasn't changed him in the slightest; he's just the same little lazybones as ever. We're not giving him any medicine, except egg whites and millet broth. Set his parents' minds at rest and tell them that I will be just as caring and attentive to their offspring as they prove to be to you—and I will not be lacking in my concern for them either.

The police chief[104]—if only he could learn to hold his tongue!—has just told me that, supposedly, the caravan has not yet reached St. Petersburg, and the reason he offers is that because of the exceptionally dry weather, the carriages have to undergo repairs at all the way stations. However, I don't go along with this, and continue to believe that you succeeded in reaching your destination on the 23rd or 24th.

Vas[ily] Ipatovich is a careful organizer, and there's no way he would have permitted such an unnecessary delay.

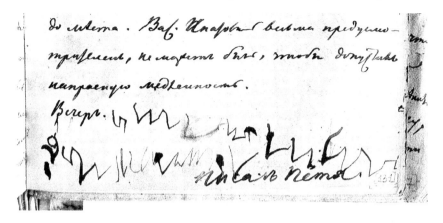

Young Pyotr's handwritten message to "Dear Mommy," 26 August 1844

✦

Evening

Petya wrote (My translation): "Dear Mommy, I'm well, don't forget to bring me toys and candy."[105]

Sasha has also written a message in her own hand, to wit: "Dear Mommy, I am well. Send me something. Polya hasn't written anything, because he's gone to bed.

Your daughter, Sasha."

After all this scribbling, the children went to be bathed. Sasha was eager to go yet again.

The doctor has asked me to give you a message to pass on to Vas[ily] Ip[atovich] and the Al. Sem. Romanovs, *that their children are all in good health*. This, as he put it, was because Al[eksandr] Ip[atovich],[106] supposedly, had written that Lydia was not well, which is not true. It's just that she lost a little weight after the diarrhea, and her peritoneal blockage has disappeared. Now she has recovered and is looking more like her old sweet self.

Oh, how I miss you, my dear wife! You will soon forget me there in St. Petersburg.

I'm so thankful to my dear Nad[ezhda] Tim[ofeevna] and Nastenka, they are doing their best to divert me. But for all that [indecipherable]

May God preserve you from all harm, my incomparable one! You must be tired after all your running around St. Petersburg. Sweet dreams.

✦

27 August. Sunday morning.

How happy I was when I woke up this morning and remembered that I was expecting a letter from you—but the post came and there was no letter from you. I felt cold, and I have to say, annoyed. Happily, I was told that some merchants from here had seen you in Nizhny. I sent the police chief himself round to all the merchants. Meanwhile, Usolka[107] came by and said that two days before the fast, that is, on Monday, the 14th of Aug[ust] he saw you with his own eyes, and that you and Kolya were well, and that the next day V[asily] I[patovich] intended to continue the journey. Thank God, it was only then that I could stop worrying.

✦

Evening

I'm pleased that I was able to get some news of you from eye-witnesses, but how come there's no letter? Could it have been that you didn't have time to write, or that you were too busy to attend to such a trifling matter? No, I'm sure that can't be the reason; probably you wrote, but put the wrong address on the envelope; you should always write to *Kamsko-Votkinsk,* Vyat[sk] Province, but don't put the "district," otherwise the letter will be placed in the *bundle* for Sarapul and will end up in the wrong post office. This is a secret I've just learned from the postmaster.

I've just seen off some guests. There was Father Vasily, the doctor, Olyshev, Semennikov, among others; later on Captain Iossa[108] arrived. He had been invited to inspect the factory by Anosov,[109] manager of the Artinsk factory,[110] who's wife's maiden name is Ivanova. He brought me greetings from everyone except Shiroshkin,[111] and mentioned that he was well and that he had recently seen him. I'm really surprised at such behavior. Ask Pyotr Ivan[ovich] if he has been paid back.

I have been following you, my Angel, my cherub, my cherished treasure, I've been following you like your shadow. Today you went to see Zina at the institute. Oh yes, Al[eksandr] Ipatovich has told me that the Penns[112] have been writing to say that Zinochka is in the infirmary. Although this news is not too pleasant, I hope to God that this recurrence is not serious. Anyway, please don't try to keep anything from me, and tell me in what state of health you found her. If you had in fact found her in the infirmary when she saw you and Kolya, she must have gotten better on the spot. You spent a little more than two hours at the institute, and from there you went with Mommy and Lisa to see Karl Fedorovich[113] and had dinner there, and perhaps you spent some time with uncle Nik[olay] Mikh[ailovich].[114] You should turn to him frequently for advice. After dinner, if there was any theatre going on, you went there—for practically the first time. Kolya was surprised and delighted by it all.

✦

28 August. Monday evening.
The children are well. With Polenka the scratching is still continuing, and that's why he's sometimes restless at night. The doctor is treating him, and we're watching him very closely. He's gotten used to the oat gruel and is quite willing to eat it. Petya and Sasha are always playing together and constantly bickering; of course, it's Sasha who gets the better of it and hurts his feelings. I'm always having to get them to kiss and make up. Both of the combatants are very sweet. Today the factory received a visit from some councillor of state. His name was something like Mi . . . di, but I can't remember it. He had asked for a carriage in order to come and see me at the factory. He is the official in charge of all the land surveyors in Perm and the province of Vyatsk. I saw him in the morning, but didn't invite him to dinner. Sasha and Petya have composed a song, "Our Mother Is in St. Petersburg,"[115] and Sasha has just run in to ask me to let her write a letter to you.

✦

29 August. Tuesday morning.
Today all the Votkinsk people went to Galevo[116] in spite of the gloomy weather. I'll soon have to seal this letter. This will now be the fourth you'll be receiving around the twelfth of September. I'm praying to God for Him to preserve your health which is so precious to me, and also for Zina and Kolya; please bless them for me and give them a big kiss. Kiss Mummy's hand, and give my kisses to Liza as well as

Vas[ily] Andreevich and the children. And give my greetings to Pyotr Ivanovich, Aleksandr Bogdanovich, and Nikolai Ivanovich Krasnov, tell him that I consider him a true friend, and no backbiter. And my respects to each and every one of my friends and relatives.

Your faithful friend
I[lya] T[chaikovsky]
Father Vasily sends his respects.

✦

Dear Aunty,[117]

I surely hope you haven't forgotten us! You've no idea how long we've been waiting to hear from you—if only one line. We felt sure there would be something for us in this post, but once again there was nothing, and you can't imagine how much we, poor things, have been missing you. The children are well. Petya and Sasha are playing right now. Polya has just been having his tea, and he has been the focus of the care and attention of all of us, and we've been doing everything the doctor has advised. Please convey my warmest respects to Amalia Grigorievna[118] and Lizaveta Andreevna, my Aunty, my Angel, please forgive me, I adore you.

A thousand kisses
N. Popova.
Kiss dear Zinochka and Kolechka for me.
Nadezhda Timofeevna is looking after Polenka right now; she sends you her warmest regards.

✦✦✦

14. ILYA PETROVICH TCHAIKOVSKY TO ALEKSANDRA ANDREEVNA TCHAIKOVSKAYA

[Votkinsk Factory,] *30 August 1844, Wednesday,*
St. Aleksandr's day, noon

Today is a holiday, I meant to go to church but I had such a bad toothache that I absolutely had to refuse invitations to two name-days, but to avoid giving offense, I persuaded Nadezhda Tim[ofeevna] to go to Al[eksandr] Pav[lovich]'s[119] party, and Nastenka to Al[eksandr] I[patovich]'s[120] party in my stead, but said that they should spell each other. I, however, have settled down to chat with you, my priceless friend, and I'm sure I'm having a better time than those who prefer to go and eat birthday cake. I wonder where you are right now, my dear? Probably running around visiting people and shopping; you must be very busy. But I'm sure that wherever you may happen to be, and whatever you may be doing, you never stop thinking about me and the children, in just the same way that we, and especially I, are following closely in our thoughts every step you take, and whatever you happen to be doing at any given moment. I'm praying to God for only one thing, that He keep you in good health as well as dear Kolya, who is not yet familiar with the St. Petersburg climate. The Penns have written to tell Katya Semennikova[121] that Zinochka was in the infirmary because of a pain in her cheek. It was probably a gumboil, or something of the kind. If so, I'm not too worried for the moment. God is merciful, and it will pass. The children have just asked me if they can go out for a ride; it's a fine day, and I was only too happy to agree. In fact, instead of going visiting, I have a mind to join them for a ride, only to some place where no one will see me. I've come back from the ride. Al[eksandr] Ip[atovich] has just been here and I gave him a hundred rubles.

◆

Evening.
Polenka isn't yet allowed to go out. I've just been playing horses and dogs with him, which he likes and calls "Am-Am." We're feeding him strong broth, sago, blancmange; everything that won't bring back the diarrhea. From time to time we're giving Petya and Sasha children's powder, which, as you know, they never refuse, to make sure that their stomachs are always clean. At 5 o'clock, that is, only two hours later, they were out riding again on the long droshky, and I rode beside them on horseback.

The weather is wonderful, better than I've ever known it in May, the pond is as smooth as a mirror, although there's not much water in it: that's an important factor in the running of the factory. And, by the way, on the business side, everything is going well for me. Olyshev is making an effort. Sonechka is still sick and is in bed. The general's wife is expected. The doctor was here visiting from 7 to 9 p.m., well past my bedtime. My teeth aren't hurting as much now after all the exercise I've taken on horseback. The reason he wanted to spend so long here with me was that, like me, he didn't feel like going to his friend's name-day party. We talked and talked about pretty well everything until we'd had our fill of talking; the children had already gone to bed, and supper was ready. Nad[ezhda] Tim[ofeevna] and Nastenka are at home and opposite, beyond the pond, all the windows are brightly lit.

✦

31 August. Thursday evening.

After dinner I had just lain down to rest for a while, when in walked Nad[ezhda] Tim[ofeevna] and announced that someone looking like an official courier had come with a letter for me from you and wants to deliver it in person. It was as if a bolt of electricity had run down my spine from head to toe, as if I were hearing a chord of sweet music. I ran out in a hurry, and sure enough the courier handed me a huge envelope addressed in the hand of Vas[ily] [Ip]atovich, and announced: "the lady told me to convey her greetings." I opened it and your dear little hand flashed before my eyes, a letter *from you* with accounts, calculations, and documents of various kinds! Of course, before reading it, I pressed it to my lips. Then I called everyone in and put on my glasses, and read it aloud. Thank God! You and Kolya are well. On the 15th you were both in Nizhny, so I was quite right when I figured that you must have arrived in St. Petersburg on the 23rd or 24th. Thank you, my busy little thing, for running all these errands. I'm pleased with everything you've done. It's just a pity that you didn't buy any mirrors. A mirror is a domestic asset. I would dearly love to have even just a pair—it would decorate the rooms so nicely. I wouldn't be bothered by the price; something good cannot be bought cheaply. To send for things from St. Petersburg is bit far, but still, I'll leave it to you to think about it in St. Petersburg, Moscow, or Kazan, if you happen to find yourself there on your way back. In any case, I'm not put out, and don't intend to be; I accept your accounts as my own, and whatever you do will be fine with me, and whatever pleases you also pleases me. I'm very pleased with you for saving money on the purchase of supplies. Of course, I like to live high on the hog, but for that you need money, and I'm not a rich man. The supplies will arrive towards the end of September, but I don't intend to open anything before you arrive, and in that way the royal sardines will be in perfect condition by then. As for the gas lamp, and anything else of that kind, please buy them in St. Petersburg. And please make a point of replacing that hard chair on which I'm sitting right now, which, I have to say, is hurting my backside. We are so happy to have received your letter that it's been decided to celebrate. We've sent for coffee and have each drunk a cup to your health and toasted you. Then I've given orders to prepare the long droshky and to saddle the horses for riding, and off we go to the factory. We can hardly restrain ourselves from cheering out loud, but we're afraid of scaring people. The weather is just as great as yesterday. The general's wife has arrived. Before leaving for the office, I went to see her. Sonechka was up on her feet when I saw her, but she was very pale. Her problem is that she's highly strung.

. . . but the young people are insensitive unlike myself . . . you remember? At tea time—6 o'clock—the general's wife called on us, that is to say myself, Nad[ezhda] Tim[ofeevna], and Nastenka, and joined us for tea. The doctor has gone to Nizhevka; tomorrow I'll give him your regards, and please try to see his Nikolasha, and write and tell me how you found him. I talked about governesses with the general's wife. I hope to God that you manage to find one who's suitable. If you're having trouble finding one by yourself, then please go to *Aleksandr Grigorievich Obodovsky*,[122] the inspector of the Foundling Home. He runs the school where governesses are trained.[123] Consult him. He is intelligent, affable, and a gentleman. His wife is called *Aleksandra Dimitrievna*. Please convey my respects to her. I would be very pleased if you could visit the Shatelens,[124] but to save yourself the trouble of searching for them, I suggest that you send one of your people to the Gostiny Dvor. Once inside, he should enter by the gate from the Nevsky Prospekt and find the shop or warehouse of the Kaidanov (formerly Olkhin) paper mill and ask someone, or better still send a note as follows: "Al[eksandra] And[reeevna] Tchaikovskaya is anxious to see Aleksandr Karlovich Shatelen in the Ordonansgauz in El[izaveta] And[reevna] Shobert's apartment." He will appear as soon as he gets this message. Convey to him my affectionate greetings and tell him that I still love him and Anna Karlovna as much as ever. Through Shatelen you may be able to see Kaminsky.

At eight o'clock this evening we received a visit from Semenov and his wife and daughter along with one of the engineers—Captain Baron Klodt, an extremely cultivated gentleman who plays the piano and sings very well. The general's wife wants to get Sonechka[125] to sing a duet with him, but Olyshev won't hear of it because she is still unwell and weak. Tomorrow they are going to have a dinner party, and have borrowed my cook, Ivan—I am very much relieved that the event doesn't entail any invitations. The children are well.

✦

1 September. Friday morning.
Today I had the following visitors: Semenov, Baron Klodt, and Sagon. I offered them a cup of coffee and a pipe, and just after they had left Semenov's wife arrived; I left for the office, and went from there to the factory. When I returned home I found Liz[aveta] Avg[ustovna] waiting, and conveyed your respects. I would be very pleased to learn that you had found some travel companions on your return journey. I would also urge you to return by way of Vologda and Ledengsk and call on your sister Kat[erina] [Andr]eevna. In this way you will have done all the things you wanted to, and then, my dear, you will no longer have to spend so much time cooling your heels on the Votka. If you happen to see Tikhmenov in St. Petersburg, please tell him to ask Glinka[126] about being appointed to the post of district police officer at the Votkinsk factory, that is if he's tired of living in St. Petersburg. I'll be happy to agree to that. Please convey my respects to them.

If you should tire of St. Petersburg any time soon and want to come home, then halfway through the month I'll start preparing the rooms, which I haven't yet been able to do anything about because the painters at Iv[an] Af[anasievich] are still at work in the church.

✦

Evening.
The doctor came and spent an hour or so with me and then left for Olyshev's. Olyshev showed up a little later to report, and asked permission to set off a small firework from the big boat for the benefit of the general's wife. He then hurried home where he had guests waiting. I didn't go there, first because no one was formally invited

except the guests, and second because I had promised not to go out anywhere until you returned. When you're away, I don't enjoy being anywhere except here at home with the children around me. I've only just begun to realize that my attachment to you, or rather my love for you, is boundless, and that my life is so closely interwoven with yours that I cannot live without you, and that when I let you go I am making a sacrifice, my only consolation being that I have done something to please you, although by so doing I have deprived myself of the keenest pleasure of my life; and although it may be only for a short time, it seems long to me, unbearably long. For all this, however, I do urge you not to be put out by my missing you—there's no need. I'll pull through somehow, and I want you to do all the important things you set out to do on your trip: bring back a governess for the children, and also Zina; breathe the air of your birthplace, see your nearest and dearest, enjoy the pleasures of socializing as much as possible, kit yourself out with dresses and all the accessories—and then be on your way. Don't forget to apply for a permit for three horses for the journey to Kazan or to Vyatka. Although you have written that I should expect you at the beginning of October, I think, and rightly so, that you will stay there the whole of September, and set out at the beginning of October. I will be happy to agree to that. In any case, please make sure to decide on a definite date for your departure and calculate as precisely as possible when and where you will be on the various stages of your journey, and in particular let me know the day of your arrival in Kazan or Vyatka where I am supposed to meet you.

The children are well. Petya and Sasha have spent the whole day larking about outside; Polya has stayed indoors, he has gotten used to it now and no longer asks for "giddy up." Although the diarrhea has gone away, from time to time it's apparent that he is going more often than usual. We're keeping a close watch on him and giving the diarrhea no chance to make a comeback. The little one is growing more and more attached to me, that's why I never leave him, although I do my best to see to it that he spends more time with Augusta. Now he's getting more comfortable with her, and sometimes won't be parted from her. Nad[ezhda] Tim[ofeevna] and Nastenka always stay close to him.

✦

2 September. Saturday evening.

Sasha just ran up to me and insisted on writing to you. You will see that her handwriting has improved, and she no longer holds the paper the wrong way round, but follows the instructions of her teacher, Petya, and writes straight. You must now be sitting at Zina's, or rather at Aleksandra Ivanovna's, where she goes for piano lessons, while Kolya is sitting nearby listening with his mouth wide open. I think, or at least I hope, that Zinochka will have learned something in three years, particularly because that's something I want to see. Your encouragement means a lot, and if she plays poorly now, out of her love for you she will have improved in the last two years, and will be playing well. Whether she can sing, you'll have to see and decide for yourself. As to who should teach her the piano and singing, well. It's not for me to say, it's for you to decide. If you're satisfied with her playing, give her a kiss from yourself and a bigger one for me. You can buck her up by telling her that in January 1847, when she graduates, we'll all come out to see her, and then she'll see all her brothers and her sister; she should just pray to God that they will all be in good health, and tell her to look after herself too. She has grown into a high-spirited girl, a real little *Undine*[127]—there's no other name for her. Petya has grown up too; he's a nice boy. What nice hats Yukhaev has sent them, soft, gray, downy ones, trimmed with blue velvet and pink feathers. I'm absolutely delighted with them. The only pity is that they're on the small side. Kolya's hat barely fits Petya. Sasha has appropriated Petya's, and Polya doesn't like his, and refuses to wear it. Beautiful weather today too.

Before dinner the children went out for ride in my droshky, and after dinner we went for our usual ride; the children in the long droshky and I on horseback. The carriages have all been fixed and now look very nice. I'm also thinking of giving the coach a new coat of paint. Because the bathroom is being renovated, Sasha and Petya are not being bathed, but the big samovar has just been used to give Polya a bath, and all the necessary precautions were taken.

Badaeva[128] has left for the Kushva.[129] Her granddaughter is suffering from diarrhea, and it's such a bad case that she has already developed symptoms of dropsy, and her life is in danger.

Vaska is in perfect health, as are all the other members of the household.

✦

3 September. Sunday morning.

After getting out of bed and getting washed and dressed, I was just sitting down at the table for tea when they brought in the post with your precious letter, my darling! Your letter from Moscow! My pleasure, my delight is so powerful that I'm sure you can feel it from where you are!

You write in great detail, holding nothing back. My divine angel, I'm so sorry that your long journey is so tedious, and that you have been so totally neglected by the person who is supposed to be looking after you. He's going to be in big trouble if he dares to let you travel from Moscow with only one team of horses; I won't just curse him, he'll feel the back of my hand. What a grasping, self-seeking low-life! But more about that later. I'm surprised you could be so naive as to be polite and civil to him; you should be simply telling him "I want to leave now" and without mincing words, and replace that coachman with another one who will make you feel at ease and will look after you. I'll write to him right away tomorrow and insist that he send Pyotr Korobeinikov[130] to accompany you on your return journey. I'll also write to An[drey] Khr[istianovich] von Ziegel.[131] My dear, don't be the shrinking violet that you present to the world. When you're travelling on a major highway and armed with an order for fresh teams of horses, you have nothing to fear unless the station supervisors try to hold you up because of the horses, in which case, I advise you to contact Nikolay Ivanovich Kriskov and ask him to obtain a voucher for you from the Post Road department. Then the station master will do what you ask, and you will encounter no difficulties at any staging post. If you should encounter the slightest unpleasantness, put the station master in his place and make a note of the name of the station. You can be sure that with all these precautions, your journey will be as smooth as possible; just make sure to pay the tolls in full at each staging post, and remember to tip the coachmen. Andrey Khristianovich will probably be making a side trip to his birthplace, but that shouldn't bother *you.* You can obtain a new voucher for post horses very easily, simply by sending in an application to the district treasury together with the money, and once you are in St. Petersburg, Nikolay Ivanovich[132] will get you your voucher for fresh horses. Judging by the way you feel now, I think that you won't really be needing to spend much time in St. Petersburg, but I won't put any pressure on you, my Angel, and you can feel free to do as you wish. I just have one request: don't forget the main purposes of your trip.

Today everyone has gathered for a picnic at the Otrada.[133] They will be feasting on more than thirty pounds of fresh sturgeon. I didn't go. The only people dining with us were Sofia Ivanovna and her husband.[134] After dinner we went for a ride to the factory. Sofia is still sick, the poor thing, and came to our place without telling her doctor, who didn't go to the Otrada either. We spent a pleasant evening at home and we talked about you; you were no doubt at the theater.

✦

Monday morning, 4 September.
Polenka didn't sleep very well last night. He had a tummy ache, but don't worry, he'll get over it. It's too bad that our little boy is so delicate; there's always something or other wrong with him. The doctor seems to think that he is more scrofulous than other children. Let's hope he gets it out of his system in his infancy, instead of growing up with it. He's feeling better now and is sitting in Nastenka's lap and playing. Petya and Sasha, touch wood! are growing and filling out. They've just clambered up to me on the table and are playing with the sand. Lidenka is taking a lesson, Pushin comes to tutor her every day, but is not too satisfied with the results—she has been reprimanded for that in the past. Nad[ezhda] Tim[ofeevna] is not feeling well.

Goodbye. I'm on my way to the office; as always, I plant an imaginary kiss on your brow.

✦

Evening.
The doctor said to serve Polenka only meat, because today he was fed only hazel-grouse and broth, which apparently is fine with him, and said we could give him kvass; right now other kids are eating watermelon, but poor Polenka mustn't. And you, my delight, what are

you up to now? Spending the day going from dacha to dacha. Please take the train back to Pavlovsk,[135] or, if you're afraid, hire a carriage, take anyone you want and go there to hear Hermann's orchestra,[136] and then tell me all about it. Go to the Nobility Assembly Hall and take a look around. You should visit the Hermitage and show all the treasures to Kolya. In a word, don't miss a thing, and try to get a glimpse of all the sights. Be sure to take Kolya to see the Tsar, the Heir to the Throne, and the Imperial Family, and particularly the soldiers and the military band.

This letter will be speeding to you in St. Petersburg. It will arrive on about the 18th of September, and you're not likely to be there much after that. Nevertheless, I shall continue to write for another two weeks, and after that I'll write to you in Nizhny, and, just in case, I'll send you a brief note in Ledengsk in order to keep you up to date wherever you may be, and if my letters get to wherever it is after you've left, it's not the end of the world, even if they get lost. Now I'm thinking of writing to Romanov and von Ziegel.

✦

Tuesday morning, 5 September
Everything is fine here at home. The children and everyone here are in good health. Kiss the hands of Mommy, Lizochka, and Vasenka for me. A hug for my precious friend Nikolay Ivanovich Kriskov, and my thanks to him for being there for you. If you see the other Nikolay Ivanovich, i.e. Rozanov, give him my regards. And kisses to Petenka Evreinov, Mashenka,[137] Agrafena Alekseevna, Aleksandra Ivanovna, and my regards to everyone.
Your friend,
I[lya] T[chaikovsky]
Please put the letters I have included with this one in envelopes, address the envelopes, and mail them.

The mirrors should not be framed, I'll take care of the framing here. The measurements of the glass for each mirror should be: width, about 70 centimeters, height, about 140 centimeters, although for the height, we could make do with sections instead of a whole sheet of glass; it's a little cheaper.

✦

My dearest Aunty![138] It's been a month now since we saw you off. We've been missing you so much, please come back soon. I kiss your little hands.

Petechka and Sasha are very sweet, and always together. Almost every day Petenka mentions Kolechka. Polechka's favorite thing is catching flies with Augusta.

✦ ✦ ✦

15. ILYA PETROVICH TCHAIKOVSKY TO ALEKSANDRA ANDREEVNA TCHAIKOVSKAYA

Thursday, 13 September 1851, St. Petersburg

My dear, good genius and Angel!

Yesterday I was at the Board of Management;[139] I was the first to see Eisemont, now elderly, and insincere, but the conversation had hardly had time to get going when in walked Albrecht with his snub-nosed son. After some talk about the fine weather, I was asked whether I had read the decision of the board on the assignment to the factories of board member N. N. Manzei because of some alleged disturbances and special expenditures. However, no one was able to explain to me what these disturbances and expenditures were, the point being that they were dissatisfied with my management on the grounds that I have been building new factories and machines. After reading the decision, I rose from my seat, bowed, and said that there was no point in my making a long speech or arguing my case, and that obviously I must tender my resignation from my post, and with these parting words I was leaving the room, but I turned back and asked them what they intended to do about the mechanical engineer whom I had brought with me in order to look out for better machinery around here or on our way here. Albrecht promised to send him back, but on the very next day he called him in and sent him to his own village to build a sawmill to saw planks without water and without wood; I believe that's known as trying to get blood from a stone.

So my friend, *l'homme propose et Dieu dispose* [Man proposes and God disposes]. Although I was out for a definite "yes" or "no," I never expected such stupidity and such barefaced duplicity from Albrecht and the other owners whom he had managed to recruit as accomplices in his foul play. As I was taking my leave, he asked me whether the money for the Nevyansk factories had been recovered from me to be given to Myagkov.

"No, what money is it that you would be wanting from me?"

"It's the salary you have received."

"Surely you're not expecting me to have worked for you without pay?"

"No, you have already received your pay."

"I'm sorry, but you haven't assigned me any salary, all I've received is my travel allowance."

"What do you mean?"

"Precisely that, and what you're asking me for is ridiculous. I have been the one running the Nevyansk factories for the last couple of months, not Myagkov."

"We never made it official with the proper documentation."

"Yes, but you told me to replace Lebedev and Bogatyrev[140] on orders from the ministry. I acted as instructed and took charge myself until the arrival of Moskvin,[141] as I duly informed you."

"Very well, I'll return the money to you, but only if the Court of Equity rules accordingly—and the court will rule against you."

"Maybe so, but let the court decide by all means, and I will provide the court with evidence of what you actually said and did." And here you have my very last "interesting" conversation with the unscrupulous Albrecht.

In situations like the one I have just described, you are always worried about me. I want you to set your mind at rest, just as I have done. When you receive this letter, please start to put things in order and prepare to leave Alapayev, and I will be joining you without fail at the beginning of October. It has been agreed that I have the right to leave three months from the date of my resignation, and I tendered my resignation to them today, the 13th of September, so on the 13th of December we'll leave for Yekaterinburg, or straight to St. Petersburg if you like. Don't let what has happened get you down, and don't let it upset you, and don't let your feelings show in front of Nik[olay] Nikolaevich. Kokar has not returned from Moscow yet, but the moment he does, I will wind up my affairs and leave immediately in order to get away as fast as possible from those scoundrels.

As for the business about Nikolinka,[142] I'll leave that until March when the request has to go in. Ivanov[143] has promised to do his best to help. Until then I'll just arrange to teach him Latin and Slavonic.

Yesterday, I got an exit permit for Petya for three days and took him to Markova's[144] wedding—she's marrying Zheltukhin. It was Markov himself who invited me. What great people they are! The wedding was *en grand* [French: a sumptuous affair]. There I unexpectedly met Nikolay Ivanovich Kriskov; I talked to him nonstop.

As for the tasks you've assigned to me, my dear, I'll only be able to carry out half of them at best. When you're here, you will know better than me what to buy and what to do.

Today, I'm taking Kolya from school, tomorrow is a holiday (Holy Cross day), and we'll be spending this evening at home. Petechka is sleeping with me. Liza[145] came, and dined with us yesterday. On the way here she lost her handbag with all her money. She had already travelled to Zaitsev, a distance of about 112 kilometers, and had to travel back alone by post-chaise and found all her belongings intact. She started out again with Captain Sevastianov—quite an *aventure* [French: adventure]—what else can I call it? Yesterday, Lieutenant Grigoriev came to see me and told me that Boris Krivonogov had met an extremely tragic death, having struck his wife's cheek just before. I'm sorry for Nastenka because now she has to go the Votkinsk factory.

Bless you.
Your Father.[146]

✦✦✦

16. ILYA PETROVICH TCHAIKOVSKY TO ALEKSANDRA ANDREEVNA TCHAIKOVSKAYA

21 September 1851, St. P[eters]burg

On Sunday, 23 September, after taking the children back to their schools, I'll be coming to you, my friend, my Angel, my own dear wife! I didn't manage to do anything about Nikolinka; that business will have to wait until I get back.

Entre nous soit dit [French: Just between the two of us]: I've finished with Kok[ar], he'll be living in Tsarskoye, but his reward, or rather his pay, hasn't yet been determined. However, no matter how little it may be, let's hope it will be enough for him to live on. I was offered the

Orenburg pro[vince], exactly the same kind of place as Kharitonov's, but because it's all so new, I can't make up my mind . . . The children are in good health. I promised to be in St. Petersburg by Christmas so as to start work in January. Incidentally, it's not entirely certain whether it will be Tsarskoe Selo or another town since, although that was the idea, it might be changed, so it's better to keep quiet. We will be living in Tsarskoe, and I'll look for an apartment there.

I'll fill in the details when I see you. If I leave on the 23rd and travel without stopping, I should arrive home around the 16th of September. I'll stop over in Moscow for five hours, but nowhere else. Petya has been with me since I first arrived; good old Berard[147] released him until my departure. Yesterday, Kolya, Alyosha, Liza, and Pav[el] Nikol[aevich] came to dinner with me. Goodbye. We'll see who gets there first—this letter or me.

Bless you all.
Your Father

Fanny Dürbach; place and date unknown

2　Letters by Fanny Dürbach to Pyotr Ilyich Tchaikovsky and His Brothers

FANNY DÜRBACH (1822–1901) was born in Montbéliard, an old French town with a complex history of religious clashes between Protestants and Catholics. The Dürbachs were Lutherans, but Fanny's closeness to both French and German culture served as a natural foundation for her upbringing and subsequently for her teaching. Like so many foreigners, including Tchaikovsky's maternal grandfather, she came to Russia to find employment. As it happened, her godmother in Montbéliard was related to Aleksandra Tchaikovskaya's stepmother in St. Petersburg, and that is how the paths of Fanny and Aleksandra crossed in 1844 when the future composer's mother visited her relatives in the Russian capital.

Fanny Dürbach became a governess for the Tchaikovsky children and lived with the family for the next four years in Votkinsk. In nineteenth-century Russia, the lot of a governess was the same as it was in the rest of Europe. But, in the social hierarchy of the Russian Empire, this customarily ambiguous position between masters and servants was marked by greater equality with those "upstairs," because the people "downstairs" were serfs. In addition to this general factor, Fanny found herself in a very favorable environment: Tchaikovsky family dynamics were built on feelings of love and affection. As she described many years later, "the genuine and patriarchal character of their relationships put me immediately at ease and made me feel as if I were almost a member of the family."[1] The youngest member of her new Russian family was little Pyotr Tchaikovsky, whom she called Pierre, and Mademoiselle Fanny became his special friend, teacher, and mentor.

When the Votkinsk period in the early life of the composer came to its end in 1848, so did his studies with Fanny Dürbach. But the deep-rooted connection between the governess and her pupil cast a lifelong spell on both of them and was reaffirmed by their final reunion at the very end of Tchaikovsky's life.

♦ ♦ ♦

THE LETTERS OF FANNY DÜRBACH TO
PYOTR ILYICH TCHAIKOVSKY[2]

1.

Montbéliard, 4 April 1892

Dear Pierre!

I hope you don't mind my calling you Pierre. Otherwise, I wouldn't feel that I was addressing you the way I used to when you were my dear little boy and I was your teacher. This morning my sister came up to my room with a letter in her hand and said: "Well this is something that's really going to please you!" Frankly, I had already given up hope of ever knowing the joy of seeing your handwriting again. When the pupils I have now insist that I write to you, I tell them: "I'll see him in heaven!" Since you come to France almost every year, please come soon so that I still have a chance of seeing you and talking to you about all those people whom you and I both loved so much. We'll have so much to talk about! I know enough of life to know that there will also be a lot of sadness. We'll have so many memories to share as well, some of them painful ones. You know how kind to me your dear parents were and how much I loved you all, and I hope that you will enjoy talking about them with an old friend whose life has been blessed with such sweet memories. How I long to hear about the paths the lives of all of you have taken! I often think of Nikola,[3] such a tall, handsome boy, of your sister Zina,[4] of Ippolit[5] and Lidiya.[6] Do they still have good memories of their old friend? Would you believe that I still have the little pieces you wrote all those years ago?[7] I have kept what you used to call your "fun" exercise books. You used to write in them in the breaks between your lessons. I've also kept the things that Venya wrote.[8] Do come; we have so much to talk about! The pupils whom I have now, or rather the ones I used to have, know you from your music; some of them are great admirers of it. Oh, if only you would come, you won't feel like a stranger in our town, but if you prefer peace and quiet, there is a hotel here with a garden, and the owners are very nice and decent people, and will make you very comfortable. In Russia hospitality is always possible, all the circumstances favor it, but it's not the same here. We live very simply and modestly in a small old house that we own, and we have a small garden and everything we need. Nevertheless, we thank you for thinking that things might be different, so thank you again. Thank you for your nice letter and for your photograph;[9] the more I look at it, the better I remember you. I myself have never had my photograph taken,[10] and anyway now a photograph wouldn't tell you very much. Don't think that I was scared by your proposal—I'm no longer in this world; I have seen so many much younger and stronger people leaving it that I often wonder how someone in such poor health as myself is still here. I was sixty-nine on the 29th of October. Your last letter, which I treasure as one of my most precious possessions and which I have read over and over again, was written in 1856[11] when you were sixteen. In it you told me of the death of your mother. Did your father live to enjoy your success?[12] And what about your dear Sashenka.[13] Did she have a happy marriage? Write and tell me about your younger brothers, but most of all I want to hear about you. Permit me to hope that I will soon be hearing from you even before we meet—something I'm so looking forward to.

Here I am writing to you so spontaneously, but when you are actually here, your presence will remind me that I should no longer be treating you as the dear beloved child that you were to me then, but will have to treat you with all the respect owed to all the honors that your fame has brought you; for now, I'll just give you a big kiss and pray God that he will bless you and grant you happiness.

Your old teacher and friend, Fanny Dürbach.

My sister[14] asks me to convey to you her deepest respects. Do you remember how hard you worked for a whole week in order to be awarded the red ribbon on Sunday? Now you can wear it every day, but I wonder if it will give you as much satisfaction now.

I hope so from the bottom of my heart!

♦ ♦ ♦

2.

Montbéliard, 26 April 1892

My dear Pierre!

How thankful I am that you didn't keep me waiting for a reply. I was very much afraid that after so many years of separation you would find me too different a person from the one you imagined me to be. You, however—and I'm happy that I've found you again—have stayed just the same. Dear Pierre, I don't want you to think that you alone are to blame for our lost contact; it's really I who am at fault. In your last letter you gave your address only in French, and I was worried that my letter wouldn't reach you by post, so I gave it to a professor of French who intended to stop in St. Petersburg on his way back to Moscow, and promised to deliver it to you. Since then the only news about you has come to me indirectly. Of course, several years later your ever increasing fame took care of that, and also my pupils kept me informed of your success. I should have written to you then, but I didn't know if you were still that child I loved so much—my dear little poet. I decided it was safer to just to live with my memories than to take the risk. I can only thank God for enabling me to love you just the way I have always done. How distressed I was to hear of the death of your dear sister Sashenka—if it's not too painful, please tell me some of the circumstances. Do you remember the wonderful dreams you had about the future when Venichka said he would become a naval officer like his father? Is that how he ended his life? The poor child! God rest his soul! Please tell me about Lidiya (I don't like people who are always asking questions, but I suppose I'm one of them). Is there really no hope of a cure for her? How sorry I am for those who love her! Tell Nikola and Ippolit how pleased I am that they—and you especially—are all in good health, and that you want to come here. The time you mentioned is a particularly good time for a visit to our city. The days are still long, and you can take long walks or go for long rides in the surrounding areas, which I think are very beautiful. But I don't want to be selfish about this, so if you can't come at that time, you can rest assured that we will always welcome a visit from you at any time. I don't like to think that you're taking on too much work, but, happily, you are in good health. Why don't you say a single word about the kind of work you're doing?

Maybe you think I won't understand it? That really doesn't matter, so please tell me something about it anyway. And that nice Sestritsa[15] of yours, she is one of the most devoted persons I have ever known. I am convinced that she has had the good fortune to have been a sincere and devoted friend to you all in good times and bad. Please tell her that Fannichka still has the fondest memories of her. I can't forget Votkinsk, and think of it often when I remember your sister Olkhovskaya, her family, and the rest of you. I'm sorry for pestering you with so many questions and wishes, but won't you write me a few lines about Nikola? If Anastasiya[16] would like to write to me, my sister would translate the letter for me, although with every passing day, to her great regret, she forgets a little more of her Russian.

Goodbye for now, dear Pierre, I can't wait for your visit. How much we have to tell each other. Surely you won't leave me without news until then?

May God keep you in good health and happiness; this is the sincere wish of your

Fanny Dürbach.

✦ ✦ ✦

3.

Montbéliard, 26 May 1892

Dear Pierre!

I'm sure that you are not one of those people who forget, but still, I blame myself for opening up old wounds.[17] Please forgive me and have no doubt of my deepest sympathy for you in the loss of all those family members whom you mourn. The further we advance in our lives, the greater the number of our nearest and dearest in heaven, while here on earth the smaller the number of those whom we loved while they were here, and who preceded us in our true homeland. Since we'll soon be seeing each other, I won't be asking you any more questions about anything. So just write whatever you feel like and whatever occurs to you. Although you write in French with the greatest ease and your French is perfectly idiomatic without a trace of anything foreign, I wouldn't like to feel that our old friendship is causing you nothing but distress. It's often much easier to speak than to write, especially when one is overburdened with work. Here at least you will be able to rest. Have you ever lived in a small town?

Votkinsk wasn't really a town, but something quite different. You will see, and if you like, you might enjoy observing our way of life, since my former pupils move in the best circles and some of the girls are musicians, and would all be delighted if you were to visit their families. Of course, you must do whatever you feel like, but the main thing is don't tie yourself down. The organist at the local church we attend is also a good friend of mine, and if you feel like playing the organ, it would be easy to arrange, since I have the key to the church, which is also used as the Sunday school.[18] What I am trying to say is that you won't be bored here. Yesterday, May the 26th, Ascension Day, the weather was beautiful, a splendid day for a holiday. I think that this year your Easter falls on the same day as ours, and I thought that perhaps you were enjoying the same fine weather. In the morning we went to church and before the sermon the choir sang, and everyone found the music beautiful. In the afternoon I re-read the letters from your dear sister Olkhovskaya;[19] they are so friendly and affectionate. Dear Zina, how soon she completed her journey in this world.[20] In one of her letters, Lidiya writes that she dreamed about me the whole night long (I had written to tell her that I was leaving Russia). Please tell her that she is in my thoughts and send her a big kiss. I'm very happy that you all love her. I thought that your poor Sestritsa was not leaving you after Alapayevsk. How kind of your sister Sashenka to give her a home in her sad old age. My dear Mr. Tchaikovsky, why do you make yourself out to be old. When I was living in your house your father's hair had turned completely gray, but he was still not old. In 1856 you told me: "Papa has not aged at all." So please don't try to make yourself appear old; leave this privilege to those who have earned it by years and experience. As I look forward to my meeting with the eminent Mr. Tchaikovsky, I kiss my dear little Pierre whom I love and will always love with all my heart.

Fanny Dürbach.

In a letter from Votkinsk, Mrs. Carr wrote: "I read all Pierre's inscriptions on the walls of Otrada.[21] Nothing could be more beautiful than M [indecipherable] it was a really charming place"; do you still remember it?

✦

3 June.

My letter should already have been sent, but I'm afraid I am writing to you too often. So please don't feel duty bound to answer my letters when you are unable to. I am quite free now, since I only teach two hours a day—it would be too depressing to give up teaching entirely. So I have the rest of the time to myself and for that reason I never have to fall behind in my correspondence—but this does not apply to you.

Goodbye for now.

Adele, my childhood friend, her daughter, and husband are all dead. The only ones left are the son, the grandson, and the son-in-law, and the eighty-year-old aunt.

✦ ✦ ✦

4.

Montbéliard, 13–19 July 1892[22]

Dear Pierre,

When I saw the word "Vichy" at the top of the page of your letter of the 7th of this month, you can't imagine how happy that made me; you were so near to us and would soon be coming to Montbéliard. Even though I was holding your long letter in my hands, my happiness was so great that I couldn't read it. But even before reaching the end of the first page I saw that all my hopes were dashed, and I was overwhelmed by such a powerful feeling of disappointment that it still weighs me down, although I know very well that everything that happens to us in life is ordained by God. I'm also aware that you were only doing what you had to do. You were kind and considerate to your ailing sister-in-law,[23] and it gave you great satisfaction. Now I am following your travels in my mind and praying to God that they come to a successful conclusion. It was so hot when you started out, but they say that the waters at Vichy have a very laxative effect in the beginning. Perhaps you will find it possible to write me a little something when you arrive. I understand that your brother has been appointed to a very important position,[24] although a very demanding one; let's hope that the administration treats him with the proper consideration, then your brother will have no trouble producing his report. I'm sure you are very fond of your younger brother? This is what you wrote to me in 1850 from Alapayevsk: "Here is some news which will cheer you up a little (I was far from cheerful at the time): on the night of the 1st of May my two twin brothers were born. I've seen them several times now, and every time I set eyes on them I see two angels sent from heaven." I would so much like to know your little favorite. Does he look exactly like his dear mother? Tell me something about him and how old he is. I hope your brother-in-law[25] would enjoy keeping you there with him in the country—why do you want to work so hard when everyone else is enjoying their summer holidays? Of course, your compositions must bring you so much happiness because they give so much pleasure to others, but I fear that it means that you are seriously overworked. I understand that you have also been taking the cure at Vichy in addition? Was there any need for this? And where have you been going for recreation? I'm sure you must have asked Nikola to write to me, since I have received a very affectionate letter from him which gave me so much pleasure, and I answered it at once. It was dated 1/13 June.

My sister intends to spend two weeks in Mondorf in Switzerland. It's a beautiful village on the shores of Lake Zurich, but since the 12th of July it's been raining all the time—fortunately for us, because our gardens are parched, the streams have dried up and the surrounding rivers are depleted. I was pleased to read in the newspaper *Tempo* that many parts of Prussia are expecting a good harvest—please God.

Goodbye for now, my dear Pierre. Until now, I had never truly realized how quickly time passes; this time I don't want to celebrate prematurely, and will wait patiently, while asking that you maintain something of the old friendship of your devoted teacher who kisses her little Pierre, but looks forward to greeting the famous man he has now become.

Yours, Fanny Dürbach.

✦ ✦ ✦

5.

Montbéliard, 9 August 1892

My dear Pierre,

Your letter was a nice surprise for me since I wasn't yet expecting to hear from you, and I was anxious to know if you arrived safely. Thanks also for the news about yourself. I hope the cure at Vichy has been good for your health, and also that of your nephew;[26] but I can't help thinking that you should really rest a while longer. I would imagine that this is what your doctors should have been recommending. I know very well what it is to be overstressed and I hope that you won't be working while you're here. We will have plenty to talk about. You will tell me everything that's on your mind, and we'll talk about all those people we love. This will all make me so happy—I only hope that this goes for you too, if only a little. I must tell you that now I'm actually pleased that you couldn't come to visit me after Vichy, because the joy it would have given me would now be behind me, and, as it is, I can now look forward to it. But please tell me why you thought that I wouldn't agree with you! My little Pierre always trusted me and I trusted him, and still do: now we need to learn to understand each other again. You also told me about your sister-in-law's arrival. Your brother Modest must be a very good and devoted person to have undertaken to raise a deaf and dumb child.[27] I believe that being a teacher is the noblest of callings (especially for a woman), and I understand all the difficulties involved. I can well imagine how much self-sacrifice is called for when you're trying to teach and bond with a deaf and dumb child. You will be telling me a lot about your brother who has already earned my deepest respect. When you come, bring some photographs to show me: I would so much like to see you all, but above all, please don't forget Paul and poor Lidiya whom I think of so often, and also her son, Nikola. So get hold of photographs of all of them. They won't take up much room. There is a Russian young lady who is spending her summer holidays in one of the small villages around here, and she is addressing all the envelopes for my letters since my sister is not here. She came here with a French lady who gives French lessons and another lady from Switzerland. She promised to come again, but I still haven't seen her. My sister had a wonderful trip and the weather was splendid. She tells me she is coming back next Thursday. I'm a little surprised that she still likes traveling; as far as I'm concerned, nothing short of absolute necessity would get me traveling.

I often suffer from insomnia (although no one could tell it from looking at me). I'd better give you the address of the hotel in case I forget next time: M. Rahn, Hotel de la Balance, rue Belfort. Our address is 28 rue de Grange. My letter has been delayed for reasons beyond my control, but I hope it finds you in good health and free from stomach complaints, something which can lay low even the bravest of us. You promised me a long letter, and I would venture to remind you of this promise, and want you to know that I am always fondling little Pierre in my mind and coming to love the grown-up Pierre more and more every day.

Your old teacher and friend.
Fanny Dürbach.

✦ ✦ ✦

6.

Montbéliard, 1/13 January 1893

Dear Pierre,

You made January the 1st such a happy day for me,[28] but I can't even send you my best wishes for the New Year because I don't know where you are at a time when it's so cold in these parts. Was your concert a success? I'm sure it was, but I would like to hear about it from you yourself. The time we spent together went by so quickly. There was so much more that I wanted to hear from you. How little you spoke about yourself, about your work, about your life in Klin and St. Petersburg.

✦

27 February.
I wanted to tell you right away that I received your dear photographs yesterday morning, Sunday.[29] I'm particularly grateful to you because I don't think that I could have brought myself to entrust them to the post, and I hope to have an opportunity to return them to you in person, or at least to some member of your family. All the pictures taken in 1848 or 1849 are engraved on my heart, but in any case I am

happy to see you all together in a group photograph, and little Polá, as Sashenka used to call him, nestling so snugly against his father's chest where all of you had once snuggled in your turn.[30] Emilia Kun,[31] who has just left, is certain she recognizes you in the photograph. I love the way you are posing; it reminds me of my dear Pierre as you were then. Your mother is the most recognizable of all. The best photograph is of your sister Sasha. Mrs. Grossman [the mother] told me what a beauty she was considered in St. Petersburg. In the 1881 picture, Nikola and Ippolit look very alike. It's a pity you're not with them in the picture.[32] It looks as if Polá is protecting his dear sister just the way she was protecting him when he was little. I love the faces of your younger brothers. Anatoly looks like Nikola when he was young. It would be so kind of you—and Nikola—to think of making me the gift of an album containing photographs of you all. You need bring me only the photographs because I have a big album with plenty of room left in it. It's a great satisfaction to know that you are now in your very own favorite retreat. If you could—and would—only take refuge there from all your worries. It would appear that you place no value on the excellent health granted you by God because you don't seem to worry about losing it by over-taxing yourself. If only you knew how impatiently I am waiting for a chance to see your handwriting. At your age time passes swiftly, but at mine it's the opposite. Recently it's been very cold here, and where we live we are not very good at protecting ourselves against the severe winter cold, and I've been afraid for you. I was happy to hear of your triumph in Brussels.[33] No one has been more convinced than I have of your talent because I saw it developing in you as you grew, although I saw you more as a poet (which I would have preferred). Nevertheless, I bless God for your success, and believe that He granted it to you to make up for all those famous people who were never recognized in their own lifetime.

I have received some letters from poor Jenny Grossman expressing her despair; first there was her father's illness, and then his death a few days later. Before that, the poor girl had known nothing but enjoyment in her life. She told me about your latest opera with great delight.[34] She was in raptures over Sarah Bernhardt, but now what kind of life will it be for her and her mother? I think Rudolph was in government service, but I don't know in which department, or whether he was entitled to any kind of pension at his age. I believe he was only forty-two. I feel particularly sorry for his poor father. He is still alive and lived through his son's last moments. The poor young man made his last wishes known to his family and received the last sacraments. On the only Sunday he spent here, he wanted to go to church. I have been corresponding with his mother for many years, and this death deeply distressed me and everyone who knew Mrs. Grossman and her daughter during the short time that they spent in this town.

My sister was very pleased to hear that you were in Kharkov.[35] She lived there for a long time and still has good memories of it. She sends you her friendly greetings, to which I also add my own, and your older friend sends you a kiss from deep in her heart—like the old days in Votkinsk.

Goodbye for now
Fanny Dürbach

Mr. Duvernois has written a very interesting book about our old Montbéliard. It was a present to me from my pupils; when you come here you might like to look at the portraits of the princes and engravings with which it is illustrated. Mrs. Ellen plays your music, she finds it very difficult.

Goodbye for now.

✦✦✦

7.

Montbéliard, 25 March 1893

My dear former pupil,

Yesterday, I received a visit from Mrs. Rahn and her aunt, an officer's wife who, after the misfortune of losing her husband and children, came to work as a companion to an elderly lady. Mrs. Jacques, the name of Mrs. Rahn's aunt, also ran the lady's household and supervised the servant. Unfortunately for her, the family of the person in whose house she had been living for two and a half years have now made different arrangements, and Mrs. Jacques has to leave. Her wish is to find similar employment with a family in Russia. She would also be willing to care for a sick lady or to work for a widower and look after his children while they are growing up, but not as a teacher, but rather as a governess who would accompany young ladies on social occasions. I had never met this lady before, but Mrs. Kun has said she comes with the highest references. She tells me that Mrs. Jacques is a delightful person in every respect. She has a pleasant appearance and has clearly moved in respectable circles. The lady is about fifty, able-bodied, and to all appearances in good health. In response to my question whether she is afraid of your climate, she replied that she was undaunted by the heat of Africa, and has no fear of the cold of Russia. Mrs. Rahn is also so sure that with your connections you will find it possible to help her aunt that I have yielded to her insistence and would ask you if you could possibly recommend Mrs. Jacques.

The weather here is splendid. Tomorrow, Sunday. Everyone who can find transport will be taking a trip to a small hill several versts from here to pick flowers. This hill is covered with lovely flowers; it has become a major event which lasts as long as the flowers are in bloom. I do wish you could be here to enjoy the fine weather and this trip.

My sister and I wish you a happy Easter, and please accept our cordial best wishes.

Your old and devoted teacher and friend
Fanny Dürbach.

✦ ✦ ✦

8.

Montbéliard, 6 April 1893

My dear Pierre,

My sister and I want to congratulate you on your great success in Kharkov[36] and wholeheartedly share your gratification. On Easter Monday, I went to see the Misses Duvernois who played me some of your pieces which they are particularly fond of. I only wish I were more musical so that I could better appreciate them. Nevertheless, I have to say how pleased I am that your music is known and loved even in such a small and remote provincial town. We are distressed to learn that you are suffering from headaches. I know they won't go away in a matter of days, and I should add that whenever I have succumbed to a headache I have had to combat it with anti-neuralgic pills. Hasn't your own doctor been prescribing them? What I'm really sorry about is the cause of these headaches. I remember that when you were here you wanted to know what the time was on your watch. I thought it was a very beautiful watch, and even wanted you to show it to me. Couldn't it be the one that you lost? I remember how tormented you were by the thought that an innocent person might be blamed, and I can imagine how hard you tried to prove his innocence. Do you think that the actual culprit will ever be found? I would certainly hope so.[37] Why are you so unhappy about your brother-in-law's marriage?[38] Surely you don't think that such sincere and constant devotion to your dear sister could end within our own short lifetime?

Of course, your nephews and nieces will find it difficult to get used to seeing someone else taking the place of their adored mother; however, with that sensitivity which you yourself recognize, their father is bringing to his bereft family home a person belonging to your own family whose qualities you cherish.[39] Undoubtedly, your cousin knew your dear sister, and must have been just as fond of her as everyone else who knew her; those motherless children will talk to her about their mother, and she will understand their sorrow, give them her affection and focus their thoughts on that land their mother now inhabits where we will all eventually be reunited with her. With your tender affection for them, you better than anyone will be able to make them understand why their father has acted in this way.

It may be that this letter will be too late to catch you at Klin, and as I very much hope you will be spending Easter with your family, and I wish you all a happy time together. Give my greetings to your dear Nikola and his family and also to your brother Modest if I may be so bold. Tell me how your nephew George is growing up?[40] Does he like his lessons, and has he learned to enjoy playing games as much as his papa?

On the fifth, the very day when I received your letter, I went to see Mrs. R to tell her what you wrote about Mrs. Jacques. These ladies understand that the best thing for Mrs. Jacques would be to go to St. Petersburg, but that would cost a lot of money without any guarantee of success. I have strongly advised her against doing that! After twenty years in Algeria it is highly unlikely that this lady will be able to stand the northern climate, although she does not agree. These ladies thank you for responding to their request so quickly and for the kindness you have shown them, and have asked me to convey their regards.

We have also had an extremely severe winter. There was 30 degrees of frost, something that no one here can recall. In Paris it was never more than 16 degrees. I am sorry that I wrote to you about our wonderful spring, and your 10 degrees made me shiver with cold; but I know that in your country the temperature can change very suddenly, and I hope that you are now having some good weather.

Do you have a garden in Klin? Here the good weather is continuing and the pear trees are full of buds, and even blossom, but it's so dry that the farmers and gardeners are complaining.

When you see your cousin Lidiya, please remember me to her. I will be very glad if you write to me soon since I would like to know if you have got rid of your headaches. As you know, everything about you is of interest to me, especially your health. Unquestionably, traveling is better for you than sitting at a desk working. The different impressions you get when you travel change your outlook. I also intended to travel during the Easter holidays. I was to have gone to Belfort to visit my cousin who broke her leg during the black ice, but my sister came down with influenza and couldn't come with me, and in any case I find the whole business of traveling very hard to organize.

My sister is better and I join her in sending you her best wishes for your health, and I send you kisses from the bottom of my heart. I do hope you sometimes think of your promise to come again to Montbéliard; I think of it a lot, and so much look forward to your visit, as you can easily believe.

Goodbye for now, my dear, dear Pierre.

Your old and devoted friend kisses you once more.

Fanny Dürbach.

✦ ✦ ✦

9.

[Montbéliard, March–April 1893]

Dear Pierre,

I didn't ask you to deal with Mrs. Jacques's problem entirely of my own free will, it was just that Mrs. Rahn asked me to, and was so sure that I wouldn't be imposing on you, that I just went along with her. Knowing as I do that you are not particularly fond of writing, perhaps you could just show people my own letter, although it was interrupted three times and therefore may not make a good impression. If you think you can help Mrs. Jacques find a position with one of your acquaintances, please be kind enough to reply soon, if only by a post-card. My sister thinks that if Mrs. Jacques had to supervise a domestic servant, she wouldn't be equipped to do it, not knowing Russian.

After what I have written to you, you may feel that I'm not very obliging, but what I fear is causing you trouble. When artists in distress turn to you for help, it's almost their right because fame of any kind carries with it obligations, and I am sure that you are besieged with appeals for help, and that's why I now regret having taken the steps I did. However, if it is really not putting you to too much trouble, and you want to respond you can send your letter directly to Mrs. Rahn at: Belfort Street, Hotel de la Balance. I have scrawled this letter to you in a hurry.

Goodbye for now, my dear, dear pupil, and do try to write me a little something yourself.

When are you going to come? We are having such wonderful weather; it makes you feel like traveling.

A kiss from the bottom of my heart from your old friend,
Fanny Dürbach.

Let me know if you have any news from your nearest and dearest.

✦✦✦

10.

[Montbéliard,] 1 June 1893

Dear Pierre,

Today is the day of your big concert,[41] and I am thinking about you a lot. It was so kind of you to send us news of yourself before you left for London. Your letter which arrived on the eve of Holy Trinity was for us like a ray of sunshine on a gloomy day. At that very time a ter-rible thing happened to the pastor of our parish. His son, a young man of twenty-seven or twenty-eight, was on leave and had come to see his parents and to take a rest after a spell of very hard work. He is a lieutenant and loves military service more than anything. On the 29th of April he went to observe some military maneuvers, and in order to get a better look he climbed up onto a very high rock. I don't know exactly how it happened, but it appears that he sat down, and as it was terribly dry, he started to slide down, and it seems that in spite of all his efforts—his hands were covered in blood—he couldn't stop himself from falling. His almost lifeless body was brought back to his father, who happened to be very sick himself at the time, so it was a terrible blow; but the worst of it was that when the young man had begun to recover, it was discovered that he had lost his mind. His father could not stand the shock and his condition deteriorated, and on Saturday we attended his funeral. Words cannot express how badly we feel for our pastor, his widow, and their seven children.

✦

8 [June]

I am wondering why I wrote about all this to you, when I should have been writing about something quite different. It's probably because you have such a compassionate heart, and also because Pastor Gordon was a man who deserved my tribute. He was only fifty-eight, but had been suffering terribly from his illness for five years.

You have stopped mentioning your headaches. I very much hope that they have disappeared completely. Please let me know.

By now I am sure that the solemn ceremony of conferring on you the degree of Doctor of Music has already taken place.[42] One more honor to add to the rest that you have earned. Our sincerest congratulations; my sister is even more delighted than I am. Please tell us all about it! Were you very tired? Did you enjoy your stay in Cambridge? How did you like the English? I think they can be likeable, and they are easier to judge in Cambridge than in London.

I think I read somewhere that [Camille] Saint-Saëns once disappeared from the musical scene in order to rest, only I don't remember where! If you too were ever to feel like disappearing from the capitals of the world and spend a little time in our small, quiet Montbéliard which would be so relaxing for you and where I would be so happy to chat with you! We've been having splendid weather here for three months now, to the delight of strollers, but to the dismay of farmers, for whom one can only feel sorry. I don't know when you will be in Klin, but since you travel around at such lightning speed, maybe you are already there. I join my sister in offering our congratulations, and kiss you warmly.

Friend of your early years
and ever yours
Fanny Dürbach

It's been a long time since you mentioned Anastasiya; please let me know what she is doing. I was hoping that your brother Nikola would write to me from his country place. If his George[43] were to send me a little letter, it would be my pleasure to reply to it. Also, please write to me about Lidiya[44] and her children.

✦ ✦ ✦

11.

Montbéliard, 24 July 1893

My dear Pierre,

If only you knew what a pleasure it was for me to hear of your stay in the country, with the steppes all around you where you can take a real break and enjoy total freedom. My sister is very proud to hear that you like the area of which she cherishes such good memories. I have never seen such a beautiful sunset as those I saw in Russia where the skies were bright with the most spectacular colors; I was particularly impressed by those quiet, mild evenings towards the end of summer. The fishermen's boats rocked gently on the mirror-smooth surface of the pond which reflected the sun. From our balcony we could hear sad and tender songs which were the only things to break the silence of those wonderful nights, when none of you wanted to go to bed; surely you remember them. If you still remember any of those tunes, why don't you use them in your music; it would delight those who are unable to hear them in your country. [Alexander] Pushkin, your poet of years ago, said that he would like his songs to be loved even in the meanest shanty, and indeed everywhere where Russian is spoken; a noble aspiration, but you could aim even higher because the language you speak is more universal.[45]

Thank you for the details of the solemn ceremony at which the degree of Doctor of Music was conferred on you. I would love to see my little Pierre arrayed in his splendid robes.[46] When you were a child, you wanted to go to England. You also wanted to speak to your sovereign, and now these childhood dreams have come true. I also want to congratulate you on the success of all your concerts, and especially on your splendid health. It's great that you are able to rest in a train compartment! But I would rather that it were one of those tarantas carriages with a good suspension. I wanted to tell you not to return to Klin too soon because I fear that you will be working when you're there, but perhaps the people around you will manage to restrain you; I very much hope they will. The English must be very pleased that you hold them in such high esteem. I also believe that whole nations, as well as individuals, are the happiest when they are Christian, because for them, regardless of life's adversities, it is religion which mostly governs their conduct.

Do you know that in your country the exams for your young ladies are, I believe, much harder than in France? Jenny Grossman has told me about her exams, and I came to the conclusion that people everywhere want women to be educated—and how rightly—since life is becoming daily more complicated.

You tell me that you will be coming again, and I think that is the best part of your whole letter.

The grape harvest in France this year is excellent and abundant—come and sample it. There used to be vineyards on the hills around our town, and I think that harvest time was the best time of the year. But although those vineyards have disappeared, the grapes are still eaten.

Goodbye for now, my dear Pierre; please give my best to anyone in your family who still remembers me even slightly. I join my sister in sending you our best wishes, and I kiss you warmly.

Fanny Dürbach

✦

26 July.
Tell me a little about Klin. Do you still like to go horse riding? Do you have a nice garden?

✦✦✦

12.

Montbéliard, 13 October 1893[47]

Dear Pierre,

I have just received your letter, but you cannot imagine how disappointed it made me—to think you are now in France. I read in the newspaper *Tempo* that the opera is holding a reception in honor of Russian sailors which will feature music by three Russian composers—yourself, [Mikhail] Glinka, and [Anton] Rubinstein—and three

French composers. Another article mentions only you, and that you will be staging one of your own operas chosen by you. But there's not a word about it in your letter; can it be that you have decided against it? I would be quite upset if that were the case, although not so much for myself, but rather for my country. The poor French tend to overdo their enthusiasms, but to sensible people this enthusiasm may appear ridiculous. However, you, who have long been a student of our short-comings and have learned to take them in your stride, shouldn't be so unyielding. I still hope you will come, and even have the impression that you won't want to act otherwise. You are used to traveling and have no problem with it, and there will be a lot of travelers in France. I learned from one of my correspondents that all the hotels in Toulon are fully booked, and that the cost of renting window space is becoming unbelievably high. Even in our small town, major preparations are being planned, but it appears that sensible people have imposed some restraint. They are making fun of the town council, which has Russi-fied all the names, and have said that since the time when Montbéliard gave Russia an empress, a little Russian blood has been flowing in their veins. As you can see, there are cool-headed people in our country, so for their sake, please forgive the hotheads.

If you wrote to me while you were staying with Nikola, your letter must have been particularly interesting, but I never got it. Your last one was dated 1 July and a lot of time seems to have passed since then.

I can't believe that Lidiya wouldn't want to write and tell me about herself and her children. And what is Anastasiya[48] doing? If you come, I have so much to ask you! I know Mrs. Edelman, and am pleased that she has found happiness in Russia; she fully deserves it. She has given her children a good upbringing, which cost her a great deal. If you see her again, please give her our regards.

Don't you feel that little Nikola is still too young to be separated from his parents? I feel sorry for those poor children who have to leave their parents' home. Are they allowed to go home for the holidays? Of course, you will be visiting him often.

I am delighted to learn that you are still feeling well. In July I suf-fered badly from insomnia. On my journey to Switzerland I enjoyed the company of some ladies who were going to Flühli. On the way back on the train I met a Russian family traveling from Lucerne; there were two children, the father, the mother, and a grandmother. It was from the Russian shirt of the older boy, who was about the age you were when I left you, that I recognized that they were Russian. It was the same national dress of that time. It gave me great pleasure to hear that they were speaking your language.

I read the names of all those naval officers who were to come to France, hoping that I would come across the name of your brother Ippolit, but didn't find it. My sister says that my letter will arrive too late to find you at home,[49] but I'm still hopeful, and that's why I want to post it today. I can assure you that I am very pleased to know that you are well, and still hope that you will be coming. I implore you to write me a few lines. My sister sends you her heartfelt greetings, and so does your old friend who loves you perhaps more than you would like.

Fanny Dürbach

✦ ✦ ✦

LETTER FROM FANNY DÜRBACH TO
NIKOLAY ILYICH TCHAIKOVSKY[50]

Montbéliard, 26 February 1894

My dear pupil, I too thank God from the bottom of my heart for restoring your son to health.[51] How worried you and his dear mommy must have been when he fell sick. Please tell me as much about him as you can. The portrait of Pierre which you sent me is a remarkably good likeness. You were quite right when you told me this; the one I have, and which I cherish, is a poorer likeness. Please accept my profound gratitude for this new evidence of your friendly feelings toward me. You did very well to leave St. Petersburg after such a difficult time.[52] I very much feared that your grief would get the better of you, and your silence worried me. Now that your mind is at rest about George's state of health, we can only hope that you too will feel better. You asked me for the letters and poems Pierre wrote as a child, so that you can copy them. What I would prefer would be for you and your brother Modest to come to Montbéliard so that I can read them to you before giving you the letters themselves.[53] There is a great deal in them which your brother Modest will find it hard to understand. I am sure that he and his ward travel a lot, so why couldn't they also come here? If your dear George is well, might you not think of bringing him with you? If you and his dear mommy[54] could bring him, the journey would only benefit his health, and it would be such a pleasure for me to see you all again. You could stay at the same hotel where Pierre stayed. It's very nice there in the spring because of the hotel's beautiful garden. If my wish does not come true, then *you* will have to explain to your brother why little Pierre's letters are full of regret. Do you remember your happy life in Votkinsk? Do you remember that when we left St. Petersburg (it was the 29th of October 1844), it was my twenty-second birthday, and I had just left nine orphans after spending three years with them? They are still alive to this day. Pierre was four on the 7th of May, and I believe it was on that very same day when we were beginning lessons that your mother, although she was against lessons for such young children, could not withstand his tears and pleas, and brought him to the class, because he wanted "to take lessons just like Nikola and Lidiya."

From that day on he had the same lessons as you, and did the same homework, and it was impossible to let him off any of them. As well as his progress and intelligence, he also had an excellent memory, and soon caught you up and stayed level with you. At six he was already reading French, German, and Russian well, and learning was no problem for him. After Venichka's[55] mother died, your father, who was his godfather, put him in our class; our lessons were already well organized, and you made progress; but all three of you were very nice to Venichka, and each of you wanted to keep him abreast of what you were learning; in this way he had three teachers, not to mention a governess. Since Venichka was very hardworking, he was soon able to keep up with you. Pierre was always his best mentor. So you all became a very pleasant little class to teach. We had our own rules, and all of you tried to get the best marks without a trace of envy among you. Do you remember how whoever came top of the class was so proud to win and wear the red bow on Sunday. I'm reminding you of all these details because I want to ask you to impress upon your brother Modest how lonely poor Pierre felt when he was left to study by himself. Since neither you nor I were any longer with him, he sought consolation in music. This is what he himself wrote about it to me: "I try to sit at the piano as much as possible, it's a comfort to me." I never forget that he was a born artist, but he was a poet as well as a musician. I'm telling you this because I don't want to see the child I loved so much misjudged. I have some letters of your mother, and I should really keep them myself, but if I send them to you, read them yourself, but don't let anyone else see them.[56] You were more fortunate than Pierre; after you left Votkinsk you went to a boarding school where you were among fellow students of your own age, you continued to work hard, while he was suffering from your absence. It was not surprising that he grew indifferent to everything. By then Lidiya had become a grown-up young lady, and preferred the company of other young ladies to Pierre's. Polá was still too young for him, and even Sashenka, who was always so protective of her dear little Polá, as she called him, could not replace you as his companion.

✦

7 March.

I had to interrupt this letter, and was only able to continue it today. You have also asked me for Pierre's exercise books. I have only one of these, which contains passages from selected stories. It belongs to you. You were doing the same work. If you find that the work was rather hard for such young schoolboys, I can tell you that you were just as advanced in our language as young French boys of your age. It was your mother's wish that you should know French as well as possible before leaving your parents' home. Until the day when your father recruited Mr. Blinov,[57] you had only one teacher of Russian, and I taught all the other subjects.

I also have some letters from Lidiya,[58] which I will also send you. As for Anastasiya's[59] letters, except for the most recent, please return all the others. You may give one or two of Lidiya's letters to her children. Everything relating to Pierre must stay with me until after my death. These dear little pages which I am sending to you are the best part of my memories. If any of you come to Montbéliard, I will tell you about the pranks and things he got up to—I find them charming, they are just childish pranks. Pierre was "a child" in the fullest and best sense.

Let me know soon if you want the things I am offering, but forgive me for repeating: if possible, try to come to see me yourself. There's just one thing I'm afraid of, it is that you might say "it's not worth it."

I know that everything I can tell you is of greater significance to me than to others, but if you would like, I will share with you some of my memories of your brother, but as you can see, I cannot write any more. If, when Pierre was here I didn't seem as old as I really am, that was only because for the two days we were together, I was so happy. He looked just the same.

I've never had my photograph taken, and my eyes are rather weak, but if you send me a photograph of yourself, then I will have one taken of myself for you. Also please send me photos of your wife and son. Thank you for the details you have given me about who will inherit ownership of your dear brother's works and royalties, and about his nephew.

I think it's a sacrifice on your part to accept nothing that belonged to him, but his memory will remain more alive for you all if everything that embellished his life is preserved just as he left it.

Goodbye for now, my dear pupil; please convey my sister's and my own greetings to Mrs. Tchaikovsky and your cousin Olkhovskaya, and also accept best wishes from, believe me, your deeply devoted friend.

Fanny Dürbach.

I hear that St. Petersburg is now enjoying a thaw. Here we are having horrid rain after some good days.

◆ ◆ ◆

LETTERS FROM FANNY DÜRBACH TO
MODEST ILYICH TCHAIKOVSKY[60]

1.

Montbéliard, 1 September 1894

Dear Mr. Modest,

Your nice letter was an unexpected pleasure for us since, I must confess, I hadn't expected to receive it so soon. I thought you would have had to stay in Paris for a longer time. Have you been satisfied with your stay there, and did you find everyone you wanted to see? I am sure all Pierre's friends gave you a very warm reception. I am very pleased that you found your nephew[61] in good health and were able to devote an evening with him to the memory of your dear brother.

Do you know that after you left, I was a little ashamed that I hadn't given you Pierre's old exercise books, but I have to confess that I couldn't bring myself to part with them; I felt that they wouldn't be staying with me for much longer, and no one else could cherish them as much as I do—they bring back so many memories . . .

When you see your brother Nikola, please show him Pierre's letter to your cousin Amalia,[62] and also the one to your aunt Liza[63]—it will remind him of Votkinsk in particular; the arrival of General Glinka[64] was always a major event, especially for the children. I so much wanted to write to Mrs. Anastasiya before, but I didn't do it even after you left; I was unwell, and then one of our cousins came with her two grandsons and her niece. They all stayed at the Red Lion Hotel, but after two days they went to stay with one of their relatives who lives beside the canal; because of the children our cousin wanted to stay in the country. They came into town often, and I was very glad that you had come before them. They spent ten days here, and we had things to attend to.

You asked me the reason for the punishment I wanted to impose on Venichka, and I'll give you some details on the subject. For several months when Nikola Romanov[65] was giving lessons to my pupils and spending time with them outside the classroom, he felt it was a pleasure and an honor to teach them some games he knew from the St. Petersburg boarding school which he had just left. He was very good at gymnastics and indeed all physical activities, and loved wrestling with one or other of his schoolmates to see who was the stronger; but your mother, who insisted on proper behavior even when it came to games, strictly forbade fighting. Well, once when I was giving a lesson to Sashenka and Polinka, I was unpleasantly surprised when Carolina, the German nursery governess, rushed in from the garden all upset, and told me that Nikola and Venichka were going at it hammer and tongs, and that it was a real battle, and they wouldn't listen to her, and Venichka in particular refused to stop fighting. I was really astonished, because Venichka was normally so obedient and sensible for a boy his age.

Before Carolina had time to leave the room, the three boys appeared. Lidiya was sitting at the piano; each of them was supposed to practice in turn while I was giving the young ones their lesson, and the others were left to amuse themselves in their own way until tea, which we took first at 6 p.m., so that the children could do their homework and prepare their lessons. This would take them at least two hours. Without uttering a word, my pupils sat down on the divan facing the school bench. "It's very unpleasant for me," I said, "to discover that I can no longer trust you and won't be able to give my lessons in peace. Since you, Venichka, can no longer do what you are told, go to the coachman and tell him to harness the horses and take you home."

Hardly were the words out of my mouth, when I regretted them. The poor child was sobbing. It was then that Pierre got up, came up to me, and said: "Mrs. Fanny, a mother doesn't send her child away, and Venichka has no mother. You have to stand in for her, so don't send him away." "So, Pierre, you mean that my pupils can disobey me at will, and get away with it without being punished?" "Then punish us, all three of us want to be punished, but don't send our friend away." But Venichka only said: "Forgive me, and Nikola too." What could I do but forgive them, although I did want to send him away for one day, but still I had exceeded my authority.

I want to remind you of your promise to translate Anastasiya's letter for me. She was someone who showed me all the kindness she was in a position to, and I would like to have something to remember her by. How happy I was to learn that your dear cousin Lidiya was with her during her last days. Tell me frankly, did I offend Nikola in my letter? Maybe he thought that I was unfair to him, but I was actually very fond of him and still have extremely good memories of him. Please ask him whether he remembers what year it was when the Duke of Leichtenberg[66] came to inspect the Votkinsk factories. Pierre marked the occasion by composing a speech of welcome. I don't remember whether he knew how to write yet, but he did recite it to us, and your mother was very much amused.

Please do tell me something about your work, it interests me very much, believe me. I would also like to hear about all the people in your family, especially your dear nephew who Pierre was so fond of. I quite understand that you wanted to stay in Klin, but if you lived there alone, you would be doing just what your brother did, and you would spend too much time working. In St. Petersburg you will find many members of your family, and you will be able to keep up with the literary life. I wish you a pleasant time there.

✦

20 September.

The Duvernois family were deeply touched to hear that you remembered them; they are away right now, and we hope they are enjoying their stay in Switzerland a little since the weather there now is nice and warm. Where we are there's been a lot of rain. My sister sends you her warm greetings. She has prepared a bottle of our Kessel Water for your journey, but forgot to give it to you. If only you knew how sorry she is about that. Please come next year so that she can make up for her forgetfulness. The last letter I got from Pierre is dated October 7th. He was in Klin after spending a few weeks with his family. You must all still have a vivid memory of him. In his memory, and in return for your kindness during those few days that you spent I have the warmest feelings for you, and kiss you from the bottom of my heart.

From an old friend of your family, Fanny Dürbach.

✦ ✦ ✦

2.

Montbéliard, 1 October 1894

Dear Mr. Modest,

I am so sorry for the delay in sending you this letter which caused you some concern over us. However, it was precisely because of this delay that I got this nice letter which you sent us. Thank you for your kindness which I very much appreciate.

Mr. Vladimir Davydov sent me the delightful letter from Mrs. Anastasiya to which he added a few lines of his own. You are both wonderful and kind young people who have affection for the elderly—something which has gone out of fashion. Tell your nephew what a pleasure it was for me to receive his letter, and give him my thanks for the news it contained. I would like to write another letter to Mrs. Anastasiya; he told me to do so, but I didn't want to risk naming in my letter all those she loved the most, for fear that it would bring back painful memories to her. Tell me if I could write to her again. Tell me something about your work on your brother's biography. Are you thinking of publishing it in installments in some review or in a single volume, since you are gathering all the necessary material. Tell me, is Lidiya taking an interest in your work? If so she could give you a lot of information, provided that she has preserved all the memories. Perhaps her memory of those early years has not failed her.

Nikola too has lots of memories of his brother, they shared everything—their lessons, and they also played together. The only difference was that Pierre preferred reading and playing the piano to noisy games, although he was not allowed to indulge this preference because of concern for his health, which, I should say, was good in Votkinsk, like that of all the other children.

✦

9 October.

I have received all your letters. It was so kind of you to translate for me Anastasiya's letters which she wrote to me in 1848.[67] You can see that I must have enjoyed my time in Votkinsk because my memories of it are among my best. I cannot explain why my dear Venichka behaved in that way,[68] and I can't wait for you to meet him. I am sure you will find that he was really a true friend of Pierre. He doted on Sashenka and was always willing to play the horse, or to play the father to her doll. Nikola was quite different, even then he was a handsome boy, very attentive to his appearance and to good manners, while Venichka was a very simple boy, but hardworking and a good friend. He was so fond of your father, who was his godfather, that I simply fail to understand why he never went to visit him; but if there were differences among my pupils, there was also total harmony among them. We were all so fond of each other.

I'm also wondering why you didn't stay longer in Montbéliard. I wanted you to stay longer, but didn't dare to try to make you. If you come again and I'm still in this world, I hope we can make up for lost time. Apart from "L'Education Maternelle" by Mlle. Amable Tastu, I also had "Family Education" by Mrs. Edgeworth in several volumes. In natural history, I also had a small illustrated copy of Buffon. For reading—the "Tales of Guizot" and also Schmidt's "Canon," and my class books, which I also used. One of our favorite volumes was "Celebrated Children" by Michel Masson; we read it and recounted it in the evenings and on Saturday.[69]

Ask me anything you like, and I will be happy to tell you anything you want to know about your dear father. Yesterday, the 10th, I once again went through the few letters to my mother which I still have, to see if I could find anything about the incident which made your parents invite a music teacher to your home. I was so frightened when I saw the damage Pierre had done to himself while using the glass in the gallery as a keyboard to tap out his best inspirations, that I was sure I had written about it to my mother, but I didn't find anything. All I can tell you about it now is that M[ariya] M[arkovna][70] was already living in your parents' home while they were away in St. Petersburg, because I remember very well that Nikola was amusing himself by giving her French lessons while your parents were away, and probably missed them more than any of the others did and was quite down-hearted. I don't remember M[ariya] M[arkovna's] maiden name, but she became Loginova by marriage. Pierre told me that her husband was a drunk, and that was probably why she turned to Pierre for help. I think that all that correspondence was the work of that lady's daughter.

I do urge you to go and see Venichka yourself; I'm sure he will be happy to see you and talk to you about his friend—that's what he and Pierre called each other. Please be good enough to tell him that I have never forgotten him.

After my return to Votkinsk, we were so happy to see each other again that he practically never left my side.

Please tell me about your pupil, do you live far from him? In St. Petersburg, distances are not a problem, and I hope that you do see him. Will your nephew be leaving St. Petersburg when he becomes an officer—you would be very lonely. I congratulate him in advance on his promotion—please tell him.

✦

11 October.

I have just re-read my letter. As regards school books, we also had the "Geographical Atlas" of Meissas and Michelot.[71] It served us well then, but it is now no longer used in schools, and has long since been frequently replaced by other books. For German we followed the Ahn method,[72] which has also been superseded. When Pierre was here he told me: "I want you to know that I haven't forgotten German," and we had a conversation in German. I told him: "Now you speak better than I do; do you like the language?" "I like *them*," he replied. He liked Germans, and the English too. Well, he liked everyone. I very much hope that in the biography of him that you're writing you succeed in making people like him as much as he deserved. It was impossible to know him without feeling the warmest affection for him.

Tell Nikola that I cannot wait to hear from him; his silence is hard to bear, especially since I could talk to him about Pierre, because I'll only have to say: "Do you remember?" and I'm sure he will. And tell me also how his wife and son are doing. Has your brother Ippolit settled in St. Petersburg? Please give my best to him, and also to my dear Lidiya. I would also like to hear about your sister Zina's children. Are they in St. Petersburg? The Duvernois family has returned, and the young ladies sometimes come to chat with me, and I have given them your regards. That old lady you saw in their family was a good musician and a great admirer of your brother.

My sister sends you her friendly greetings, and I send you my heart-felt kisses, and I apologize for my thoroughly bad writing.

Without any doubt, you and your nephew both possess a good style in our language, and I really should try harder in my letters to you, but the time for that has passed; all I can do is just push the pen along.

Goodbye for now! May God bless your work—and one more kiss.
Your old devoted friend
Fanny Dürbach.

✦ ✦ ✦

3.

Montbéliard, 26 February 1895

Dear friend,

You will no doubt be upset to learn that I have not received a letter from our dear Venichka—or should I say "Colonel Alekseev," although I can't bring myself to. He, like your dear brother, and all the others, have always been and will always remain for me my beloved pupils, although, of course, I am delighted with his distinguished career. Perhaps I will get a letter from him some time; he was always so persistent that I am sure he will find it possible to write in French, however hard he may find it. Tell me once again how happy you were to find him; remember how I told you that he was not one of those people who forget, and he was so attached to your whole family. When he came to us, everyone welcomed him with open arms, especially Pierre, who thought losing your mother was the worst thing that could happen to anyone. He wanted to share with him all his childish treasures, and also the box in which he kept all his books and notebooks, but when I praised Nikola for keeping his so neat and tidy, I immediately heard Pierre say: "Venichka, tidy up, I hate untidiness." I had better end this letter right now if I don't want it to arrive bearing a date that is two years old. Although I was actually waiting for a letter from Venichka, I would still have written to you sooner, if I hadn't been unwell. At the beginning of the winter I was suffering from an abscess in a tooth, and then it was a bad cold that I caught from my sister, which finally turned into neuralgia, which I hadn't had for a long time, and on top of it all there was the real winter weather: snow, high winds so strong that people could hardly keep their footing. However, Christmas day turned out to be fine. We had the same weather as when your dear brother came to Montbéliard, only not so cold. I will always remember the two days we spent together with him, but I hope that your visit here is rapidly approaching.

Soon, you in Russia will also be celebrating Christmas; I wish you all a happy one. Please convey to all the members of your family who are in St. Petersburg our sincerest best wishes, especially Nikola and his family as well as your cousin Lidiya. Perhaps your nephew will go and spend Christmas with his folks—won't you be going too? It would be more cheerful with him than without him. Don't forget to tell Mrs. Anastasiya that I think about her a lot. It was very nice of your brother Anatoly to send us his good wishes, thank him for me, and also my dear Polá. Keep us up to date about everyone. As you must know from the newspaper, France commiserated with your national mourning, and now our country associates itself with all the hopes you place in your new Sovereign. God grant that he follow in his father's footsteps for the well-being of both our countries, and indeed for the happiness of Europe. Thank you for the offer you made to Venichka— to translate his letter for me; that was really kind of you when you have so much business of your own to attend to. Please tell me about your work, if only a little. You know how interested I am in it. Don't let me wait too long for your letters. I am always so pleased to hear from you.

The Duvernois family send you their greetings, they are all well. I join my sister in extending to you our best wishes for your health and for the New Year, and sending you our warm kisses.

Your old friend
Fanny Dürbach.

✦ ✦ ✦

4.

Montbéliard, 26 February 1895

My dear,

It was so kind of you and your nephew to wish us a Happy New Year the way you did, that I also wanted to send you our best wishes for your New Year, but my sister and I were not well. There was an outbreak of influenza in our town, and very few families were spared. Before this I never really knew what it was like to be sick because my sister would take such good care of me that there was no need to feel sorry for me. However, this time she was the first one to fall sick—and quite seriously; of course, she was also the first to recover, whereas my condition was exacerbated by bronchitis. My sister has already begun to go out, and I'm very much looking forward to doing the same. I can't tell you how kind to us the Duvernois ladies have been, as well as my other pupils who have been sending us so many tasty treats. Our cousin, Mrs. Kun, was also sick at the same time we were. I do hope that you and your nephew have been in good health. Please keep us up to date about your brother Nikola, and tell us whether his son has recovered from his whooping cough. Give them our best, and tell Nikola what a pleasure it is for us to get his letters, and that it wouldn't take him much trouble to write me a little something. You know, when I see the sun for the first time again in the spring, I still hope that you and your nephew will come for the holidays. You told me that travelling is no problem for you, and we would be so happy to see you again. Please let me hear about your work; you know how much it interests me, and how much I hope that what you write about your brother will fully do him justice; you loved him enough to be able to do that.

When I'm feeling better and have taken care of the backlog of all the letters which have piled up, I'll write to Venichka. Tell me about him and his first meeting with Nikola. I am sure that my dear Lidiya will also be nice to him. In Votkinsk everyone liked him although he was so shy.

Here in our little Montbéliard, things would have been very quiet were it not for the ball and the concert to celebrate the opening of the hospital. The concert was particularly successful. All the artists from around here took part.

Although the papers say that it was a very bad winter everywhere, I don't think it was as bad for you as it was for us with our climate, because you are better organized for protecting yourselves against the cold than we are. The good weather is slow in returning to us. Goodbye for now Mr. Modest and dear Mr. Davydov, please let us hear from you soon, and give our best to all the members of your family, including your brother Ippolit and his family.

Be assured of our deep affection.

Your devoted friend
Fanny Dürbach.

✦ ✦ ✦

5.

Montbéliard, 1 May 1895

Dear Modest,

It's such a pleasure to hear from you that I want to reply right away. It's so kind of you to send me news of your family and of all those to whom I am so devoted. I'm so pleased to hear what you say about Colonel Alekseev, and many thanks for all the details you have been willing to share with me. Venichka also had two delightful little sisters, please ask him about them. Thanks also for telling me about your work. I can't wait for you to finish it. You know how much it interests me. I hope God will let me live long enough to see your book translated into French. Perhaps you will need to come to Paris; if so, please do come to Montbéliard. You made some real friends here, and both the Duvernois family and Emilia Kun would be happy to see you and your dear nephew. You could use Emilia's garden in the mornings and could go out all together in the boat. My sister's garden is not so overgrown as last year, and both she and I would be glad to see you on our little terrace. Please try to come both together. If you are economical, you won't need to spend very much, and we could talk about the people we both love. Please tell me about anything that interests you, and allow me to share your thoughts, just as Pierre used to. Jenny Grossman writes to tell me that she and her mother will be going to the Crimea, and from there on to the Caucasus—a somewhat longer journey than coming to France. I very much hope that poor Mrs. Grossman will recover. Jenny writes that since the death of her husband, her mother has never been herself; because of that I am more worried about the young daughter than the mother.

I would like to hear more about Nikola and his family; I keep on hoping to get a letter from him. Tell me how you spent that long, harsh winter. Perhaps you will soon be going away to the country, which will be better for you than the town. How much I would have liked to spend that evening at Venichka's together with all of you. Tell me what my dear Lidiya and your brothers Ippolit and Anatoly are doing, and give them my best. I think about all of you, and especially your nephew whom I have taken such a liking to, both for himself and for his late mother.

I hope you are now enjoying good weather, it returned to us yesterday. Last week it rained every day, and on Friday we had a thunderstorm and hail around here which inundated everything and did a lot of damage, but wasn't so bad as it might have been a month later.

Goodbye for now, my dear, write to me soon. My sister asks me to convey her cordial greetings, and I send you a heartfelt kiss.

Fanny Dürbach.

Didn't you promise to send Lucie Duvernois a piece of music? Allow me to send you a small album with views of our town.[73] One of my former pupils has written to tell me that your Easter is exactly at the same time as ours. It's so nice to think that we are celebrating this important holiday at the same time as you.

✦ ✦ ✦

6.

Montbéliard, 8 October 1895

Dear Modest,

You won't believe how eagerly I waited for your letter. I know you are very busy, but I don't understand why Nikola couldn't find a spare moment to write me a few lines; after all, in the country during those long summer evenings, he surely could have found a few minutes to talk to me about what is close to his heart. I wish he would tell me about his wife, who, as you have said, is so nice, and about his son, who was no doubt spending the holidays with his family. Please tell him that I am deeply hurt by his silence, and if I have done anything to deserve it, I wish he would tell me what it is.

I'm so glad to hear that your biography of Pierre interests your friends.[74] Recently when I was looking through *his papers,* I found the following written on one page (he must have been barely eight years old at the time): "Why on earth did this almighty God create me?" I want to send you this page. I wonder how many fully grown people may never have asked themselves this question, when here is a small child asking it! What I am afraid of in your account is that you will attribute a vastly too important role to me. I was very happy when I was with your family and so what I wanted was to do my best to give back to the children what I had received from their dear parents. You didn't have the good fortune to know your mother well enough to appreciate the nobility of her character—that would have made you love her even more. I must tell you that she was even more scrupulous than me when it came to matters of conscience and tactfulness, and she demanded from her children nothing less than total honesty. I don't have to remind you of the part your father played in the upbringing of his children. My duties in your household were a source of great happiness to me.

Tell me what Nikola thinks of the biography of his dear brother, since both he and Lidiya are better able to speak about him, and have more to say, although Pierre did tell me that after her husband died, your cousin Lidiya lost her memory. I am sure that Venichka and even Polá have some good memories. If only you include something about how often your dear brother neglected himself because he was busy thinking about others. Please write soon telling me something about yourself. You didn't say anything about where you spent the summer, and whether you were with your nephew. Give my best to him and all the members of your family.

The Duvernois family spent part of the summer in the Auvergne. Because the summer was so splendid, I had hoped you would have taken advantage of it, although I would have been sorry if you had come when they weren't here.

Mrs. Kun's garden was a pleasant place for her friends; when the heat was at its greatest they were able to enjoy its refreshing cool. She, i.e. Mrs. Kun, is alone now; both of her sons are away doing their 28-day military service in Belfort. Victor, the director of a savings bank, comes here every week on business.

My sister and I send our warmest regards to you and everyone who has the pleasure of knowing you.

Please accept the expression of our strong attachment to your family from your sincere and devoted friend.

Fanny Dürbach.

If you mention me in your biography of Pierre, you will, of course, refer to me only by my initials.

♦ ♦ ♦

7.

Montbéliard, 9 January 1896

Dear Modest,

In the first two days of this new year, I have been recalling our dear Pierre's visit to us. I have been receiving visits from the same people as three years ago, but Pierre himself is now in a better land than the one we are living in now, and that should be a consolation to us, although the emptiness he left behind him is still the same; there is still that sense of loss which will stay with us as long as we live. After that we will all be reunited forever. I hope this letter will find you in St. Petersburg; perhaps you will all be getting together for Christmas and the New Year. If so, remember me to your whole family, and tell them that my sister and I wish you all the best for a happy new year. If you see dear Lidiya, tell her that I think of her often, and that I was pleased to hear from you about her family. I sincerely hope that Nikola's business will prove successful. Please be good enough to tell him that I am always pleased to hear news of him as well as of his dear wife and son. Mention me also to Venichka. Don't forget anyone, I'm always thinking of every one of you. Perhaps your nephew has gone to join his family for the holidays; if so give him, as well as Ippolit and his family, our best wishes. You wrote to tell me that you wanted to get some information about the School of Jurisprudence in Pierre's time. Mr. Benjamin Favre would certainly be able to help you in your research. He lives in Avenue de Fosse. Perhaps you would also prefer to approach his friend Mr. Duvernois, who could get from him the information you require. Or perhaps you will wait until you come to Montbéliard. How happy we would be if you would think of us during your trip. It wouldn't be much fun for a handsome young officer to come to see two little old ladies, but I would talk to him about his mother, and tell him that she can be summed up in two words: kind-hearted and intelligent. I would also tell him what fun we had in the evenings arranging Sashenka's wedding, when your parents were out. She had a beautiful little carriage with two beautiful horses harnessed to it. Polá wasn't the horse, but the bridegroom. So much time has passed since then, but the memories of those times are still alive, and what happy times they were!

The Duvernois family are all in good health. They were traveling a lot in the summer—which was very useful for them, especially for Mrs. Ellen, who spent the whole of last season in the south staying with her rich relative. They all send their regards to you, and we are all eagerly looking forward to our forthcoming meeting with you, God willing.

What made you think that my family might have felt that you're not as favorably disposed to me as you should be? I'm afraid that precisely the opposite is true. You were all too nice to me. Our family is shrinking; in August there were five deaths in the family. One of them was a favorite cousin of ours, who died while staying with one of her former pupils. I must confess that of them all, it was the death of a delightful five-year-old boy which upset me the most. He had come to us for the holidays with his mother and two sisters. He died of meningitis! His poor parents were inconsolable. They are the Struzes, a bourgeois family from Paris. My cousin had taken her children to her parents for the holidays, and they called on us on their way back. Their little Robert was so sweet and so clever that he captivated us.

My sister joins me in wishing you the very best and a happy New Year. She never forgets the important days in your calendar. Goodbye for now—and a heartfelt kiss to you.

Yours, Fanny Dürbach and her sister.

♦ ♦ ♦

8.

Montbéliard, 31 July [18]96

Dear Modest,

Your long awaited letter finally arrived. I had hoped that it would announce that you would soon be with us, but you don't say a word about that. Could it be that the death of your brother-in-law is preventing you from making the trip which you had encouraged us to hope for? What a blow that death must have been! Pierre told me that Mr. Davydov enjoyed good health, and also that he was a model husband, and consequently a wonderful father. How sorry I am for your nephew and also for poor Lidiya—how much trouble she has known in this world! Please convey to them our heartfelt condolences in their grief. Please tell us about each and every one of them. How I long to be able to express my sympathies to them—and to the young widow—in person! As you know, everything that affects everyone in your family is close to my heart.

Your brother, Nikola, must have felt very sad about letting his wife and child go down to the country when he couldn't go with them. I'm sure you see each other very often since you are so close. Please give him my warm greetings. I am full of admiration for the zeal with which you are pursuing the noble task you have undertaken, but I fear that you may no longer be able to prevent the book swelling into an enormous tome. Unquestionably, all of Pierre's letters are interesting. They came from the heart, and it's the heart that they speak to; moreover his descriptions and observations have a particular appeal. The letters he received undoubtedly include many appeals for his help and intervention; people turned to him in particular because they knew that he was incapable of turning them down. My greatest wish is to see you keeping alive . . .[75]

♦ ♦ ♦

9.

Montbéliard, 20 March 1899

Dear Modest,

Two days ago, on the 18th of March, I received a very nice letter from professor Knorr[76] in Frankfurt am Main. He says that he had the pleasure of knowing your brother personally and was an admirer. A society in Berlin has commissioned him to write a biography of the great composer, and because he wants his work to be worthy of his subject, he is trying to gather as much relevant material as possible for the purpose. You, of course, with your usual kindness responded with your help and even encouragement by suggesting that he ask me if I would share with him some of my memories of Pierre's childhood, which he promises to return to me in full and in perfect condition. Those of Pierre's papers which are in my possession no longer belong to me, and are ready to be sent to your family after my death. I am happy to act as their curator, but, as I told you in Montbéliard, they are to be returned to you. I cannot bring myself to entrust them to the postal service—unless, of course, you yourself ask me to do so. Nevertheless, I would be very happy to see a biography of our dear Pierre published in German. Seven of the girls I used to teach are still living in Germany. Two are unmarried, but all the rest have families, and I would love them to have the opportunity to appreciate your brother by reading his biography. If the comprehensive biography which you are authoring is written for musicians and scholars, what about another one for a wider public including school libraries? This would highlight the noble spirit of the poet and the great artist that he was. To produce a work of this kind would inspire people to love and respect humanity, and would be a noble endeavor, and if professor Knorr feels that the material concerning your brother that I have in my keeping would be of some use to him in his work, then he should come to Montbéliard, as you did. However, there is one thing I'm afraid of; that is that what is very important to me and what I value very highly may not seem so important to him. Furthermore, I am now very old, and in this day and age the elderly are not particularly popular. So would you mind writing to Mr. Knorr, and with all your natural tact and delicacy inform him of all the reasons for my refusal—I also expect to be sending him a few lines.

As you know, my sister and I, and even the Duvernois family, love to receive every one of your letters, so please do not keep us waiting too long for the next one.

I have the deepest respect for the humanity of his majesty, the Tsar of Russia; may God bless him for being a lover of peace. Please send me the address of your brother, Nikola, and also the address of Alekseev.[77] Send me news of all your family, I love them all, and am always thinking of them just as I did in Votkinsk. Pierre has taught me to love you also, my dear Modest, as well as your brother Anatoly. May God preserve you!

Your devoted Fanny Dürbach—teacher from Montbéliard, France, (Dube)

Don't forget to remember me to my dear Lidiya and her family.

✦ ✦ ✦

10.

Montbéliard, 22 May 1899

Dear Modest, Your nice, affectionate letter deserved a quicker response, but my state of health is the reason for this involuntary delay.

Ever since Easter I have been suffering from influenza, and it's taking me a long time to recover. First of all, let me congratulate you on buying Pierre's house, a peaceful retreat which he loved so much and where he did so much of his work. I'm sure you will say that when you are there, you are surrounded by cherished memories which make your work so much more gratifying.[78] I'm also convinced that everyone who loved your brother will be coming to see once again his favorite place to stay.

Dare I ask you why you still haven't sent the first volume of his biography to be published. Would you mind telling me something about your work—but you will when you come and we'll be able to sit down and talk face to face, if only . . . If only you knew how eagerly I look forward to my meeting with you and your nephew. My sister shares my feeling, and she was flattered to learn that you have some memory of her kitchen garden; tending it is still her favorite occupation. She would very much like to see your own beautiful garden and pretty house, as well as those parts of your country where she once lived, but now she can no longer face the prospect of traveling—even in France.

Thank you, dear Modest, for all your news about yourself and your family. You know how interested I am in hearing anything about them, and I'm happy to know that Nikola and his family are in good health.

✦

25 July.
Many weeks have gone by since I started this letter; my health has not yet been restored, although there have been better days when I could have written to you, but I was waiting for professor Knorr to return two of Pierre's letters which I sent to him with your permission. Pierre's letter also includes a letter from Nikola, the only one written to me when he was a child, and a letter from Pierre himself in which he describes how you all celebrated your father's name day in Alapayevsk. Perhaps I will only get those letters back when Mr. Knorr's book has been published, but I wanted you to know where those precious letters are right now. If I didn't send him any of Pierre's poems, it was because I had to detach from the notebook those pages which contained the ones I preferred, and you know how afraid I am of entrusting any of these papers to the post.

The Duvernois family were deeply touched to learn that you remembered them, and are all eagerly looking forward to seeing you again. I join my sister in sending you our best wishes, and I add my own best wishes to all of you. I can assure you that I never forget any of you. At my age people write their memoirs, and the memories I have are very precious to me. Please remember me to my dear Lidiya and her family.

I am sure that Paul, my dear little Paul, is tremendously proud to be a grandpa.[79] Congratulate him for me. Please don't make me wait too long for your letters. Give my love to your beloved nephew and, once again, to all the members of your family, whom I love so dearly, from your devoted

Fanny Dürbach.

✦ ✦ ✦

11.

Montbéliard, 16 July, 1900

Dear Modest, it will be two weeks tomorrow since I received that lovely parcel from professor Knorr, but so far I have been unable to express to you the delight I felt when I first looked through the book. In its foreword, Mr. Knorr extends his thanks to all those friends and admirers of your dear brother, and to you in particular, dear Modest—but still in spite of my own pleasure in being able to read this biography in a language I know, and in realizing that many people in this country whom I know and love will also be able to read it, I can't help regretting that your own book was not the first to appear. Please don't be angry with me, but I do think that you should have been the first to write about Pierre, because no one could have done it better than you. What trials and tribulations poor Pierre had to overcome in order to achieve fame; but that's the way life always is—never a crown without a cross!

✦

1 August.

Many days have now passed since I started this letter. I have been having terrible headaches because of the torrid heat, and this has prevented me from taking up the pen.

You have said that you would come in February, and we've been looking forward to your visit ever since. We also think that you will be coming with your nephew to the exhibition. At the beginning of the winter, the weather was so bad that perhaps you couldn't face the prospect of traveling—to Italy. I am sending this letter to Klin, since it is the only address I have, and with the weather like it is now, it's nice to be at one's dacha in the country. How I would like to hear some news about you all. It's so easy for you to write to me. How delightful it must be to be staying in Klin, and how much you must treasure it! I gave the Duvernois ladies a copy of your dear brother's biography. You can't imagine how happy it made them, not to mention myself, we talk about you often. They are going to Switzerland, but I do hope that they won't be away when you come here. Please, please write me a few lines! You write with such facility. Tell me about your nephew, your brothers, and about your dear niece and about all of you. You know I always remember all of you. My sister sends you her affectionate greetings. We had a terrible December, but with the New Year my sister began to feel a little better, but now she is suffering from the heat, but I mustn't complain. God sends us so many blessings, and I should be grateful for them.

Write us a few words.

With sincere affection
Your ever devoted
Fanny Dürbach

When you see my dear Lidiya, remember me to her. How many memories it brought back when I saw the picture of that dear house in Votkinsk. I would also like to hear some news of your dear sister Zinaida's children.

✦ ✦ ✦

12.

Montbéliard, 9 November, 1900

My dear Modest,

I would have been so pleased to get your nice letter, if it hadn't contained news of your dear nephew's illness, although you did express your hope for a swift recovery. Pray God that this nice young man will get well soon. Stomach ailments are not dangerous, although very painful; I am troubled less by them in the winter than in the summer when it is so hot.

How happy we will be to see you if you come to Montbéliard as you intended.

If time destroys everything and takes away one's health, it has no power over those sincere affections which, like our most treasured possessions, we will carry with us beyond the grave.

If only you knew how happy I was to hear of the warm reception you were given in Leipzig, where I spent my first three years abroad, and of which I still have good memories. So strange that none of my former pupils chose to settle there.

What makes you think that Pierre's name enjoys less renown in France than in Germany? Judging from what I have seen in Montbéliard, our small town, it's my impression that quite the opposite is true. How is your biography progressing? I'm very pleased to hear that it's going to be translated into German, but I hope it will be translated into French too. Have you received a copy of Mr. Knorr's book? I hope you are happy with it; I am reading it with the keenest interest. Pierre's sister Sasha really loved him, and it was her company he sought when he needed comforting and cheering up. From her earliest years she had the gift of winning the trust of others, and was your mother's little friend. What a bitter loss it was for her children to lose such a mother at such a young age.

✦

14 December.

It's been many days since I started this letter, and I was even tempted to tear it up, but you will see that I was thinking of you. My sister came down with bronchitis again, but it was not as bad as last year and now she is much better, and we have God to thank for that, because I'm not much use these days. I expect you will be going to St. Petersburg and will be seeing my dear Lidiya there, and, of course, her dear daughter, Katya, will be with her. Please give the ladies my best, and also my dear Polá—already a grandpa; I would so like to see all of you again, and even those who have forgotten me. I have received a postcard from Moscow with only enough space for a few words; if your brother Nikola could send me one like that, I would be very grateful to him. Would you mind telling him this? If only you knew how much France has been blessing God for restoring your universally beloved Tsar[80] to health—a lot more so than Russia herself has!

Winter weather hasn't arrived here yet; we have had rain together with thunderstorms; flooding has been feared, but so far the cold has not been severe. Perhaps you will be spending the winter in Italy where you will enjoy constant fine weather. But if you are in Russia, please give our warm greetings to your nephew, your sister-in-law, and her daughter.

And if you're not too busy, and you get news of my dear Zinaida's children, please tell them that their late mother's old friend is thinking of them. I took the liberty of presenting the Duvernois ladies with Pierre's biography and was thrilled to hear that they had so much pleasure in reading it. We often talk about you, about Pierre, and all of you.

Goodbye for now, God willing!

I join my sister in sending you our heartfelt greetings, and I wish you all the best. I remember everyone, and Nikola and Venichka are in my thoughts.

Your devoted and grateful friend
Fanny Dürbach

♦♦♦

LETTER FROM FREDERIKA DÜRBACH TO MODEST ILYICH TCHAIKOVSKY

Montbéliard, 16 October 1901

Dear Mr. Tchaikovsky,

It is now a year since we received your last letter. At that time you were in Berlin with your sick nephew; I hope he has fully recovered. That is my heartfelt wish, and I am praying to God for it. You must have received the news of my sister's death[81] that I sent you. God took her from us on the 1st of May. Without the opportunity to do any more teaching life had become a burden to her, and it was her wish to leave us without delay for that place from which there is no return. She wasn't even very ill, just a little weak, with some difficulty in breathing. She got up every day and made her own bed and remembered you and your whole family very often. She prepared everything she had kept as a memorial to your dear brother. Be so kind as to let me know the address to which I should send you these keepsakes, as well as the letters your dear brother sent her, if they would be of value to you.

Recently, the October number of a Swiss review published a biography of your beloved brother in French. I obtained a copy, and both my acquaintances and I very much enjoyed reading it.

The Duvernois ladies are in good health and have friendly memories of you, and whenever they visit we talk about you a lot. Mr. Duvernois is getting older but is always going out for walks, since so far the weather here hasn't been terribly cold, just rather damp. I hope that your brothers, and nephews and nieces, as well as your sisters-in-law[82] are all in good health; please give them all my regards.

Thank God, my health is not bad, and I try to maintain it as far as possible. I imagine that your biography, if not yet completed, is well advanced. We haven't received any advance announcements, and I don't know whether you will be sending one to us, as you had intended. However, since I have Mr. Knorr's biography, as well as the one in the Swiss review, I will wait for yours patiently.[83]

Goodbye for now, dear Mr. Tchaikovsky; if you should ever come to Montbéliard, it will be an enormous pleasure for yours faithfully,
Frederika Dürbach.

Pyotr Tchaikovsky; Moscow, 1868

3　Letters by Pyotr Ilyich Tchaikovsky

THE MAJORITY OF Tchaikovsky's letters presented in this chapter are addressed to his younger brothers, the twins, Modest and Anatoly. When they were born, Pyotr Tchaikovsky was ten years old. As he wrote to his "chère et bonne M-elle Fanny" on 2 May 1850, "Je les ai déjà vus plusieurs fois; mais chaque fois que je les vois je crois que ce sont des Anges qui ont descendu sur la terre [I have already seen them several times, but each time when I see them I believe that they are angels who have descended to earth]." The boy's moving welcome to his baby brothers marked the beginning of a passionate lifelong bond between Pyotr, Modest, and Anatoly Tchaikovsky. Even though the composer was sincerely devoted to his other siblings, Nikolay, Ippolit, and especially Aleksandra,[1] he enjoyed an exceptional closeness to the twins, who were just four years old when their mother, Aleksandra Tchaikovskaya, died. Tchaikovsky's emotional attachment to the boys went hand in hand with a deep sense of responsibility for their well-being. Here is what he wrote to his sister in September of 1862:

> I got up at an uncommonly early hour today: I was woken by Tolya and Modya, who were leaving for school. By the way, I should remark here that my affection for these little fellows, in particular (and this is confidential) for the former, increases every day. I'm personally very

proud and fond of this finest emotion of my heart. At the sad moments in my life I just need to think about them and life becomes dear to me again. I try as much as possible to replace a mother's care and caresses, of which fortunately for them they don't carry the burden of remembrance, with my love and it seems I'm succeeding in it.[2]

The school where Tolya and Modya studied was the same School of Jurisprudence that was earlier attended by Pyotr Ilyich.

Anatoly Ilyich Tchaikovsky, upon his graduation in 1869, began the career of a civil servant and, over the years, steadily advanced to increasingly higher positions. Pyotr Ilyich always expressed great interest in all aspects of Tolya's life, including the turns in his brother's career. The composer even occasionally used his personal connections in order to foster it.[3] At the same time, he was very aware of Anatoly's doubts about his choice of profession and lingering dissatisfaction with his life:

> It really grieves me that you are so depressed. I won't try to console you, because you say yourself, and with reason, that at bottom, you have nothing to complain about. But, since I'm a few years older than you, I think I can claim the privilege of offering you some advice. I couldn't be more familiar with the feelings you are having now. As I see it, there are two reasons for your low spirits. 1) it's your nerves, and that's something which can always put you in a black mood without any particular reason, and 2) wounded pride.[4]

Despite his bouts of melancholy, Anatoly Ilyich had been firmly placed on the career ladder and continued to move smoothly up.

A succession of government appointments took him to many locations in the Russian Empire, and his older brother visited him often. In 1885, Anatoly Tchaikovsky received yet another appointment and moved to Tiflis (now known as Tbilisi, the capital of Georgia). There, he began his service as state prosecutor but soon was promoted to deputy governor. By that time he was married, and his newfound family life as well as his career advancement brought a great deal of emotional balance to Anatoly's life.[5] When, in the spring of 1886, Pyotr Ilyich made his first trip to Tiflis, he wrote that Tolya "has a very happy, contented air about him, and it is apparent from his dignified demeanor and confidence, which weren't noticeable before, that he is a bigwig here."[6]

Tchaikovsky also found that his music was well known and loved in the Georgian capital. The Imperial Russian Musical Society at Tiflis and Anatoly Ilyich, who served as a board member of the society, didn't spare any effort to turn the composer's visit into a glorious event. The theater where the celebration of Tchaikovsky took place "was decorated with greenery and flowers and the composer's box was immersed in his beloved lilies of the valley. The adornment of the theater created an extraordinarily elated, festive atmosphere [. . .] for the entire audience. Tchaikovsky was, as it were, a guest of the whole of Tiflis."[7] Following his initial trip to Georgia, Pyotr continued visiting his brother every year until he died in 1893. Anatoly outlived Pyotr by more than twenty years, and he died in 1915. He held the rank of privy councillor, the third-highest office in the Russian Empire.

Modest Ilyich Tchaikovsky, who received the same education as both Anatoly and Pyotr at the Imperial School of Jurisprudence, didn't follow his twin brother's career path. Although he worked for several years in the judicial system, he left civil service after receiving an offer to become a tutor to a deaf-mute boy from a wealthy family named Nikolay Germanovich Konradi (1868–1922). Modest Ilyich turned to the study of a teaching method for deaf people, which he then used to educate his pupil; eventually he taught young Nikolay to talk, read, and write, and later became his legal guardian. This employment allowed Modest to have a relatively flexible schedule and to devote more time to his somewhat eclectic though adamant literary aspirations. Early on, Pyotr Ilyich didn't support Modya's ambitions:

> I don't really like your melancholic mood, but I perfectly understand it—I've experienced the same when I was your age. I'm just afraid that by yielding to gloomy feelings you will stop your studies. Yet I assure you that work is the only salvation from emotional pain. You had the misfortune to be born with the soul of an artist and you will always be drawn into that world of sublime spiritual joy. But because, along with the sensitivity of your artistic nature, you are not endowed with talent, for God's sake, be careful not to submit to your inclinations.[8]

Later, however, the composer acknowledged his brother's predilection for writing and became much more appreciative about Modest's literary talents. He wrote to Anatoly in 1878,

Yesterday, [. . .] Modest read me two chapters of a novel he's been working on bit by bit for some time now. I was amazed. It's so good, clever, subtle, interesting and fresh that I couldn't believe that the author himself was sitting there right in front of my eyes. Modest has serious, undeniable talent.[9]

Gradually, Modest began to succeed in his literary career. His articles on theater and music appeared in various periodicals; he also published some of his prose writings, including a short story printed in one of the leading literary journals, *The Russian Messenger.* Another medium he tried with reasonable success was drama—a few of his plays were performed and favorably received in St. Petersburg, though arguably Modest Tchaikovsky has earned his most notable recognition as an opera and ballet librettist. His first foray into operatic libretto resulted in sharing success with his famous brother. That opera, *The Queen of Spades,* premiered to rave reviews in St. Petersburg on 7/19 December 1890.[10] The following year, the brothers collaborated on the next and last of the composer's operas, *Iolanta.* After 1893, Modest Ilyich continued writing libretti for Russian composers, including one for Sergey Rachmaninoff's opera *Francesca da Rimini.*

What became the main focus of his life, however, was shaping the legacy of Pyotr Ilyich Tchaikovsky. Modest Ilyich's role was instrumental in the founding of the Tchaikovsky House Museum in Klin. He created an invaluable archive containing his brother's vast correspondence, manuscripts, photos, memoirs of his contemporaries, and other documents. The high point of his work on the composer's papers was the writing of *The Life of Pyotr Ilyich Tchaikovsky,* a three-volume biography published in 1900–1902.[11]

Notwithstanding the importance of Modest's unique contribution to Tchaikovsky studies, it is not a secret that he assiduously cultivated his brother's image as a musical genius whose creative brilliance was fully matched by his unblemished life and remarkable personality. For the sake of such an idealized portrait, Modest concealed everything that was related to the composer's homosexuality and even made a number of deliberate cuts in the original documents kept in the Tchaikovsky archives.[12]

Modest Ilyich Tchaikovsky died in 1916 in Moscow and was buried at a cemetery near Klin.

✦✦✦

1. TO ALEKSANDRA ANDREEVNA TCHAIKOVSKAYA

[St. Petersburg, 21 September 1851][13]

Dear Mommy, I kiss your lovely hands and fingers and everything.
P[yotr] T[chaikovsky]

✦✦✦

2. TO MODEST ILYICH TCHAIKOVSKY

12 October [1869, Moscow].[14]

My lovable little brother!

I'm just so busy that I can hardly find the time to write to you, and that's the only reason why you've so rarely had the pleasure of hearing from me.

Here's what I've been so busy with:

1) Arranging Anton Rubinstein's overture *Ivan the Terrible* for piano four hands.
2) Finishing work on, and correcting the folk songs for piano four hands.[15]
3) Writing the overture to Romeo and Juliet.
4) Preparing the lectures for my new course on musical form.[16]

Apart from all this, I have to sacrifice a good deal of my time for Konstantinov[17] who arrived from Odessa for a short stay and has simply taken me over. I've been staying at home a lot, although I go out almost every evening. Mostly with Bibikov[18] who comes to pick me up. By the way, don't think badly of me; the two of us just support one another on the prickly path of virtue and try to stay as pure as doves. I hardly ever see Gruzinsky or Petashenka;[19] Petashenka used to drop by with the criminal intention of observing the Cadet Corps, which is right opposite our windows, but I've been trying to discourage these compromising visits—and with some success.

The Italian opera is in full swing here: the *Marquisio* sisters[20] are wonderful singers, but after Arto,[21] I can no longer enjoy listening to anyone else. Incidentally, that extraordinarily charming woman is in

St. Petersburg and has been living there for one and a half months (I don't really know why); try to see her, and when you do, just think that I came so close to tying the Hymeneal knot with her.

I'm really happy that you liked Menshikova.[22] I've always been one of her few admirers here in Moscow. As for my opera,[23] not a whisper; I'm beginning to think it will never be performed; by the way, I've just written a letter to Gideonov[24] asking him for a definite answer about the fate of my opera; I now think that if I had been more aggressive and practical, it would have been put on by now.

The other day, your old friend Petrovsky[25] showed up drunk; Agafon[26] did very well not to let him in. I've received just one letter from Volodya[27] in Paris; he is well and having a good time with Ryumin.[28]

Kisses, my dear Modka, I insist on a letter from you.

Yours, P. Tchaikovsky

Bibikov sends you kisses.

◆ ◆ ◆

3. TO MODEST ILYICH TCHAIKOVSKY

[St. Petersburg, 30 August 1870][29]

Modya! You make me furious. How could you squander that money so irresponsibly, you scoundrel? Haven't you got any shame? I implore you to get back to work energetically; and this is what I mean by "energetically": do exactly what you're told; behave respectfully in the presence of your superiors, even if you don't mean it; if necessary, pay court to their wives, in short—do everything you can to draw attention to yourself. Adamov[30] has written, or is about to write to Kreitern,[31] so you make sure to go to him in the event of any doubts or misunderstandings. Wouldn't it be better for you to transfer to *Tambov*, where you could live with the Kartsevs,[32] and wouldn't that also be more economical? By the 1st of October, I'll buy you some warm clothes, and if possible, before I get my official appointment I'll send you a little something to help you out. Write to me in Moscow.

An affectionate kiss, and say hello to Valuev,[33] and tell him from me what *"a disreputable drunk"* he is.

Once again, a not unaffectionate hug!

Your revered brother, Pyotr.

Think about Tambov, and write to me—that is, if you feel like it.

I kiss you, while at the same time I'd like to give you a thrashing for throwing away that money.

Grrr! Grrrr!

✦ ✦ ✦

4. TO PYOTR IVANOVICH JURGENSON

Moscow, April/May 1873.[34]

Jurgenson!

I'm sending you the prologue to The Snowmaiden.[35] I'll finish the rest on Sunday. If you can, send me 15 rubles in silver, which will save me and my "family"[36] from certain ruin, for I don't have a fucking cent in my pocket.

P. Tchaikovsky

✦ ✦ ✦

5. TO ALEKSEY IVANOVICH SOFRONOV

Kamenka, 7 June [1876][37]

My dear Lyonya!

I've really been missing you and it frightens me to think that I won't be seeing you for a good three months. How are you? In good health, I hope? I left Moscow on the 27th in the morning and went straight to Nizy.[38] I just spent three days there and then left for Kiev where I spent one night. The heat was awful and I bathed twice in the Dnieper. The next day I arrived here in Kamenka by steamer feeling quite ill. I was feverish all day, and it was so bad that even now I haven't quite recovered. I'm going to stay here for two weeks and then go abroad to see my sister. I'm really hoping to get a letter from you; if you've already written to me in Nizy, then the letter will be sent on to me here. If you haven't yet written, do so right away and be sure to copy my correct address abroad.

"France. Vichy. Poste Restante. M. Pierre de Tchaikovsky"

Goodbye, dear Lyonya, big kiss. Stay healthy, don't mope, and write to me.

Yours P. T[chaikovsky]

✦ ✦ ✦

6. TO ALEKSEY IVANOVICH SOFRONOV

Vichy, 3/15 July 1876.[39]

My dear Lyonya,

I've been here in Vichy for three days now, and I'm taking the waters. I'm terribly bored and not an hour goes by without my thinking of you. My God, if only I were rich! I would be sending for you right this minute. I left Kamenka on June the 18th, and arrived in Vienna on the 20th. I've been here a week waiting for my sister who has moved here with her whole family to her country place. I spent just one day with her, saw her off, and went straight to Lyon to meet Modest. I spent three days in Lyon without leaving his and his pupil's side. I had a great time with them, but now it's such a drag that I can't find any peace of mind. If it hadn't been for my health I would be taking off for Moscow right this minute. Today I got a letter from Nikolay Lvovich[40] who says he went to our apartment and wanted to take the newspapers, but the doorman said that you had come and taken them. Is it true?

Why were you in Moscow? I got your letter and Misha's[41] while I was still in Kamenka. I was overjoyed. I was hoping to find a letter from you waiting for me at the address I sent you, but obviously my Lyonka was taking it a bit too easy in the country[42] and didn't care to give me the pleasure of getting even a couple of lines from him. At the beginning of August I'm returning to Russia to see my sister in the country; please write to me there. *Kiev province. Cherkassky District. Village of Smiela.* And from there *to P. I. Tch[aikovsky], Kamenka, care of Lev Vasilievich Davydov.*

Kiss Misha for me, and tell him that I'll write to him next time. Big hug.
Yours P. Tchaikovsky
Say hello to your mother, Olga,[43] and your sisters.

✦ ✦ ✦

7. TO MODEST ILYICH TCHAIKOVSKY

28 September 1876 [Moscow][44]

Dear Modya! I've lost your letter, so I can't respond to your arguments against marriage point by point. To me many of them didn't hold water; on the other hand, many were completely in line with my own thinking. I remember that you predicted the same fate was in store for me as that of Kondratiev,[45] Bulatov,[46] and *tutti quanti* [Italian: all those others]. You can rest assured that if ever my plans are carried out, I certainly won't be following in the footsteps of those gentlemen.[47] Next you say that I shouldn't give a damn about *qu'en dira-t'on!* [French: what will people say]. That's only true up to a point. There are people who can't look down on me for my failings simply because they grew fond of me before they suspected that I was a man who had as good as lost his reputation. Sasha is a case in point![48] I know she has guessed the *truth* and forgives me *unreservedly*. The same goes for a great many others whom I love and respect. Do you really think that it doesn't weigh heavily on me that I am aware that they *pity* me and *forgive* me, when in actual fact I haven't done anything wrong! Can you understand how it kills me to think that people who love me can sometimes *feel ashamed* of me! It's happened a hundred times, and will happen a hundred times more. In short, what I want is to get married or openly have an affair with a woman in order to shut the mouths of all those scum whose opinions I don't give a damn about, but who can cause pain to people close to me. In any case, don't worry about me, my dear Modya. It will be longer than you think before my plan is carried out. My habits and tastes have become too much a part of me to be cast off like an old glove. I'm very far from possessing a will of iron, and since my letters to you I've already given way three times to my natural *proclivities*. Just imagine! Only the other day I made a trip to the village where *Bulatov* lives, and whose house is nothing less than a male brothel. And not only did I go there, *but I fell madly in love* with his coachman!!! So you're quite right when you say that people are totally incapable, no matter how hard they try, of not yielding to their weaknesses.

Nevertheless, I'm going to stand by my intentions, and you can be sure that one way or another I will see them through. But I'm not going to rush into anything or do anything impetuous. Whatever happens, I'm not going to *tie myself down*. It's either going to be an official marriage or an affair with a woman, but only in a way that won't interfere with my peace of mind or my freedom. However, for the time being, I have nothing specific in mind.

The other day Al[eksandra] Ar[kadievna] Davydova[49] was here. I met her twice—she's a lovely person. The rehearsals of Vakula will start at the beginning of October. I have no worries about that. Will we be seeing each other? Now, I think you can give me a positive answer. Before I end this letter, I just have to tell you that I adore Kolya *passionately*,[50] I'm just *crazy* about him. Somehow or other I just have to see you both this winter.

P. *Tchaikovsky*

Say hello to Mme. Kondratieva and Fofa[51] for me.

✦ ✦ ✦

8. TO ANATOLY ILYICH TCHAIKOVSKY

12 January 1877 [Moscow][52]

Dear Tolya,

I got your letter this morning.[53] It was very upsetting. Why have you taken to moping? I really don't understand. Women adore you, you're successful in your career, and everyone who knows you loves you! The only thing missing is money! Can this really be the only reason why you are so down in the mouth? If that's really the way it is, I'll just have to drown myself, because it's hard to imagine that anyone's affairs could be in a bigger mess than my own. The thing is, Tolya, I really need to see you. Is there any way you could possibly manage to come here for a whole week of Shrovetide? Perhaps because Papa is so old and sick I should really find an opportunity to go to St. Petersburg. But after *Vakula*, our capital has become really repellent to me,[54] and as you can easily foresee, I'll have much less time to spend with you in St. Petersburg than in Moscow. And, of course, living in Moscow won't cost you a penny. I'm waiting for your answer. If you prefer to come not for Shrovetide, but earlier, so much the better. I'm really anxious to see you.

I won't be going to see Glamsha[55]—unless I'm invited. I've seen her a few times and have been very attentive. She's a very good looking woman, but alas, that means nothing to me,[56] and, to be frank, I would be very pleased if I didn't have to pay her visits. Incidentally, I have accumulated a lot of business to attend to, and apart from that I'm preoccupied night and day with the thought of going to Paris in March to give a *concert*, something which everybody here and in Paris is advising me to do. For this concert I'm going to need no more and no less than—2,000 rubles! And where can I get that kind of money?

In any case, all the arrangements have been made; and if I don't get the money—I'll have to cancel.[57] There's no point in hesitating and playing for time. Please don't say anything to anyone, except Modest, about this for now. Do come, dear Tolya.

Yours, P. Tchaikovsky

✦ ✦ ✦

9. TO MODEST ILYICH TCHAIKOVSKY

St. Petersburg, 8 July [1877][58]

Modya! I have the feeling you're worrying about me, and I feel the need to put your mind at rest. I was married on the 6th of July.[59] Tolya was present. I must confess it was a very difficult day for me, if only because I had to go through the ordeal of a wedding ceremony, a long wedding breakfast, and a ceremonial send-off and all that stuff. I slept wonderfully well on the journey. We spent quite a nice day yesterday, went for a drive in the evening, and enjoyed some entertainment at Krestovsky Island;[60] the night too passed very peacefully. No deflowering took place, nor is it likely to happen any time soon. But I have arranged matters so that that is something I won't have to worry about. My wife has one great quality: she is blindly compliant with my every wish. She is of an extremely equable disposition, content with everything, and wants nothing more than to be a support and comfort to me. Do I love her, well, that's too early to say; but I already have the feeling that I may come to do so once we're used to each other.

Anyway, this is what I want to ask you, Modenka! Until August my wife and I will be inseparable: here in the country at her mother's,[61] in Moscow, and wherever. On the 1st of August, I'll be leaving Moscow and going straight to Sasha's[62] where, whatever happens, I'll spend a few days. I can't tell you how much I'm hoping that you will extend your stay until I come; what a pleasure it would be to see you there! But if you can't stay for a few more days, then wouldn't you agree to come to Sasha's later than the 15th of July as you had planned. In any case, do try to arrange it so that we can meet.

I wrote the *better part* of *Onegin* in Glebov, and very much hope to complete it before the start of the school year—but I don't know if I'll be able to do it in time.

My most tender kisses; there's nothing more to write for now. I love you, and in the midst of all the little troubles I'm having right now, it's the thought of you that gives me something to look forward to.

Yours, P. Tchaikovsky

Kiss Kolya for me, and my greetings to Alina Ivanovna, her husband,[63] and dear Sofia Aleksandrovna.[64]

❖ ❖ ❖

10. TO ANATOLY ILYICH TCHAIKOVSKY

St. Petersburg, 9 July [1877][65]

My dear and precious Tolya!

Yesterday was a day of constant mood swings ranging from total calm to unbearable anguish. I was tormented by the same old anxiety and despair over you in spite of the telegrams from you and Kotek,[66] who told me that you had left in good spirits.

How unfeeling and heartless it was of me to tell you that I would not go to Laroche because I was worried about the 25 rubles.[67] How could I have been so selfish! Well, I did go, and thank heavens I did. In the first place he greeted me like a Jew welcoming the Messiah. Clearly he was at the very brink of ruin, and clutched at me like a drowning man at a straw. Well, I want to be that straw and do everything possible to rescue my drowning friend. Secondly he stayed for dinner and spent the whole evening with us: he was very nice to my wife, and, most importantly, he acted as a buffer between us, easing the strain of our *tete-a-tete*. I should say that this "strain" was only on my part. She seemed to be perfectly happy and at ease. In the evening we went to the Kamyenno-ostrovsky theatre and then went back to my place for tea and beer (in very small quantities). His presence really raised my spirits. Last night there was the first attempt—a rather feeble one: let's say that it didn't meet any resistance, although of course the attempt itself was pretty feeble. However, this first step helped a great deal. It brought me closer to my wife because I resorted to various manipulations which established a certain intimacy between us. Today I feel immeasurably freer in my relations with her.

The weather is awful. I don't know to handle this evening, but in any case, Laroche will be there. I promised to go and see him at 3 p.m. Yesterday I had two encounters. The first in the morning when I was walking arm in arm with my wife and I met Niks Litke[68] on the Nevsky Prospekt. I spoke to him, but for some reason couldn't bring myself to introduce the lady as my wife. The second in the evening on the way to the theatre when I ran into Konstantinov.[69] I didn't say anything to him either, and this time emerged from the encounter only five rubles the poorer. The money is trickling through my fingers like water. I think the first of August is going to be the happiest day of my life.[70]

Yours, P. Tchaikovsky.

✦ ✦ ✦

11. TO ANATOLY ILYICH TCHAIKOVSKY

St. Petersburg, 13 July 1877.[71]

Tolichka, yesterday was perhaps the worst of all the days since the 6th of July. This morning I felt as if my life had been destroyed forever and I was in a state of total despair. By 3 o'clock a lot of people had come round: N. Rubinstein, his sister Sophie,[72] Malozemova,[73] K. Yu. Davidov, Ivanov,[74] Bessel, Laroche. We dined together. In the evening we first saw off Nikolay Grigorievich to Moscow and then Malozemova and Sophie to Peterhof.

After returning home with my wife and Laroche, we ordered roast beef, vodka, and beer as usual. Now, every evening I've begun to drink a little so that I can get some untroubled sleep. Finally, Laroche, who has become very cheerful after his bout of depression, left. It was the moment of the day that I dreaded the most, when I was left alone with my wife. We walked round with our arms around each other and I suddenly felt calm and content . . . I don't know how that happened! No matter what, from that moment, everything around me suddenly became bright and clear, and I felt that whatever my wife might be, she was *my wife,* and that there was something absolutely right and normal about this . . .[75]

For the first time I woke up this morning without that feeling of despair and hopelessness. There's nothing the least bit unpleasant about my wife. I'm already beginning to feel about her the way every husband does with a wife he's not in love with. Most important of all, today I've begun to feel entirely at ease with her, don't feel I have to entertain her with conversation, and am quite calm. August the 1st no longer seems some kind of distant harbor where I'll be moored for a while before embarking once and for all on some ocean of despair. Now I am simply focusing on the delightful prospect of seeing you again. So you may congratulate me.

Today, I have finally weathered the crisis. I'm on the mend. But what an awful, awful, awful crisis it was. If it hadn't been for my love for you and all those closest to me supporting me throughout my *unbearable inner torment,* it might all have ended badly, that is, in sickness or madness.

Today we are going straight to Moscow. My wife has heard that the money due to her from the mortgaging of the woods is waiting for her. Then we're off to the country.[76] Then, I'll steal a day or two from July and wait it out until God grants me the joy of seeing you.

Big kiss.

I give you my word, there's no need to worry about me. I'm fully and truly convalescent.

♦ ♦ ♦

12. TO ALEKSEY SOFRONOV

16/28 October 1877, Clarens[77]

The address: Switzerland. Canton de Vaud. Clarens. Pension Richelieu. M. Pierre de Tchaikovsky.

My dear Lyonya!

Just got your letter, and can't tell you how happy I was to get it. Up to now, I had heard nothing from you and was very worried about you. Thank God you're in good health. My precious, look after yourself and don't fret. For the moment, I still have no idea what to do about the apartment.[78] I'm waiting for various letters and replies; I first have to decide whether I'm going to stay here for long and what I am going to do about Antonina Ivanovna. In any case, you will stay in the apartment until the 1st of December, but not a day longer. By that time either I will have returned to Russia or sent for you to join me here. *Tolya* will be returning to Russia at the end of November, and if I decide to leave the apartment, I'll get him to make all the arrangements. He'll be seeing Ant[onina] Iv[anovna] and, if she wants, she can sell off everything she bought. Our things we'll move to the Conservatory. In any case, I will no longer be living with Ant Iv (*but don't tell any-*

one!) and when I return to Moscow you and I will live together. Now, Lyonya, you'll have to be patient for a little and things will be dull for a while; but you can be sure that I will never leave you and until my dying breath I will always love you like my own brother. Write to me and let me know if you need any money. If you do, I'll give you a note for Jurgenson and you'll get some from him. Please Lyonya, don't stint yourself, eat to your heart's content, and if you're bored, go to the theatre or the circus. I'll take care of all the expenses. Now, here's what I want you to do for me. *Take the hard-bound music manuscript book which contains my symphony—the one we took with us to Kamenka: inside that book you'll find another soft cover music manuscript book where I had started writing out the score.*[79] *Take all that to Jurgenson, who will send the music on to me.* Be very careful with it.

Goodbye my dear, my precious. I send you countless kisses.

Yours, P. Tchaikovsky[80]

Write back right away.

✦ ✦ ✦

13. TO ALEKSEY SOFRONOV

[Clarens], 27 October/8 November [?] 1877][81]

Lyonya!

Deliver the barrel of white wine to Nikolay Grigorievich Rubinstein's apartment.

I have written to Nik[olay] Lvovich[82] to tell him how to arrange for you to travel here. Follow all his instructions. At the end of December[83] I'll send you your fare to *Vienna.* And I'll wait for you there. Thanks for your letter I kiss you, my precious

✦ ✦ ✦

14. TO ANATOLY ILYICH TCHAIKOVSKY

Venice, 8/20 Dec[ember] 1877.[84]

Tolichka!

Nothing special happened today. The weather has taken a turn for the worse, and I can hear the sounds of a storm at sea in the distance— even behind closed windows.

Yesterday evening I got into a row with Alyosha.[85] It all began when I noticed that when he thought I wasn't looking, he was putting some kind of ointment on a cloth, and it wasn't the first time this week that I had noticed it. Up to last evening he had been trying to put me off the scent by talking about some kind of pimple which had appeared somewhere on his body. But yesterday he suddenly blushed, and I began to suspect that there was some problem with his genitals. I started to press him on the details, but he refused to answer, and I lost my temper. I tore up a tie, a shirt, and broke a chair, among other things. While I was busy with these strange gymnastic exercises, my eyes suddenly met his. He was scared stiff, and went all pale, and gave me such a pitiful look that when he finally managed to stammer out a few words like: "What's wrong with you?" and "Calm down!," I calmed down right away. That's when he began to cry, and I had a hard time trying to make him stop. This, of course, was followed by a reconciliation scene. Tolya, you can't imagine what a nice and good person he really is in spite of his apparent rough manners and indifference. It turned out that it was just a common or garden boil, and he was just trying to hide it from me because he knows how upset I get when anyone around me is the slightest bit sick, and preferred to keep me in the dark. You have to know him as well as I do in order to appreciate his endearing qualities. But what really bothers me is that he didn't bring any books (except Evtushevsky's *Arithmetic* and the Bible) and he has nothing to do. Two days ago I made him write a letter to Modest, corrected all the mistakes that I could, explained the rules, and made him rewrite it. Today, he's going to write a similar letter to Nik[olay] Lv[ovich].[86] How do you like that Nik Lvovich! Would you believe that he took the letters that came to me at the apartment, and actually opened them and read them!!! When I sent him a letter from Clarens about Alyosha he tried to get him to reply to me that he, Alyosha, was *sick* and couldn't come. In fact, he did everything he could to persuade him not to come by frightening him with everything under the sun. The old fool is not the most scrupulous of men.

My work is in full swing,[87] and I'm finding Venice harder and harder to take every day, and the food is uneatable. I'm expecting a letter from Modest. Why haven't I heard from you yet?

✦

Friday, 9/21.

Today, I finally got my hands on some money. After breakfast I went to the banker and he paid me the whole sum in gold. It would seem to be a tidy sum, but in fact it's hardly enough to live on. I sent *Kotek* a money order for 300 marks, but that's hardly likely to last him very long. The hotel bill for one week came to 247 lira; although that included the telegrams! But if you figure that apart from the hotel, I'll be spending 5 fr[ancs] a day on cigarettes and coffee and other odds and ends, it looks as if I'll be able to make ends meet, but only just. And I won't be surprised to find you telling me to send you money to pay off some debt or other. I'm afraid you'll be getting very little for *Vakula,* and won't have enough to cover my basic necessities! Actually, it seems I'm getting to be more and more like *the old woman* in Pushkin's fairy tale about the *golden fish.* The more money that heaven sends down to me, the more money I want. God knows what I would do without Mme. von Meck! May God bless that woman a thousand times over! Again no letter from you today; I'm starting to get a little worried. However, good old Kotek writes to me every day.

His throat problem has cleared up completely.[88] He heard Sarasate[89] play, but was not impressed. Today I bought *A Hunter's Notebook* and Belokha's *Geography*[90] for Alyosha. How the latter book found its way onto the shelves of a smart bookstore on St. Mark's Square is beyond me. Beyond that, nothing much to report, and I won't write any more in my diary until tomorrow. Alyosha is very, very sweet. But how execrable the food is!

✦

Saturday, 10/22

The first movement of the symphony is almost finished. I worked very hard today and I'm very tired. This morning I received a letter from Modest. He wants to live in San Remo (near Menton). I'm very much in sympathy with his choice. I sent him a telegram to this effect. At the end of the week I'm thinking of going to *San Remo* to prepare everything. I'm hoping it will be possible to make the same arrangements as in Clarens.

I'll be leaving Venice with no regrets. Yesterday evening I felt like a little carousing. I went to the *Birarria di Genova*,[91] where there's singing and gambling every night—a kind of *Café-chantant*. It was a waste of time, the singing was laughable, with pretensions to seriousness, the beer was awful—a total bore. I drank a mug of beer and went home. Today the streets are full of action. Christmas is in three days and gifts are on sale everywhere, people crying their wares, shouting, you can hardly shoulder your way through the crowd. I've just bought from a bookstall for 6 lira a hefty tome of a French illustrated history of Napoleon.[92] I'm drinking some tea and want to take a look at the book. I'm in excellent health, have no worries, and I'm cheerful.

Goodbye! A tender kiss. I'll be sending you the next letter on Wednesday.

P. T[chaikovsky].

♦ ♦ ♦

15. TO ANATOLY ILYICH TCHAIKOVSKY

Sunday, 11/23 Dec[ember] 1877.[93]

Today, I finished work on the hardest part of the symphony, the first movement.[94] After breakfast we went to the Lido[95] and had some coffee in that same restaurant by the sea and spent a long time collecting sea shells. Alyosha was so taken with this activity and was having such a good time that I even found myself sharing his pleasure. He collected just about a pood.

The way back was quite eventful. A fog suddenly descended and was so thick that it was literally impossible to see two steps ahead of us and we went off course and got lost, almost colliding with a barge. We had to stop and ran aground. To make a long story short, it took us a whole hour to get back instead of half an hour. The cold was brutal. I haven't yet received a reply to the telegram I sent to Modest.[96] It's now eleven o'clock. As usual at eight o'clock we had some tea. At nine o'clock I felt like going for a walk and went out. Some *ruffiani* [Italian: pimps], you know the kind, guessed what I was looking for, and wouldn't leave me alone. The bait they were using to hook the prey (i.e., me) was a delightful young creature. I had to put up some fierce resistance because the bait was working. But I didn't let it get the better of me. I don't know whether they wanted to blackmail me, or just screw some money out of me, but I didn't let myself get taken in. To put them to the test, and to give them the impression that I was biting, I followed the bait. When it finally reached one of the main squares, with me following on behind, I stopped outside a café. I had hardly had time to move into the shade when both the *ruffiani,* who had been following, kept on flitting back and forth. In order to put a stop to all this, I intercepted one of them (you remember, the one with the curly hair) and let him have it straight. "Stop all this nonsense! I know exactly what you're after, but you're very much mistaken. If you don't stop harassing me, you'd better watch out!" They didn't know what to say, and I left the field triumphant.

But what a marvelous, attractive bait! No need to worry though, *my word of honor,* I won't let temptation get the better of me.

As a tasty tit-bit, I've left for last my thanks to you for your nice, supremely comforting letter which I received today. It made me so happy to read it. It makes things look so much brighter. I won't take up Sasha's suggestion that I come to live in Verbovka. I'm sure you can understand it would be a little strange, neither one thing nor the other. And, in any case, right now there can be no question of my returning to Russia: Modest is coming to stay with me here! The summer is another matter. The prospect of coming to live in Verbovka is really appealing.

Until tomorrow, Tolya. Big kiss!

◆

12/24 Dec[ember] 1877.
In your letter yesterday you said: *"I'll write again tomorrow."* Well, today I waited a little anxiously for your letter, but it never came. I did, however, get a telegram from Modest[97] to tell me that Alina[98] had given birth and that he was leaving next *Tuesday.* I've decided to leave for San Remo[99] on Friday to look for a place that's nice but not too expensive. I'll stay in Milan for one day. Today, nothing special happened. Just worked as usual, and went for walks at the usual times. Those *ruffiani* didn't come near me today, and no *bait* was dangled. I haven't written to you about the pigeons before. Now I'm feeding them every day and have learned how to get them to sit all over me from head to toe. They even quarrel and fight while sitting on my hand or my head. I'll leave Venice without any regrets; although I have to say that it's perhaps

precisely because of the Venetian peace and quiet that I've been feeling so good the last few days (touch wood!). My nerves are in amazingly better shape, and I'm sleeping better than ever, although every night before going to sleep I do drink some beer or a glass or two of cognac. My appetite is excellent—as it always is. Of course, it is the symphony that I have to credit for all this, but it's only thanks to the monotony of life here in Venice and the total absence of distractions that I've been able to get down to work so steadily and assiduously. When I was writing the opera,[100] I never experienced the same feeling I've been getting from the symphony. With the opera I was just hoping for the best, maybe it will turn out well, and maybe it won't. With the symphony I have every confidence that I am producing something *really special* and the nearest to perfection of form of all my compositions to date.

I'm still reading *Pendennis*,[101] but alternating with *The History of Napoleon*. I'm making a point of reading two newspapers every day before I go to sleep: *Italie* and *Gazzeta di Venezia*. Until tomorrow, my dear.

✦

13/25 Tuesday.
It's Christmas Day here. They celebrate it just the same way we do in Russia—by staying at home. The streets are completely empty. After two weeks of wonderful weather, it's raining here today for the first time. I'm at work as usual. Yesterday I felt like going to the theatre, but it's no fun going by oneself, and Alyosha didn't like the idea at all. We stayed at home and drank tea; I took a short evening walk, and now I'm about to do some reading. For me this is the best time of the day. Once I've closed the shutters, I can enjoy perfect silence. Alyosha is asleep. The silence is so complete that I can hear the lamp burning. I think, I daydream, I remember, in a word, I'm at rest. There's still no letter from you, and that worries me a little. I got two letters from Kotek—and real ones.[102]

Good night.

✦

Wednesday, 14/26 Dec[ember].
Finally got your second letter today.[103] I can't tell you how much pleasure it gave me. I was delighted to read everything you wrote, but the

best thing is that now I'm beginning to get used to the idea that I may be able to spend the summer in Kamenka, or rather, not Kamenka, but Verbovka; that's the place where I'm really looking forward to staying. When you get this letter, I'll already be in *San Remo*. Today I read the article on San Remo in the Baedeker guidebook. It's a delightful place, and I remember it from when I passed through in 1871.[104] However, it's not particularly cheap. Ever since the Empress[105] lived there, it has become fashionable. Now her Royal Highness Olga, Queen of Wurtenburg,[106] abides there; but it's full of hotels and guest houses.

Today, I worked all the morning until lunchtime, and after a short walk, right through to dinner without a break. I've almost finished the third movement of the symphony. In the evening I went to the Birraria di Genova, a *café-chantant*, pretty dismal; but I really enjoyed my two tankards of beer. I'm waiting impatiently for your letter from Moscow. You're really taking a lot of trouble for me, my dear! Nik[olay] Lv[ovich] hasn't yet sent me any report or letter.

Kisses, dear boy. Yours P. T.

♦ ♦ ♦

16. TO MODEST ILYICH TCHAIKOVSKY

[After 1877][107]

[*missing text*] Remarkably enough, the symptoms you have described to me are the very ones I've been experiencing myself recently. Irregular heartbeats, attacks of nerves, depression, heaviness in the chest area, shortness of breath, the urge to cough up whatever it is that's causing this pressure on my chest. I've been experiencing all these symptoms for some time now. The only difference is that you have been seeing doctors, but as for me I simply can't stand them and all that [*missing text*]

I should tell you that the real culprit in all this is the intolerable *stomach* which, in the case of some nervous systems like ours is incredibly erratic and capricious in doing its job. If you would like to be rid of your ailment once and for all without any help from doctors, then take the following measures.

1) Eat as little as possible; 2) eat only light food: broth, beef, boiled vegetables (except onions and cabbage); 3) don't eat just before bed time; 4) don't drink vodka at all, but if you can't refrain, never more

than one glass; 5) *don't smoke* (smoking a lot has a terrible effect on the kind of stomach that you and I both have); but since you are hardly likely to give up smoking altogether, try at least to smoke as little as possible—and that will help.

I'm firmly convinced that following these healthy rules will unquestionably prove to be effective treatment. The trouble is that it is extremely difficult to comply with them scrupulously and to the letter—and I'm not asking you to do that. It will be enough if you follow just 50 % of this advice—and everything will turn out fine. Don't forget that we are no longer young, and the longer we go on like this, the worse shape our organs will be in, and the less effectively will they function. *Moderation* in all things, but *especially in food,* will allow our organs to function without stress, calmly and smoothly, and as a result they will be able to function properly regardless of our years. It's only when we're young that we can afford to put them under excessive strain. And it really is our stomachs of which we demand too little. Everything that appeals to our noses and our eyes we stuff into our bellies, while forgetting that it is after all the poor belly that has to do the delicate and complex work of processing all this stuff into blood, tissue, fat, bone [*missing text*].

◆◆◆

17. TO PYOTR IVANOVICH JURGENSON

San Remo, 17/29 January 1878.[108]

Pyotr Ivanovich!

I've just received your letter and I'm horrified. I sent you the Glinka translations[109] on Friday, December 28/15. I'm practically going out of my mind with worry that Glinka's manuscripts may have been lost. I'm not particularly concerned about my translations, but if this piece of shit precious only because of my resounding name, is something you had only a single copy of, then I have no choice but to hang myself. I've just telegraphed to Venice, and if I don't get a satisfactory answer today, then I'll go to Venice myself. Good God!

This postal service is abominable!!! It has caused me so much hardship, precisely here in Italy. This country of lemons and oranges just stinks!

I've read your ticking off for not joining the delegation. To make a long story short, I'll just briefly expound my *profession de foi* [French: creed].

1) I am never going to go round begging to foreign big-shots in order to ingratiate myself with them.

2) I have never and will never allow the success of my music to depend on my becoming an official representative of Russian music like some prick at a name-day celebration, without money, without instructions, *without any possibility of organizing anything, since the government categorically refuses to offer any subsidy,* in other words to allow myself to be placed in such a stupid and delicate situation.

3) I would be much better off showing up in Paris not at some exhibition where any ass-hole will fall over himself to come to be heard and given a license for world-wide publicity, but to go at a normal time, as I wanted to do last year, and not as an official representative because that job would oblige me to take care of everybody except myself, but to go just by myself without any official visits, and on my own money. It would just be: "Here I am! Come and listen if you want!"

In any case, I've already made up my mind that the exhibition will be a poor occasion for garnering publicity. There will be a thousand people there hunting, just like me, for fame and fortune (which, by the way, I don't give a shit about), and there, because of my diffident temperament I am liable to go quite unnoticed.

4) You indirectly reproach me for neglecting your interests as well as my own. Well, you'll just have to forgive me, my friend. Take me as I am or forget me. I have never been any good at peddling my wares at any time, but now there's no way I'm going to be of any use in this regard.

5) The main thing is, I don't want to go to Paris, because I'm sick of it, because it's boring, because I want to spend the summer in the country in Russia, because I'm fed up with trying to be something that I simply am not, and fed up with forcing myself to act out of character, however lousy that character may be. I've simply got to the point where I want to say: "If you want to know me, love me, play me, sing me; crown me with laurels, adorn me with roses, burn incense to me, fine! If not, I don't give a shit, and go to hell!" What I'm talking about is the public, fame and all that shit.

You may be surprised to see how much shit and other foul language I am using here. I've become an angry man. I'm sick and tired of everything; my God, if only you knew how sick and tired!!!! As to the reactions in various quarters to my refusal to be part of the delegation, I've made a lot of fascinating observations.

Goodbye, my dear, forgive me!

Yours, P. Tchaikovsky

✦ ✦ ✦

18. TO ANATOLY ILYICH TCHAIKOVSKY

Sunday, 8/20 January 1878, 12 midnight [San Remo][110]

Just back from the theatre with Modest. They were doing Faust. Modest had a good laugh. After lunch we travelled the 10 versts to Bordighera.[111] Got your letter.[112] I'll reply tomorrow. There's no news. Why don't you say anything about yourself?

✦

Monday, 9/21 Jan[uary] 1878.

One of the worst days of my whole life. Alyosha came back from the doctor and said that there was absolutely nothing wrong. However, he was told to apply the ointment four times a day, and take a bath every day. In the morning, I was already in a bad mood and upset, and this news shattered me. I should tell you that Alyosha had been acting strangely all the time. The news that he had syphilis didn't scare him a bit. He was quite unapologetic, and he didn't utter a word or make a single gesture to suggest that he was at all ashamed or embarrassed in front of me. The only thing that bothered him was my intention to send him back to Russia, and he started crying when I told him. But after I changed my mind, he became as cheerful as if nothing had happened; in fact he became downright disrespectful, so that even Modest got angry; in the end Alyosha stopped doing the least little thing for me. In short I couldn't have been more dismayed, offended, and mortified by the whole thing. Furthermore, ever since the ugly truth came out, I simply couldn't bear to see him go near Kolya, while Kolya himself seemed to be deliberately hanging around him. I ended up getting a really unpleasant and nasty feeling every time I looked at Alyosha. I just couldn't believe that such a nice, well-

behaved boy, such a naïve, pure and innocent youngster was now going around with his member covered with sores. What also hurt me
was that he had deceived me, and didn't tell me anything about it
while he was in Moscow, otherwise, I would, of course, never have
brought him here. So why did he come? Wasn't the reason why I sent
for him so that he could console and comfort me? Instead, he brought
his infection here with him, and on top of it all, did everything he
could to hide it from me! I was beside myself! And, yes, I made a scene
and was so upset that I even missed lunch; instead I threw a tantrum
in my room. I have to thank Modya; he sorted out everything for
me. He ran to the doctor, had a long talk with him, at my insistence
explained to him that a place had to be found for Alyosha away from
us. The doctor promised to find a place for him in some *maison de
santé* [French: clinic]. When he got back, Modya managed to pacify
me. The tantrum I threw this morning had affected Alyosha, and he
started behaving better. Dear God! If only he had uttered a single
word of regret, of contrition, or some acknowledgement of having
acted badly in coming back here carrying that disease! But nothing
of the kind. It would have taken only the slightest word from him,
and I would have relented. I would have started feeling sorry for him,
and that would have banished all the resentment I was feeling. I just
don't know what's happening to him. With that syphilis he's become
a completely different person to me. I simply don't recognize him; a
totally different Alyosha.

Mme. Meck continues to perform the role of my caring and vigi-
lant guardian angel. Soon after Modya had calmed me down and had
left for a walk with Kolya, the postman arrived with a *letter charge*
[French: registered letter] from N[adezhda] F[ilaretovna] von Meck]. I
open it. The first thing she says is that she is glad I refused to act as a
delegate, and I was afraid that she would be angry. Then she offers the
usual thousand compliments and expressions of affection, and finally
encloses a postal order for an extra 1,500 francs, over and above the
allowance, to cover the cost of publishing the symphony.[113] Needless
to say, my current financial condition is far from brilliant. My money
has long since vanished, and all that's left is what belongs to Modya.
So the 1,500 francs really comes in handy. Who is this unfathomable
woman? Somehow she divines exactly when and how to write to me
when I need comforting. When Modya came back he couldn't get over

his amazement at the tact and refinement of her nice letter. She also enclosed some photos of her family.[114]

Alyosha spent the whole evening rubbing in his ointment. I find it disgusting and hate to go near him, but Modest is incredibly kind. Of course, he is annoyed with Alyosha for behaving so strangely toward me, but at the same time, he's sorry for him and helps him with his treatment, his lotions and all that.

I got a letter from Kotek which made me angry. He told me about the cold response he got from Mme. Meck to his letter,[115] and believes that it is the syphilis she is holding against him. Then he starts wondering aloud about who could have been gossiping to her, and guess who he decided it must have been. Yes, me of all people!!! That really annoyed me. Nevertheless, I wrote back to him right away, but said nothing about how annoyed I was, because I feel sorry for him. He asked Mme. Meck to give him the money she has been sending to his sisters, since they no longer need it. Nadezhda Filaretovna responded with a short note to tell him that she has been sending money to his father, and that he, i.e. his father, will deal with it as he chooses. That letter is bound to make poor Kotek feel bad, but that doesn't mean that his idea wasn't wildly inappropriate. And if that wasn't enough, he is asking me to tell N[adezhda] F[ilaretovna] that he didn't get the syphilis from *a whore,* but from *a singer*!!!! You know what occurred to me. Living, as I do, on someone's bounty, I must be setting Kotek a poor example. Indeed, he came right out and said as much in one of his recent letters: "If you're going to reproach me for asking Mme. Meck, then I'll have to ask, 'Then what about you yourself!!!'" I really took offense at that remark, as well as the next one: "So I will stay in Berlin and live on the 250 francs which I will get from the very same individual who gives you 1,500 francs." There's something strange about that remark; sounds like some kind of reproach! As if he's telling me that it's much more than I deserve. I really don't know if it was a good idea for him to decide to stay abroad. I should send for him so that we can have a heart-to-heart talk. As it is, it's hard for *me* to give him advice right now. He's asking me whether he should stay in Berlin to study with Joachim. Even supposing I decide that he shouldn't—can I tell him that? He's surely going to say that I'm only telling him that because I don't want to give him the money.

✦

Tuesday. 10/22

This morning I replied to N[adezhda] F[ilaretovna]. After breakfast we went to see the doctor—a very nice man. Tomorrow Alyosha will go to the *maison de santé*. He will be getting full board and lodging for 6 francs a day. They will be giving him a bath every day. I got your letter, which had a good and pleasant effect on me, although it pains me deeply that you are so depressed.[116] But why? Fall in love, Tolichka! You're still young, and that gives you the right to surrender to the greatest pleasure there is. But don't go to extremes; no melodramas, no scenes, and without turbulence of any kind! So why not just go ahead and marry Kartseva![117] But no! What am I saying! I wouldn't advise even you to get married. I'll write to you tomorrow about Ant[onina] Iv[anovna] and that trouble about the money question. If only your plans involving Panaeva as Tatiana[118] had worked out? Alyosha is be-having better today. He's beginning to show some signs of understand-ing. How hard it would be for us to do without him, but the main thing is we won't be able to leave Kolya's side!

I'm going to bed; I'm tired.

✦

Wednesday, 11/23 [January] 1878

I feel bad, Tolya. Two hours ago the *monk* came for Alyosha, col-lected his belongings, and took him away. We went with him. We had to climb high into the mountains. The home was clean and smelled like a hospital; the room was small but cozy! When we got there, the prior immediately appeared and promised that the patient would receive the best possible care. Fortunately, a Rusyn[119] from Galicia who happened to be living in the same *maison de santé* offered to act as Alyosha's interpreter; he speaks a little Russian. I was sorry to leave Alyosha there. Today I've already stopped being angry with him. He will come to us in the morning. We'll have dinner together at noon, and then go for another walk, and we'll have supper at 6:30 p.m., and then every evening there will be four applications of the ointment. Will he be cured eventually?

I wrote to tell Jurgenson to give A[ntonina] I[vanovna] her allow-ance—100 rubles on the first of every month up to the first of April, and the 300 rubles of mine remaining with the Conservatory he should receive in due course. You know about the rest of my proposals from draft of the letter to A[ntonina] I[vanovna].

Write a little more about yourself; who is the latest woman in your life; how are Papa and Liz[aveta] Mikh[ailovna]?[120]

Kisses, dear boy. P. Tchaikovsky

Tolya! Read the letter to Antonina Ivanovna which I've enclosed, and send it. If you find it stupid, then write to her yourself, but along the same lines. In a word, my conditions are final, and I won't give an inch: 1) 2,500 rubles and a promissory note, 2) 100 rubles a month, but absolutely no written guarantee, and 3) I keep the piano.

Kisses.

✦✦✦

19. TO ANATOLY ILYICH TCHAIKOVSKY

Florence, 13/25 February 1878.[121]

Yesterday, just after sending my letter, I received yours, but I'm only answering it today because I had quite a few letters to write in the evening, and I was too tired. I wanted to talk to you in a little more detail about the confession you made to me. It really grieves me that you are so depressed. I won't try to console you, because you say yourself, and with reason, that at bottom, you have nothing to complain about. But, since I'm a few years older than you, I think I can claim the privilege of offering you some advice. I couldn't be more familiar with the feelings you are having now. As I see it, there are two reasons for your low spirits. 1) It's your nerves, and that's something that can always put you in a black mood without any particular reason, and 2) wounded pride. The second reason is, of course, more important than the first, because it's that which upsets you and has a bad effect on your nerves. And that's what I want to talk to you about. Essentially, what you are feeling is an extremely common phenomenon. I don't know a single one of my acquaintances, at least those possessing a minimum of intelligence and a generally more sensitive organism, who wouldn't have suffered the very same kind of discontent, the very same frustration to which you are prey. They have all thought they were destined for some kind of outstanding achievement, and have either failed in the attempt, or, although, like you, have been entirely successful, they never reached the pinnacle they had expected. I won't get into a discussion of whether you were justified in thinking of yourself as an exceptional person, because I don't know what it was you aspired to. As I see it, you have been entirely successful. I never had any special wish to see you become a great legal scholar or a great man of any kind. I've always loved you for what you are. I have always thought of you as an intelligent, kind, high-principled, decent, and *able* man; in other words, someone who would make his own way in the world, create an independent position for himself, and be loved by everyone. Well, you have achieved all this, and your success in your career and in your social life cannot be questioned. If you tell me that your only ambition was to become an outstanding prosecutor, well, that's exactly what you have become. Indeed, that is precisely how people describe you— an outstanding prosecutor. No one doubts it. As to your being an intelligent and extraordinarily nice fellow, everyone agrees about that too. That you have a sensitive nature and are a real gentleman, that you are one of the chosen few who possess a rare depth of understanding, this is a fact that no one can deny. You are, in fact, one of those rare personalities whom others simply cannot help liking. Now if that's not enough for you, then you are not being entirely sincere when you say that all you want to be is a successful prosecutor. But here again, I repeat, I don't want to get into a discussion about whether or not you have it in you to achieve something great. As you know, no great man is great in the eyes of his cook. By extension, you could say that no great man seems great to his own brother.

I tell you frankly that I have always regarded you as a man of great natural charm, the kind of man in whom all your qualities combine to form a harmonious and well-integrated whole. I believe the secret of this charm lies precisely in this harmony where no single quality exceeds to the detriment of any other. So, just to put the matter to rest, I want to say that I have always expected a brilliant and enviable future for you, and that in my eyes you are moving inexorably toward the goal which I have always imagined for you.

If you don't give way to your black mood, and don't become dispirited, I'm convinced that you will rise to a very high position in society because you really have what it takes to make a brilliant *career* and a happy life for yourself. Since I have never observed in you any predominant talent (like music, for example, in my case), I always thought you would pursue a broader and more general course, and in that way, because of that extraordinarily harmonious and integrated balance of your wonderful temperament, which I have mentioned, you were sure to end up occupying an eminent position in life. It's very possible that I'm mistaken, and you have good grounds for considering yourself a failure—but I'm telling you frankly what I think, in the hope that it will benefit you.

So that's what I wanted to explain to you; there is nothing so pointless as suffering brought on by excessive self-esteem. I'm saying this because it's something I have constantly suffered from myself, and I have never been satisfied with the results of my efforts. Now you might be thinking that since I am often mentioned in the newspapers, I am a celebrity and should be happy and contented. The fact is that that simply doesn't count for me, and *j'ai toujours voulu peter plus haut que mon cul* [French: I've always wanted to fart higher than my ass]. I wanted to be the number one composer not only in Russia, but in the whole world; I wanted to be not only a composer, but a first-class conductor; I wanted to be an extraordinarily clever and knowledgeable person; I also wanted to be polished and urbane and shine in society— and God knows what else! It was only little by little, at the cost of all kinds of unbearable suffering, that I came to realize my true worth. And that was just the kind of suffering I wanted to spare you. It's comical to recall the extent to which I tormented myself for failing to get into high society and become a social success! No one can imagine how much I suffered and how painfully I struggled to overcome my unbelievable shyness, which at one time even robbed me of my sleep and appetite for two whole days because of the prospect of dinner at *the Davydovs!!!*[122] And what secret torment I endured before I could face the fact that I was totally incapable of being a conductor! How much time it took for me to understand that I belong to the category of the reasonably intelligent, but do not belong in the class of those whose minds possess abilities which are out of the ordinary. And how many years did it take before I realized that even as a composer—I was merely a talented person, but no extraordinary phenomenon.

It's only now, particularly after that business of the marriage that I'm beginning to understand that there is nothing more futile than trying to be the person that nature never meant you to be.

In any case, life is short, and the wise man, instead of moping and agonizing over frustrated ambition, wasting time on pointless regrets over unfulfilled dreams, should be enjoying life.

And, you know, Tolya! I'm actually glad that you don't possess any particular artistic gifts which might point you in an exceptional direction. Every single one of those people finds his way barred by a host of obstacles, intrigues, favoritism, lack of recognition, rivalry, etc. However, by taking a more common path, and simply striving through your work to achieve a position of independence, you can make a splendid life for yourself. Ambition should be reserved for those times when it serves as an incentive for advancement in your career. And in good conscience you can do your job, putting into it every effort and as much time as it takes to do it successfully. You possess the natural gift of scrupulousness, and that guarantees that you would never *stoop* to compromising your position. You should never let yourself be put out by the fact that others less able and less worthy than yourself are getting ahead of you. If in my musical life I have been able to come to terms with the fact that people less talented than myself have achieved far greater fame and fortune, then in the course of your career you will surely have to come to terms with some of life's injustices, because in a civil service career, *personal connections and luck* play a greater role than in any other walk of life.

I'm afraid that in the heat of the moment and my zeal to be of help to you, I haven't expressed myself clearly. I see from your letter that you are constantly fluctuating between belief in your possession of extraordinary powers and despondency and failure to recognize your true worth. I want to show you a middle way between those two extremes. What you have is *une nature superieure* [French: higher nature] but without any particular outstanding talent. You therefore have the right to look down from above on life, and on the inevitability of the frequent triumph of mediocrity and banality, and by coming to terms with that, to live the life of a quiet observer.

If, for example, you began to read more than you have hitherto,— how much satisfaction you would derive from it! Reading is one of life's greatest pleasures when it is accompanied by peace of mind, and not in fits and starts, but on a regular basis. Art too can give you many pleasant moments. Since you have the gift of making people like you, your *social life* too can embellish your life, provided again that you don't give way to morbid pride and ambition, and you don't try to outshine everyone else at all costs.

The social round can by very pleasant when you don't go into it with the idea of upstaging everyone else with your *savoir faire,* intelligence, and charm etc., but just in order to observe and study people, leaving aside any idea of self-promotion. In any case, if I know you at all, you have boundless tact, you can be simple, natural, and unaffected, and were born with impeccable manners, so it's not for me to teach you how to conduct yourself in society.

That's all for now. I'll continue tomorrow.

✦

Florence, 14/26

Today, I meant to continue with my homily and go into detail about one important side of your life, or rather your dissatisfaction with life. I want to tell you at some length about something I've noticed in you; a kind of drive to become well read and to acquire all sorts of information. However, I've noticed that what is really behind this drive is not just a straightforward interest in acquiring knowledge for its own sake, but rather a desire to display your knowledge and to prove that you are better informed and better educated that any of your acquaintances. But reading is only truly a pleasure when it is done for its own sake and not for purely tangential purposes driven by a misplaced need for self promotion. Yes! I was intending to go into this and many other matters, when I suddenly received your letter in the form of a diary, which made it perfectly clear to me that you are simply in *love*.[123] I was very pleased to learn this, although I was also sorry to learn that it was robbing you of your sleep. I was pleased because love was what was lacking in your life, and also because I believe that Panaeva cannot help loving you back, and I foresee something good coming of it.

What a pleasure it was to read your diary! I think it's the best way of corresponding. It's the first letter you've ever sent me which has given me a clear picture of your life. It's almost as if I could actually see you at the concert and at Palkin's[124]—and at home unable to sleep! Reading your diary was like reading a really absorbing novel.

However, I should be getting on with my own story.

Two days ago (Sunday), we went for a ride out of town—a very pleasant outing. I should mention that the monastery *des Chartreux* [French: of the Carthusians] left me with a very poetic memory. In the evening I went for a walk along the embankment in the vain hope of hearing that familiar wonderful voice somewhere.

Meeting that divine boy and hearing him singing once again has become the goal of my life in Florence. What has become of him? Yesterday morning I wrote something for the piano.[125] I have made it my business to compose something every day. After breakfast we went to the *Palazzo Pitti*.[126] In the evening, I tired myself out walking along the embankment still hoping to see that dear boy. Suddenly in the distance I caught sight of a crowd, and heard singing; my heart missed a beat. I ran up, but, oh what a disappointment! It was some fellow with a mustache singing, and pretty well too—but, of course, no comparison!

On the way home (we are living a long way from the embankment), I was followed by a youth *of extraordinary classical beauty* and dressed perfectly respectably. He even engaged me in conversation. We strolled around together for about an hour. I was pretty agitated, and was in two minds, but finally said that my sister was waiting for me at home and, after we had arranged a rendezvous for the day after next, which I will keep, said goodbye to him.

I spent the whole evening talking to Modest about you. He read me a few chapters out of his diary which he had written in the autumn.[127] It was striking how similar his self-dissatisfaction was to your own, and he suffers from periodic bouts of demoralization in just the same way as you, and thinks he is just a nobody etc. I can only tell you that in actual fact you and Modest both are positively the most captivating ornaments of the human race, and that there is nothing better or more delightful in my life than the two of you, each in your own way. Even your defects please me.

So, my dear, please cheer up, and don't be afraid of comparisons with anyone!

Just accept the fact that there are people cleverer and more talented than you, and arm yourself with the conviction that you possess that *harmoniousness* which I mentioned in my letter yesterday, and it is this quality that lifts you way above the heads of the crowd. So what, if Laroche is cleverer than you and me? So what if Apukhtin is wittier than us? I would throw myself into the nearest river or shoot myself if Laroche and Apukhtin suddenly became my brothers, and you became just a friend!

If Panaeva comes to love you, I'll write a whole set of romances for her, and simply become her grateful slave.

I'm sending this letter out of turn. I can't wait until tomorrow. Your photo has been covered with kisses. Tomorrow, I'll send it to N[adezhda] F[ilaretovna].

Yours P. Tchaikovsky.

I smother you with hugs.

◆ ◆ ◆

20. LETTER TO KARL KARLOVICH ALBRECHT

Florence, 14/26 February 1878.[128]

Dear Karlyusha!

I need to write a letter to Fitzenhagen,[129] but since I am positively unable to write in German, I must ask you to translate word for word the following letter.

> Dear Friend!
>
> You were kind enough to arrange to get my cello piece and the waltz for violin printed by Leuckardt.[130] At the time you told me that if those pieces were printed abroad there would be better prospects of sales than if I offered them to Jurgenson. I was convinced by your arguments and asked you to send the pieces to Mr. Leuckardt from whom I didn't even want to receive any honorarium, as long as they were printed well and quickly. After a while, you told me that Mr. Leuckardt would not only take my pieces, but would offer me an honorarium of 300 marks. A year has gone by, and not only have I not received the honorarium which that Berlin gentleman offered me on his own initiative, but I have yet to see the pieces printed, and to my great astonishment I have learned that the manuscripts are still lying untouched in his office. In the meantime, I have a publisher in Moscow who has not only always

been eager and quick to publish anything I offer him, but has always paid me a handsome honorarium, and never allowed the poor fruits of my endeavors to gather dust and molder on his shelves.[131] Now, in spite of what must have been the galling and indeed detrimental preference which I was incautious enough to reveal to Mr. Leuckardt, he is asking for both those pieces.

In the circumstances, I am driven to conclude that not only is there no point in my waiting until the Berlin gentleman takes it into his head to do me the honor of printing my work, but also that it is humiliating for me to be subjected to the caprices of some Dutch prick (please tone down this expression!) when I don't have the slightest need of him. So I must ask you, dear friend, to undertake the task of writing to that asshole of a sausage monger (tone this down!) to tell him that I absolutely refuse to give him my pieces, even if he offers me 300,000,000 marks for each one. I demand that the vile sausage monger (tone it down!) send both manuscripts to Jurgenson forthwith. Incidentally, be sure to add that if he ever takes it into his head to offer me an honorarium for either piece, I intend to shit on his ugly mug (tone it down!). Excuse me for troubling you, dear friend.

Yours, P. I. T[chaikovsky]

Today I received a poster with some brief comments of yours[132] which really touched and cheered me. *Merci,* my dear fellow.

❖❖❖

21. TO ANATOLY ILYICH TCHAIKOVSKY

Florence. [18 February/2 March 1878][133]

Just when I was beginning to enjoy your diary, I started slacking off. Today is Saturday, and I haven't written you a single letter since Tuesday. Still, I won't take the easy way out, and I'll give you a belated account of what's been happening.

❖

Wednesday, 15/27 Febr[uary]

I spent the day in a torment of indecision. My rendezvous had been arranged for this evening. A truly *bitter-sweet dilemma!*[134] Finally I decided to go. I spent two absolutely wonderful hours in the most romantic circumstances; I was scared, I was thrilled, I was afraid of the slightest sound. Embraces, kisses, an out-of-the-way apartment on a high floor, tender talk, what delight! I returned home tired and exhausted, but with wonderful memories.

✦

Thursday, 16/28 Febr[uary]

Nothing special. After breakfast a pleasant walk in the Cascino.[135] You wouldn't recognize it now. It's becoming lovely—a sheer delight. Leaves are beginning to appear on the trees. Birds are singing nonstop. There are solitary, shady paths. In the evening I went to the public theatre and had a great time. Imagine the most heart-rending drama performed by the most naïve and enthusiastic actors, and in it, in spite of all the horrors, a huge role is played by *Punch*. In a word, the strangest amalgam of the most far-fetched melodrama and buffoonery. The audience exploded into ecstatic applause. The tickets were incredibly cheap. We had a splendid box directly overlooking the stage, and that made the pleasure even greater. The box cost four francs. Modest came in just at the end.

✦

Friday, 17 Febr[uary]/1 March

Nothing special today either. Got a letter from Mme. Meck, who is in raptures over my symphony. How nice of her! And what a warm and affectionate letter! Note how none of my Moscow friends have yet written me a single word about the symphony. After dinner I hung about in the hope of running into my delight. But no luck. However there was another pleasure in store for me. On the *Lung Arno*[136] I came across those street singers and simply asked them if they knew that boy.[137] It turned out that they did, and they gave me their word that this evening he would be on the *Lung Arno* at nine o'clock. But today I have another rendezvous, though that's for Saturday.

✦

Saturday, 18 F[ebruary]/2 M[arch]

Didn't sleep too well. In the morning, went to look at Santa Croce church,[138] where, among others, Machiavelli and Michelangelo are buried. Just returned from a really long walk to S[an] Miniato.[139] I went alone. From there there is a splendid view of the whole of Florence. I don't know why, but I'm out of sorts today. I think there's something wrong with my stomach: otherwise I can't explain my bad mood and irritability. This happens to me sometimes. Actually, I have really nothing to complain of.

In a week, and certainly no later, we are leaving for Switzerland. I would be happy to stay here longer—but I'm spending money like water, so I'd better beat a hasty retreat. So from now on my address will be: Clarens, Villa Richelieu, and that's where not a moment will go by without my thinking of you.

How are things with P[anaeva]? I'm worried about you.

Kisses. P. Tchaikovsky

I'm really upset by Shumsky's[140] death. Masha Golovina is suffering from consumption. She wrote to me, but doesn't know that she has got it.

◆ ◆ ◆

22. TO ANATOLY ILYICH TCHAIKOVSKY

Florence[141]

Another belated letter. I'm sorry! A lot of impressions have accumulated over the last few days. I've been *living*, and not just vegetating. Whether I've been happy; well that's another matter. But I have been living intensely.

◆

Saturday. [22 February/6 March 1878]

In the evening 1) I had a rendezvous and 2) a meeting with that young boy, the singer.[142] I was looking forward so eagerly to seeing him that it overshadowed the first rendezvous. I managed to get out of the lover's tryst with some difficulty, and was totally consumed by the prospect of enjoying our youngster's singing. I arrived at nine on the dot at the place where I was supposed to meet the man who had promised to find him. The man was there, as well as a bunch of other men who were curious to see me and were crowding around our youngster. The first thing that struck me was that he had grown somewhat, and was *good-looking,* although at the time we met him we both thought he was unremarkable. Since the crowd was growing and there were a lot of people about, I continued walking toward Cascino. On the way, I voiced doubts about whether it was really him. "When you hear me start singing, you will know it was me. That was when you gave me a silver half-franc!" All this was uttered in that wonderful voice and went right to my heart. But that's nothing to what happened when he started singing. The effect on me was indescribable. I don't think you could feel more deeply moved when you hear Panaeva sing! I wept, I was overcome, I melted with delight. Apart from that song you know, he sang two new ones, and one of them, "Pimpinella,"[143] was quite delightful. I rewarded him and his companions handsomely. On the way home I met Modest, and was really sorry he hadn't been there. Anyway, we decided we would go and hear him again on Monday morning. From that evening on I was totally in thrall to this one feeling, and that person who had earlier given me so much pleasure was just blotted out.

◆

Sunday, 19/3

Nothing special. After the bad night we spent, I didn't feel too well in the morning. In the evening I went with Modest to the masquerade at the main theatre, the Pergola.[144] I had expected to see some boisterous and exuberant entertainment. Nothing of the kind. Very few people, lousy costumes, and absolutely no women, so the men were dancing with each other. Among those wearing masks was that person, but alas, for me she had totally lost her appeal. The only effect she had on me was sheer boredom.

◆

Monday, 20/4

Because it was the last few days of carnival *he* appeared in costume along with two mustachioed companions, also in costume. It was only then that I got a good look at him. He was unquestionably handsome with an indescribably winning glance and smile. It was better hearing him in the street than indoors. He was shy and didn't give full voice. I noted down all his songs[145] and then took him to have his photograph taken. The photos will be ready only after we have left; I'll send you one.[146]

✦

Tuesday, 21/5

I had arranged a rendezvous for the evening, but I decided to get out of it. Fortunately, I ran into that *person* and made up some excuse. So the evening was free and I went to the theatre with Modest where there was a carnival show with Harlequin, Colombina, and so on. It was quite amusing.

✦

Wednesday, 22/6

In the morning I got a very touching letter from Sasha.[147] Went to see the Museo Nazionale,[148] very interesting. Lunched with Modya and Kolya in *our* restaurant, you remember? (*Gille e Leta*). Went for a walk to Cascino alone; it was a long way. I picked some violets that I'm putting in this envelope with the letter. After dinner, *he* will be coming and will sing. I'm savoring the prospect. Tomorrow evening we are going straight to Geneva to Modest's great chagrin. He likes Florence. But we can't stay here any longer. I'm spending money like water.

Tolichka, try to get the money for "Vakula"[149] and send it to A[ntonina] I[vanovna].

✦ ✦ ✦

23. TO MODEST ILYICH TCHAIKOVSKY

Brailov, 18[–20] May [1878][150]

Tomorrow, I'll send this letter off straight to Grankino.[151] It's nice to think that you will find my little note I dashed off waiting for you after you arrive. My dear Modya! It would *be simply wonderful* if, while I'm here, I could think that you too are well and happy. But alas, although I know very well that you are in Kamenka, I also know that your stay there is poisoned, firstly by your forthcoming journey to Grankino, and secondly by my absence. This last assumption is not prompted by any immodesty on my part, it's just that I am pretty sure that in the same way that your absence has spoiled my stay here, you too must be suffering from my absence there. But of course in this, time makes a big difference. Already today, I'm missing you less than yesterday, and tomorrow, I'll be missing you even less than today. Yesterday, Alyosha arrived, and that was a great comfort and joy to me. In any case, you'll find the details about yesterday evening and today in the letter which I'm sending to Sasha.[152] If you don't get it before you leave there, they'll send it on to you.

✦

19 May, 7 o'clock in the evening
I had just come back from a walk in a very cheerful mood when I was suddenly handed a *message* from Kamenka from which I learned that the telegram I sent two days ago from Zhmerinka had not arrived. I was extremely surprised and quite upset. Modya, can you believe that even though I am entirely free, and no one is bothering or hindering me, I still can't manage to get through all the things I want to do, and that annoys me a little. This morning I wanted to write out a violin piece,[153] and didn't even manage to finish half of it. I wanted to write letters to Kotek, you, and Nad[ezhda] Fil[aretovna] and don't even have time to finish this page because I want to take a walk before sunset, have supper, play, and go to bed. How am I going to write the three letters I intended to?

I continue to be entirely satisfied with *Brailov.* It has no charm or character. There is nothing here to remind us of the old days—everything is spick and span and the house really belongs in town rather than in the country, but it couldn't be more comfortable, spacious, and luxurious. I am coming to like the garden more and more. Today I climbed over the garden wall, and there not far off was a small square wood, and I made straight for it. It turns out that it is what is left of a garden built by Catholic monks from the monastery that was Catholic up to 1840. Of the wall that once surrounded it, all that's left are the ruins of the somewhat picturesque gates. The trees are old and thick. The grass is overgrown and lush—a sheer delight. It's a place I like more than anything else I've seen. It gives totally free rein to the imagination. I sat under an enormous oak tree and began to imagine the monks who once walked here and how they mortified their flesh. The thought of the flesh brought me to within an ace of being overcome with desire, and I started thinking lustful thoughts about Ast[apka] and felt an overwhelming desire to feast on her delights, and . . . "Nothing . . . nothing . . . silence!"[154]

Alyosha is a dear; but more about him tomorrow.

✦

20th of May

I got your letter today.[155] If you had made up your mind to upset me, well you've certainly got what you wanted! Oh yes! I'm really hurt and deeply regret to find you once again bringing up a subject in all seriousness which I thought we had disposed of once and for all. I thought you had finally come to terms with the idea that our dreams of living together were just that—dreams, and totally unrealistic. But here you go again! Modenka, I'm going to tell you for the last time what I think about this idea; and I'll make it short.

1) If you're really going to live in Moscow, then it has to be either in my place or in the same place—doesn't matter which. Your idea of living by yourself or with the Kolreifs[156] doesn't make any sense. Now, if we're really into comparisons, then living with the unrefined but decent Konradi and his silly, vulgar, temperamental but civilized wife would be better than living with that old moneylender Kolreif, who has such a bad reputation. As for his wife, it never ceased to bother me when I saw through her sugar sweet manner and couldn't help being irresistibly reminded of how I've been—and am still paying back her husband at rates of interest that only the yids charge.

2) There's no way you can live with me for a thousand reasons. a) I'm really not so fond of Kolya as to be willing to make drastic changes in my lifestyle for his sake. b) It's my view that it's better for Kolya to be exposed to the various shortcomings of his own parents (about this you came up with the spurious conclusion that it would harm his development to be exposed to these shortcomings; after all, everyone has shortcomings), better, that is, than to be exposed to my particular defects and shortcomings, which I simply don't have the strength of character to give up for his sake. c) I'm simply *incapable* of assuming the responsibility that would suddenly be imposed on me of becoming the virtual *head of the family* that he would be joining.

d) I don't want malicious tongues to start wagging and hurting this innocent child. Inevitably, people would start saying that I was grooming him to be my *lover,* and what's more a *deaf-mute—which would make it easier to* avoid gossip and rumors.

e) I'm too touchy, and value absolute quiet too highly not to feel the constant presence of a child too oppressive, especially such a difficult and extremely restless one as *Kolya*. In any case, I'm against the idea of living with anyone at all, even with my *nearest and dearest*—it inevitably leads to *money problems*. Whenever arrangements have to be made about money, misunderstandings always arise. It would be a different matter if you, for example, came to live with me, even for years at a time, but just by yourself, and as my guest. But if you were to bring Kolya with you to live with me, and Kolya is richer than both of us, I would no longer consider you a guest, but rather an independent lodger, and this would lead to a thousand little doubts, misunderstandings, friction and arguments; and this would be no good for any of us.

But you will tell me that my reasoning is purely *selfish,* and that it's time that I stopped thinking only of my own comfort and convenience, and started thinking about yours. So now I'm going to consider the inconveniences of your separating from Kolya from the standpoint of *your* moral and material interests.

3) a) No point in beating about the bush. When you, in your eagerness to break away from Alina Ivanovna, say that you would be content with three or even two thousand, if only you could get what you want, I am astonished to the depths of my being at your naivety and your lack of self-knowledge. But that's just it, look who's talking! Regardless of all the unfavorable aspects of your difficult and trying situation, nevertheless *in view of your colossal incompetence when it comes to handling money,* I think you are extraordinarily fortunate to be able to live free of charge. There's no other way you could possibly live. There's no one except Kolya's parents who could so naturally and simply take care of your situation and see to it that all your major material needs and living expenses are covered, i.e. your apartment, your board, your servant, and your laundry. b) When you read these lines, you will suspect that I don't want to share your point of view, i.e. that I'm forgetting your hatred of A[lina] I[vanovna], but you are wrong. To this I'll respond by saying that most probably you don't hate her more than I hated *Rubinstein*[157]—and this is something I've never told anyone. In spite of this, I lived with him, because I had to, and I stuck it out until the possibility arose of moving out without friction or unpleasantness; c) friction and unpleasantness with Konradi will be inevitable if you take Kolya and leave them, and this will have a very bad effect on Kolya and completely ruin what you think of as your freedom. d) This freedom of yours will simply be *imaginary.* Being

financially dependent on Konradi, you won't become a free man, the difference being that, if you stay with them, your dependence is something *normal,* but if you leave them, it will become *abnormal.* e) If you leave Konradi, your responsibilities will become ten times greater because, no matter what you say, something that is very important for you is that while you are living with them you can go out as often as you want, but if you take Kolya with you to live somewhere else by yourselves, you'll never be able to set foot outside the house. f) Without any doubt, in the very first month after you move out *you will find yourself in financial difficulties.* As things are you have been the only one affected by such difficulties, and nothing terrible has happened, but when you discover to your horror that the lack of money is affecting Kolya, that will give you a very bad feeling—a feeling a thousand times worse and more painful than your feelings of antipathy toward A[lina] I[vanovna] right now.

Good God, I could give you a thousand more *reasons,* but what would be the point? The plain fact of the matter is that *I feel, I know, I can foresee* a host of troubles ahead, if you don't listen to me, and insist on going your own way. With your idea of moving out from Konradi's you're being just as blind as I was last year with my idea of getting married. Well, maybe not as blind as that, but almost. Tell me honestly, Modya, do you really think that it wouldn't make me truly happy to live *with you* in different, normal, and favorable circumstances? Can you really doubt my boundless love for you? Well, doubt if you want to. But about your love for me, I don't have a moment's doubt, but this is the *sacrifice* I'm asking *you to make for me.* So please, *for my sake, as a sacrifice,* stop and forget about leaving the Konradis. As far as you're concerned, the only way I can get peace of mind is knowing that *you and Kolya are staying with them.* Try to stifle your antipathy to Kolya's mother. After all, she *is* his mother. While you're there try to minimize your contacts with her, but do go on living there. This is the way it must be. As responsible, dutiful, incomparable, and yes, I would even say great, as you are when it comes to taking care of Kolya, when it comes to dealing with life, you are just as *ir*responsible. If you think you would be doing me a favor by turning your back on the Konradis and moving in with me or near me, you are gravely mistaken. This would just mean a whole lot of anxiety, trouble, and torment for me, and, believe me, I've had my fill of all those things.

Who knows, maybe things will change and fate, without having its hand forced, will find its own way of arranging for us to live together. My life in Moscow is *not predictable*. Maybe I'll come and live with you—or near you! That would be a different matter. But, for God's sake, don't make a move now. Now, if you tell the Konradis that you'll give them all the summer months, then why not just resign yourself to the status quo and stay there with them for the winter, and then in the summer, as a kind of summer vacation, come and stay with me, or Sasha, in Kamenka, or abroad, or wherever. Anyway, do as you wish. This is my last word on the subject. I'm not going to change my mind. I'll be really disappointed if you hold this against me. Whatever you decide to do, my love for you is unwavering—but I'll never come to terms with the idea that you have so casually assumed a burden which is hard for you to bear. It kills me to think, loving you and Tolya as I do more than anything in the world, that I am doomed to live far away from you both, but I have got used to the idea by now, although I still haven't given up hope that fate will one day unite us. And anyway, when all is said and done, perhaps there's even a good side to all this. How much joy and happiness it gives me when I do meet either of you! Amid the routine of everyday life, what a pleasure it is to be able to contemplate the prospect of these meetings, and look forward to them like holidays! Not to mention that my strange and irritable temperament is sure *a la longue* [French: in the long run] to prove too tiresome and burdensome for permanent cohabitation.

Now I'm going to take a ride to the factory.[158] I'll finish this letter when I return.

◆

7 p.m.

I went to the factory, which is splendid and impressive. I took Alyosha with me. Count Scipio, the manager, showed me around the whole factory; my only wish is for your good. I look upon your relationship with Kolya as a *cross* which you bear with the greatest Christian virtue. Why did all this happen? Maybe it was for the best, maybe not, but *I understand perfectly* how heavy a cross it is to bear. Nevertheless, deep in my heart there is a premonition that there is a lot of trouble ahead if you don't listen to me. Anyway, do what you feel you must. Whatever happens you will always own the lion's share of my heart.

Alyosha is a dear and funny. When he sees how everyone grovels in my presence, he too behaves more deferentially than usual with me. But when we're walking through the woods together we argue about all sorts of things, and his chatter enriches my Russian vocabulary. A *shamarova* hill means an ant hill, and a dog's corpse is known as a *trebushina* in his language—these are just some examples.

I would be in a good mood and feeling cheerful, but I am worried about you. When will this letter reach you? In the meantime, I'm afraid that the moment you arrive in Grankino you'll immediately begin to *take action,* and I have the feeling that there's trouble in store. I just have one thing to ask of you: we must meet without fail in *July:* if you want me to come to Grankino, I will. But we must also spend some time together again in Verbovka. I beg you! I embrace you passionately.

Yours P. Tchaikovsky

◆ ◆ ◆

24. TO ANATOLY ILYICH TCHAIKOVSKY

Moscow, 29 Sept[ember 1878][159]

Tolichka!

Yesterday I received a letter from N[adezhda] F[ilaretovna].[160] It was in answer to my question: how did she feel about my wanting to leave here? As might have been expected, she writes that she has long hoped for the very same thing, and had indeed anticipated that I would stop feeling that it was my duty to stay at the Conservatory. I found the letter very comforting and it cheered me up immensely. She also said that I was absolutely right not to agree with Davydov's proposal,[161] and that I need *total freedom* (with the words underlined), from which I conclude that she has no intention of ever cutting off her financial support.

This makes me happier than I can say. There is one more contribution to my complete peace of mind. Rubinstein, far from being upset by my departure, has already started looking for my replacement, and has asked Taneyev[162] to come and teach at the Conservatory, and in order to prevent the real reason for his appointment becoming known, Taneyev will for the time being be teaching piano; although he has been told to prepare to teach theory. So now I am free to leave at any time with an easy conscience. And this *any time* is much closer than you think. Don't be surprised, but I have promised Kotek to come to Berlin in December. And I will, if nothing happens to prevent me. In the first place, I feel a strong need to go abroad. The reason is that as long as I remain in Moscow I won't write a single note—and I am really anxious to get down to work in order to justify my existence in my own eyes and to make up for my sickeningly stupid behavior here. You have to agree that it's much more convenient to work in Clarens than in St. Petersburg, which is after all a noisy place, full of people, and abuzz with activity where it's impossible for me to arrange things so that I can work without distractions. But here's the thing; of course, I won't go abroad without spending some time *with you* first, or should I say *under* you.[163] In fact, I've had it in mind for some time to spend either the whole of November, or part of November and December in St. Petersburg for the special purpose of enjoying your company. After that I'll go abroad; I'll work hard, and at the beginning of spring I'll come back to St. Petersburg to live under you again. So, there it is, Tolya! Don't bother to come here—it's not worth it because *I'll* be coming to see *you*. Here I'm just camping. I simply loathe my house, and I would get very little pleasure from having you as my guest. It's this damned Moscow, of course, which has the good fortune to be the home of such a delightful personage as A[ntonina] I[vanovna]. The very thought that that reptile is here is enough to make me sick. By the way, she has dreamed up another tactic. She doesn't dare write herself, so it's that lovely mother of hers[164] who writes to me to assure me of her passionate devotion, and once again invites me to be sponsor at the wedding of her daughter Masha and persists in adding that without my blessing the young woman is unwilling to surrender to the bonds of matrimony. I responded[165] with the most studious politeness that I am obliged to deprive myself of the pleasure of meeting my *dear relatives,* as she so grandiloquently puts it.

I can't help laughing at Kotek's tragic view of my current situation.[166] There's nothing remotely tragic about it. I am just bored and disgusted, and avoid everyone by taking refuge in the outskirts of the city, or in the private rooms of various taverns. You wouldn't believe how expensive this is proving! It's costing me at least ten rubles a day.

Smacking kisses. Please go and see if there is suitable accommodation for me on the floor below you.

Yours, P. Tchaikovsky

✦ ✦ ✦

25. TO MODEST ILYICH TCHAIKOVSKY

Florence, 4/16 D[ecember 1878][167]

What the hell is going on! I find myself in the most ridiculous situation. It reminds me of a man who is taking a running jump, and while he is going full tilt, a wall suddenly rises up in his path. I haven't yet received my wretched manuscript![168] For the first ten days since I arrived here while awaiting the arrival of the first three sections of the suite, I have really been enjoying orchestrating and making a reduction for piano four hands of the last sections. But the days are passing and no package has arrived. So I'm doomed to sheer idleness, since, as you know, my temperament doesn't allow me to start work on something new until the current piece is off my hands, so my life here is just a waste of time with no work to do, and it lost its *charme* the moment I ran out of work. Yesterday, at least I got a letter from Tolya,[169] which helped to stop me fretting. From this long awaited letter I learned that he had taken the manuscript to Jurgenson[170] two weeks ago so that it could be sent on to me. So what can that old nincompoop be thinking? In a word, I'm in a bad temper and out of sorts—at least to the extent that someone who is contented and doing well in all other respects is entitled to be in a bad temper. And by the way, the weather is lousy, and there is snow in the streets and on the roofs, and it's either raining or snowing non-stop—very unattractive! But the fact is that once the weather clears up and brightens up: then you feel so good that it almost brings tears to your eyes.

Now there's something I want to tell you. After Alyosha had gone to church yesterday, I needed some paper, and while I was looking for it in one of his drawers, I came across something really interesting. It was a diary he had been keeping in San Remo last year.[171] I simply devoured it. It turns out that he only pretends to be so unfeeling, but in actual fact he was suffering and feeling terribly depressed.[172] It affected me deeply. Now he has gone into town for stamps, and I'm going to take the opportunity to copy some entries for you; they're of great interest.[173]

No. 1) January 1878.

. . . so we went to see Dr. Seki, a real bad moment—that question about what my trouble was—my head began to spin and I thought I was in a really bad way—but it passed! I finally made up my mind to tell what it is I'm suffering from! Because I was afraid that the innocent Kolya may have caught it because of me and I said that in Moscow I was suffering from a chancre, the doctor examined me and said that I had syphilis. I was taken aback! And I thought I was a goner. Mod. Ilyich told P.I. and P.I. says that you can't possibly stay with us because Kolya has been hanging around with me and might catch it, and so you should go to St. Petersburg or Berlin to Kotek. Like, I was supposed decide right on the spot, but I said I would wait a little and went to my room where I cried for a long time!!!

No. 2. . . . he replied to me that I shouldn't pick up anything with my hands! They put something on my plate—it wasn't much. I don't know what got into me, but I took some more, and he starts screaming at me, so I lost interest in the food. I felt terrible for those two days, and no one talked to me, and I put on a cheerful face like nothing was wrong etc.

No. 3.

I went to see the doctor. He gave me a very nice welcome and asked me to sit down. He took out his book and told me to rub in the ointment twice a day and that was all. He said I should come back tomorrow or the day after and that there was nothing seriously wrong and I ran home feeling really happy. When I got there I meant to tell Pyotr Ilyich everything, and he flew into a terrible rage, and starts shouting and crying, telling me to get the hell out, and let the doctor take me away somewhere, and he just wants me out of his sight. He had no breakfast—went to his room and cried and so on.

No. 4.

P. I. . . . was very pleased to see me leaving. At dinner M. I. told me about that and I took the news quite calmly. P.I. said perhaps we'll be leaving, but you have to stay here. I said nothing the whole evening and sorted the laundry. Kolya misbehaved, but I just ignored it, but when he wouldn't let me ring the bell, I pushed him away. I did what the doctor ordered and rubbed in the ointment and went to bed, but didn't feel like going to sleep, although I don't know why. Maybe it was because I was so upset or it was just a sleepless night. They went for a walk. When they came back I heard them talking among themselves. Pyotr Ilyich said, "So that's how I'm getting punished for my love; here I am, short of money, and now I'm supposed to pay for his treatment."

Mod. Ilyich said, "Well, what can we do?" and then they went to bed. I can't describe how bad I felt when I heard that! I sank my head into my pillow and started to cry.

No. 5.

. . . I was so hurt that I went to my room and drank a glass of water to stop myself crying. I packed my things and sat and waited for one of the Brothers of Mercy from the monastery to come for me. I felt so bad at having to part from Pyotr Ilyich and I just broke down and started sobbing bitterly—I don't know what came over me, but no one noticed. I saw some young man come dressed like a monk in a black robe. He went upstairs and started talking to M.I. He called down to me and told me to come up, and said that the man had come for me. I went to put my coat on and burst into tears for the last time. I washed my face so that nobody could tell I'd been crying, and then went to see them etc. . . .

No. 6.

Interesting what he says about Kolya

. . . Whenever I was with him, Kolya never let up and kept on playing up, and I began to be afraid of him like an enemy. Every time he made a movement a feeling ran through me as if he was about to hit my back and legs with a stick. I didn't want to go on walks with him anymore, so I stopped going out with them so often . . . We went to the town of Bordicher[174] and Kolya started up again, snatched my stick and kept trying to trip me up with it so that I would fall down; he hit me on the legs, poked it in my eyes, knocked off my hat, as well as other nasty tricks, but I didn't say anything. All this was playing terribly on my nerves. Although I liked Kolya, I was angry with him for being so mean to me . . .

. . . .

Modya, I trust I wasn't mistaken in supposing that these extracts would be of psychological interest to you, and that they would remind you of last year. Since I had nothing better to do, I thought I would copy them.

A smacking kiss for you, and a gentler one from me to Kolya.

P. Tchaikovsky

On 16/28 I'm leaving for Paris, but one more letter may find me here. The address is: Hotel de Hollande.

✦ ✦ ✦

26. TO MODEST ILYICH TCHAIKOVSKY

Clarens, 6/18 J[anuary] 1879[175]

Modya! Tolya proposed that I should write in the form of a diary, and I agreed to give it a try. It's most probable that my diary won't be all that interesting. But we'll see.

✦

Friday, 5/17
I got up shortly after eight o'clock. I had a good laugh at Alyosha who had a small gumboil and his swollen cheek made him look really comical. After coffee I took the same walk. These days I'm in the grip of an overwhelming sexual urge and my walks are dominated by futile hopes of meeting someone. Whenever I find myself near the Russian boarding school, my heart almost stops beating because I'm so aware of all those lovely girls within its walls, and I stand there hoping at least to catch a glimpse of one of them through the window. Some hopes! Apart from the chambermaid cleaning the room, I never see anyone. After my walk I sat down to do some work, and it was a very success-ful session. I finished a long ensemble number in the first act before the final scene. (Joan alone, with a chorus of angels.)[176] At dinner I was in a cheerful mood and joked with Marie.[177] I asked her: "Which do you like better, carrots or a man's kiss?" Without hesitation, she replied: "A kiss." After dinner I went for a walk alone, because Alyosha isn't feeling too well. When I returned, I spent two painful hours having to prepare the text of the all-important scene with Joan and the angels. It's something I find terribly difficult. In any case, I was already in a nervous state about the prospect of all the work I have ahead of me before I finish this. That's what is making me so unhappy! I'm always in a hurry, and just burning with impatience to see the moment arrive when everything is finished. Afterward I played cards with Alyosha, and such a wave of appetite swept over me that I could hardly bear to wait until supper, for which, by the way, I was served macaroni. Poor Lyonya went to bed straight after supper; he's not feeling himself right now. I wrote a letter to N[adezhda] F[ilaretovna]. After that until mid-night, I had a very enjoyable time reading *Little Dorrit* by Dickens. What a marvelous book that is! I didn't sleep particularly well.

✦

Saturday, 6/18

Alyosha woke me some time after eight o'clock. His cheek was so swollen that you couldn't look at him without laughing. Although he said he was quite well, you could tell he wasn't just by his eyes. To-day's work went remarkably well, so that by dinnertime I was cheerful again and joked about a lot with Marie. Went for a walk by myself. The weather was terrific, frosty, but with clear skies. It's fun going for walks around here because at every step when you start climbing you run across a crowd of young boys, little girls, and even grown-ups sledding downhill. Once again these greedy eyes were feasting hope-lessly on all the girls who happened to be there. I went into the Clarens cemetery. I found quite a few new graves. I sat down for a long time on a bench by the Montreux church enjoying the scene. When I got home, I found two letters waiting for me, one from Kotek, and one from P. I. Jurgenson containing a money order for 500 francs,[178] and worked on the first scene of the second act of the opera. Alyosha still doesn't feel up to scratch. I want to put him to bed right away and give him some tea. He has some fever, but I'm not worried, because to all appearances there's nothing seriously wrong with him. It's after seven now. I can hardly wait for my supper. I'm pretty pleased with myself on the whole; my work is going well, my appetite is good, and (with few exceptions) I'm sleeping very soundly. Goodbye, Modya. Kisses.

Yours P. Tchaikovsky.

✦ ✦ ✦

27. TO ANATOLY ILYICH TCHAIKOVSKY

Clarens, 9/21 J[anuary] 1879.[179]

Although it's not my turn to write to you today, but to Modest, I'm writing anyway because of my indescribable gratitude for your two wonderful letters, packed with interesting details, which both arrived at once.[180] Modest's letter on the other hand was brief and uninforma-tive, although I don't hold that against him in the slightest, since he explains to me the reasons why he had no time to write. I swear to you, Tolya, that in my whole life I've never read a novel as gripping as your letters. And it's understandable. The whole cast of characters is so fa-miliar, and, in varying degrees, dear to me. Your letters leave me with mixed feelings. On the one hand, I am frightened, horrified and non-plussed by the crazy life you live in which you are swirled around like a speck of dust in a storm. On the other hand, I often feel quite envious. For example, I would really like to be at Kolya's to see in the New Year, and to be able to get a look at you all,[181] and see how Tanya looks in her ball gown, and Olga[182] entertaining her guests, and watch Georges Kartsov[183] dancing etc., etc. But the main thing is those minutes when I long more than anything to enjoy hugging my Tolya! Such a pity that I can't spend more time in St. Petersburg! The next time I'm there, I'll do my level best, on the pretext of having to work, not to go anywhere, and just spend all my time at papa's and Kolya's. Well, we'll see.

You make me laugh with your suspicions about the disappearance of your letters. Not a single one has ever got lost. Ever since you started again to write in the form of a diary, you've been writing so much more often. You see how easy it is!

Now, let me tell you about my day, and I'll start with last night. As I had a touch of the flu, I slept rather badly and had some very strange dreams, which I have to tell you. One of them stood out because it was essentially about a *play* on words. I was at a meeting where *Renan*[184] was making a speech, which he ended with these curious conclusions: "There are four things on earth which must be treasured: *France, reve, tombeau, roi*" [French: France, dream, tomb, king]. I turned to my neighbor and asked him what it meant. He replied that Renan was a royalist, and that was why he had been executed, and for that reason after his death he didn't dare to speak his mind, but spoke only in riddles, and those four words mean: *"France! Dream of your handsome king"* (ton beau/ tombeau). In my dream I was deeply impressed by the cleverness of the dead Renan who managed to continue making a speech. Right after his speech, Gerke,[185] the lawyer, went up to him, and they started drinking beer and speaking German. Then I woke up and while still befuddled with sleep, couldn't get over my admiration for Renan's riddle. The second dream was that Annette Merkling[186] was sleeping with me in the same bed and was in tears, begging me to screw her. In order to conceal from her the fact that I couldn't get it up, I pretended to burst into tears and said that I was sorry for her, but that in spite of my passionate desire to satisfy her, I could not bring myself to commit incest. Then she started forcibly clutching at my pitifully drooping member, and I was so terrified that I woke up, and there and then resolved to tell you or Modya all about both dreams in my first letter. Pretty weird, don't you think?

I've finished the first act.[187] After taking a walk *solo* (because Alyosha still can't bring himself to go out), I came home and found four letters on the table: two from you (and how happy that made me!), one from Modya, and one from N[adezhda] F[ilaretovna]. Very strange; no letters for three days, and suddenly four all at once. How pleased I was to learn from your letter that dear Volodya Zhedr[insky] has really livened up and is dancing, putting on shows etc. Before supper, I toiled over the text of the duet for the King and Dunois, breaking my head over the rhymes. My cold has gone away. Am in perfect health.

Smacking kiss! Yours P. Tchaikovsky.

✦ ✦ ✦

28. TO PYOTR IVANOVICH JURGENSON

Clarens, 19/31 January 1879.[188]

Dear friend!

I got your letter yesterday. Congratulations to my dear friend on the birth of his daughter![189] I hope that she will remain the youngest member of her family not just for now, but forever, and also that the family circumstances of that good friend will bring him the utmost peace of mind and joy. I think that time, which usually smooths over life's rough edges, will bring its healing power to bear here too. I dare to hope that all the things that are not quite right will gradually righten themselves out (if I may so put it) and that the wounds of all those who have been hurt will heal and that everything that has gone unexplained and unexpressed will come to be explained and expressed and that peace and universal happiness will prevail . . .

What you wrote to me about the hounding and victimization of N[ikolay] G[rigoryevich] in the papers has upset me more than I can say.[190] It's not the first time that this kind of nastiness has upset me when I think about it, and I've been wondering what I can do for my part to put a stop to this objectionable persecution by the gutter press, but am at a loss as to the means.

There is probably no one it behooves more than myself to write something tempestuous about it, and I would be only too willing to do so—and forcefully—but there is a *reason* I can never get involved in controversy, especially with anonymous columnists. You know how those vermin operate. They spread gossip and bludgeon their victims with *insinuations*—and you know how vulnerable that makes me. Experience has shown how easily the lowest hack journalist can muzzle me merely by hinting at a certain matter. If it were *just me*, I would spit on their insinuations, but for the sake of the people closest to me, whom I love dearly, and who share my family name, I am backed into a situation where that is the thing I fear most in the world. So, in the circumstances, there is nothing I can do. Of course, I could always write something unsigned, but firstly those snooping vermin will find out who wrote the article attacking them, and secondly, anything I wrote defending Rub[instein], would only have any value if it bore my name.

Yesterday, I came to the conclusion that there is only one course open to me. You know that Stasov,[191] so bellicose, so unfair, and so vehement in his writing, is at bottom not really malicious, and is a decent person, although passionately and single-mindedly partisan. I decided that if one were to write to him explaining that it is the duty of every honorable man who loves the art of his people to stand up for such a figure as N[ikolay] G[rigorievich], and that we cannot permit a man who has contributed untold services to Russian music to be insulted with impunity day after day in the press, and also that this man is *irreplaceable* and that the whole of Moscow musical life will be destroyed without him—out of his sense of decency he will make Suvorin[192] call off his Moscow cur and stop him barking at N[ikolay] G[rigorievich]. So that is what I've done.

I sent Stasov a detailed letter,[193] and asked him to go to Suvorin right away and tell him what an unsavoury role his correspondent is forcing upon his newspaper, Novoye Vremya; I don't know what will come of this, but I swear to you that is the only thing I can do. Please be sure to maintain the *utmost* secrecy about all this. When Stasov replies to me, I'll let you know the results of this effort.

I went to Geneva for music manuscript paper. What a boring and dreary dump it is! I went to the Symphonic Association. Before giving you an answer about St. Croix,[194] I'll need to find out where it is. I'll reply in my next letter.

So long for now.

Yours P. Tchaikovsky.

✦ ✦ ✦

29. TO ANATOLY ILYICH TCHAIKOVSKY

Paris, 15/27 F[ebruary] 1879.[195]

You've become so good about writing! Before, I could barely expect a single letter after waiting for two weeks! Now, I just have to go to the *poste restante* (and I go at least twice a week) and there's a letter from you waiting for me! But both of your most recent letters contain the news of your illness, so are not so pleasant to read. I do hope you are over it all now. Tolinka, you really have to make some serious changes in your lifestyle for the sake of your health. There's no way you can stay healthy and keep your nerves in shape, if you continue to live like a madman. Number one; you have to be more careful about your diet, and as far as possible make sure to eat at the same times every day; secondly it's high time you made a serious effort to avoid having visitors during the day. I know from my own experience that even the most sensitive people don't realize that their visits are taking up your time. So don't let anyone in—anyone at all! At the very least, what about going over daddy's place in the mornings and doing your work there. Anyway, it's better if we talk about all this when we meet—and we won't have to wait too long for that. Do you know that I'm actually beginning to count the days and the hours before I leave! When all is said and done, Paris is not the place for me. Even in spite of the very pleasant little affair I happened to have here (which I am too embarrassed to tell you about in any detail),[196] I don't enjoy life enough not to prefer change. Of course, you will say that there's nothing to keep me here, and I am free to leave right now, but I can only tell you that it would be very unpleasant to go home without having finally completed the opera, and I have no more than about two weeks of work left—or even less. This is what I would rather do. I would leave here with the greatest of pleasure for two weeks in Clarens, but it would make me feel uneasy because of N[adezhda] F[ilaretovna]. So I'll have to stay here until 28 Febr[uary].[197] On that day, or at the very latest, the day after, I'll leave for Berlin for a day or two. In a word, in less than three weeks we will be embracing. Tolya! I really cannot stay at your place.[198] I've been too spoiled, and I've become too touchy to be content living in a place where I don't have a corner to call my own. Don't forget while I'm in St. Petersburg, it is imperative, no matter what, *to orchestrate the Suite and put a few finishing touches to it.*[199] There wasn't enough room even for the two of you, and where was I supposed to squeeze in, let alone Alyosha! And anyway, since you and I are both working in the mornings—does it really matter that we won't be in the same apartment? In any case, I'll still be having dinner and spending all the evenings with you. After all, I'll be spending at least three weeks in St. Petersburg, if not a whole month! So, please, my dear boy, think about where to put me up—to me it seems that the best place would be "La Paix,"[200] where Sasha stayed. Don't forget that I'm now getting 8,000 a year, and it's ridiculous for me to stint on such trifles.

Today, by extraordinary coincidence, I got a letter from Sasha[201] at the same time as one from Petya *Genke*[202] in which he writes that Vera fell seriously ill while travelling. You can imagine how worried I would have been, if I hadn't been lucky enough to get the letter from Sasha telling me that Vera was out of danger. However Tanya is now sick, and Sasha thinks that the others might come down with something too. Nevertheless, I was so worried that I immediately sent a telegram[203] with a prepaid reply in order to find out if the children were well. Imagine Yury[204] with the measles!! It brings tears to my eyes to think of it; I can't help it. And, as if providence had arranged it, I'm still under the spell of Dostoevsky's *The Brothers Karamazov*. If you haven't read it, rush out and get the *Russian Herald* for January.[205] There's a scene in the book where Father *Zosima* is receiving visitors in the monastery. It so happens that there's a description of a woman prostrate with grief over the *death* of all her children, and after the last one dies, her anguish drives her mad, she leaves her husband, and becomes a vagabond. When I read the part where she describes the death of her last child and the words with which she expresses her inconsolable anguish, I burst into tears and wept as I've never before wept over a book. The effect on me was just shattering.[206]

Since I've been here, I haven't been to the theatre. There's any number of interesting plays that are worth seeing, but I just don't have the energy. It's surprising how much I've lost interest in the theatre. The only time I'm happy and content is when I'm sitting around at home in the evening in my dressing gown, hearing no sounds and seeing no faces. Every day I have dinner at the *Diner de Paris*.[207] Instead of the theatre, I've picked up a new weakness: *shopping!* Yesterday, I bought eight *ties!*

Kisses, dear boy. Yours P. Tchaikovsky

I was so envious when I read the description by you and Modya of the party you gave where you played forfeits. Now, that's my kind of party!

✦✦✦

30. TO ANATOLY ILYICH TCHAIKOVSKY

21 F[ebruary]/4 M[arch] 1879. *Paris*[208]

Here is a brief diary of everything that has happened recently:

✦

Sunday 18.
I spent the morning working. After lunch I walked to the Padelou concert.[209] It was an interesting program. The main work was *Berlioz's* "Symphonie Fantastique." The soloists were the Viardot son, violinist, and daughter, singer—both pretty good.[210] I didn't stay until the end. The weather was great, and I had a very pleasant walk home. I especially enjoyed the sight of this wonderful city, full of life and glitter.

The rest of the day I spent in a daze. At 7 p.m. I had a rendezvous.

Apart from all those feelings so brilliantly depicted in the romance "Sweet Pain," in the inimitable way I have, I still find all kinds of things to be afraid of which I can't even describe, and I was in a state of all-round anxiety—which had a funny ending.

For some reason, the person I was waiting for with my heart in my mouth didn't show up, whereupon I drowned my sorrows by going to enjoy an excellent dinner. After taking a walk, I spent the evening at home. I slept badly; I was a nervous wreck.

✦

Monday 19.
Worked, and then had breakfast. Got a ticket to the theatre for a show that was said to be very amusing. I needed some distraction. I have been working non-stop, and was feeling very tired,[211] and have been constantly under stress, and if that were not enough, I was also angry with 1) Bochechkarov who sent Modest a really nasty letter, and 2) N[adezhda] F[ilaretovna] no less! Of course, as they say, "a woman's hair may be plentiful; but not her gray matter." One would imagine her to be an intelligent and sensitive woman, and I really think I have described myself to her well enough. But can you believe that

in her last letter she actually asked me why I don't see Turgenev and Viardot?[212] I found that really exasperating, because it means that I have got to explain to her all over again that I am anti-social and hate meeting people. I was enjoying myself at the theatre—although not all that much—and had to leave before the end and dash off an endless letter to N[adezhda] F[ilaretovna]. I didn't sleep too badly, and I woke up thinking of the pleasant prospect of leaving in a week, and that the opera will probably be ready by then.

◆

Tuesday 20.

I worked. After breakfast, I went to order some clothes. At two o'clock I gave Pakhulsky[213] his regular (twice weekly) lesson. Then I went back to work. At seven o'clock I had dinner, and then took a tremendously long walk and *went back to work again.* It's now midnight, and I'm very pleased with my day's work. My dear Tolya, when you get this letter I don't think it's worth writing back to this address. Better to write to me in Berlin where I'll be staying for two or three days. The address is: Berlin, Linkstrasse, 18, II Treppe. P. I. Tchaikovsky, c/o Herrn Josef Kotek. And then—hurrah!—we'll be meeting in St. Petersburg! But, oh, if only it were possible to keep out of the way of friends and relatives while I'm there. When I'm in Berlin, write and let me know where you want me to stay in St. Petersburg.

A thousand tender kisses.

Yours P. Tchaikovsky

Will you come with me to Kamenka for Easter, or should I spend it in St. Petersburg???

◆ ◆ ◆

31. TO MODEST ILYICH TCHAIKOVSKY

17 February/ 1 March 1879. Paris.[214]

I want to describe to you in a few words my little adventure. On practically the first day after I arrived in Paris as I was leaving the *Diner de Paris,* I caught sight of a nice young girl, of very pleasant appearance, dressed cheaply but cleanly, and above all with wonderful big eyes.[215] I kept my eyes on her, and I felt that she was looking back at me with some interest. She gave me the same eye treatment when we met again along the *Passage,* but when I came out, I found she hadn't followed me. For several days in a row, whenever I left the *Diner de Paris* she was right in my path, but I didn't have the nerve to go up to her. By that time I felt that I was beginning to fall for her, and during my dinner I felt agitated and my heart missed a beat whenever I thought of her. I decided to forget about the whole thing, and for the next two days made a point of avoiding the Passage. But the very next day (as so often happens with weak-willed people) I not only went there, but resolved that I must get to know her no matter what. So when I ran into her I gave her a sign that she should follow me. We struck up an acquaintance right then and there, but after talking to her learned that she was a milliner and that at the moment she was out of a job. I gave her three francs, and after telling her we would probably meet again, I took my leave. Of course I spent several uncomfortable and stressful days agonizing about whether or not to give way to my impulses. Finally, I made up my mind and went to look for her. I found her and took her to a café in some out-of-the-way side street. After talking for a while I saw that she was a perfectly decent girl and not out to rob me, and at her suggestion, took her to a little hotel in *Rue St. Denis,* and rented a room. I spent a pleasant evening, but couldn't help worrying about whether someone might come in, or something like that. We parted on affectionate terms, and when I asked her if she didn't find it repugnant being with an old man like me, she replied: *"Eh bien. Jouez: je vous aime comme mon pere"* [French: Let's pretend I love you like my father]. I told her that I was Swedish and that my name was *Frederic Odenburg,* and I found it terribly funny when she called me *Frederic.* This was on Wednesday. It's now Saturday, and I haven't seen her since. We have a rendezvous for tomorrow, but I have such a strong urge to see her that I'm going to the Passage today to see if I can find her. Unfortunately, the pleasure I might otherwise get from seeing her is poisoned (she is nice, amusing, and extraordinarily delicate when it comes to money matters) by the unwarranted but tormenting fear of *something or other,* when in fact there is really nothing to fear.

Modya! How nice it would be to know that you like my scenario.[216] I have been working as meticulously as ever, and I hope that by the time I leave I will have finished the whole thing, and I leave in less than two weeks. It's a good thing that I'm having this little affair. If it weren't for that, I would have been terribly bored. Now there's no longer any doubt about my feelings about Paris. I've really gone off it. I haven't gone to the theatre a single time since I saw *Le Gendre*.[217] I've no interest in going out anywhere: the shops, the streets, restaurants, the electric lighting, the glitter, the bustle—everything has lost its charm for me, and although I stay at home most of time, the way I did in Clarens, I just seem to have lost the habit of spending those wonderful few moments contemplating my happiness, something that I experienced every day, and practically every minute while I was there.

I was sorry to learn that you had been suffering from shortage of money. Why didn't you write and tell me? I could always have managed to arrange a small loan for you from Jurgenson. We'll be seeing each other in about 17 days.

Kisses. Yours, P. Tchaikovsky

In spite of my lovely Louise, I'm counting the days and hours before I'll be leaving here.

◆ ◆ ◆

32. TO MODEST ILYICH TCHAIKOVSKY

Paris, 22 February/6 March [1879][218]

Dear Modya!

Yesterday was a momentous day for me. To my own great surprise, I actually *completed work* on the opera—yes, completed. When you come to write the very last word of your novel,[219] you will understand how deeply gratifying it is to relieve yourself of the load you've been carrying. Say what you like, but to spend hours every single day for almost two and a half months trying to squeeze music out of your head—sometimes it comes easily and sometimes it's a real effort—just wears you out. But now I'm really going to take it easy! Now, the instrumentation, that's purely intellectual work—like embroidering on canvas from an existing pattern. Today I have already started pulling the threads together and putting the finishing touches to the suite.[220] Tomorrow, I'll finish off the remaining details of the fugue in the suite, and starting the day after tomorrow, I won't even sit at my desk until I'm actually in St. Petersburg. In fact, for someone whose dedication to his work is nothing short of a zealous commitment to reaching his goal, namely the goal of achieving the *right to do absolutely nothing*, this is the sheerest triumph!

Yesterday evening, I was finally walking around Paris an entirely free man, in fact nothing but an idler casually strolling around. And perhaps it was for that very reason that I felt that old love I had had for Paris for so many years had come back to me as strongly as when I was young, although there was one other factor which contributed to that feeling, namely a poster announcing a performance of my *Tempest* at the Châtelet concert hall on Sunday.[221] Seeing my name up on posters and in the windows of music shops made me feel right at home in Paris. However, I have to tell you that, while on the one hand it made me feel good, on the other hand it worried me. I know in advance that it's going to be a poor performance and the audience will be hissing, as has always been the case when my works are performed abroad. For that reason I would prefer it if the performance were to take place after my departure. But it's out of my hands, and I'll just have to resign myself to suffering a little on Sunday, but it will only hurt a little, for in this regard I'm a kind of old hand at this game, and I know very well that my time will come, but so far in the future that I won't be here to know it. Anyway, whatever happens there, yesterday and today I've been strutting around Paris like the cock of the walk, and consoling myself with the comforting knowledge that I can dawdle as much as I want—you wouldn't even recognize your brother gallivanting around in his new overcoat, top hat, and smart gloves.

Yesterday, *j'ai entrevu* [French: I caught a glimpse of] Mlle. Louise. I'll be spending a few pleasant hours with her before I leave.

Today I'm going to the theatre at the *Varietes* where they are playing *Le Grand Casimir*.[222] It's a big hit.

✦ ✦ ✦

33. TO ANATOLY ILYICH TCHAIKOVSKY

28 F[ebruary]/12 M[arch], *Paris*, 1879.[223]

I'm leaving today, my own dear brother, and in just a few days we'll be embracing. I'll be leaving in excellent spirits, even though I'm desperately short of money! Yes! Just imagine; I've been wildly extravagant, and I had been counting on receiving funds which simply failed to materialize. I had to telegraph Jurgenson to send me some money in Berlin.[224] I'll also be needing money when I'm in St. Petersburg. Can't you get hold of 300 rubles for me from somewhere until the 1st of April? Can't Kolya give me the money?[225] Or couldn't we get the money from Konradi? On the 1st of April I'll be getting 1,000 rubles from N[adezhda] F[ilaretovna]. Apart from that, I'll probably be getting something from Moscow for Onegin.

Now, about Onegin. Two days ago, I got a telegram from Jurgenson telling me that on Saturday, Onegin was performed right through with an orchestra for the first time, and that everything is going splendidly, and that it will be performed without fail on 17 March.[226] I've made up my mind that, no matter what, I will be at the performance *incognito*. You and Modest will, of course, both be there. Don't forget!

I'm sending you a cutting from the paper from which you will see that in keeping with my habitual exaggerated pessimism about the success of my works, "The Tempest" was by no means a dismal failure. It so happened that only one gentleman booed, and he also booed Saint-Saens.[227] I've totally come to terms with this unpleasant event. There's just one mournful little note in my symphony of satisfaction that haunts me. I'll be taking my completed opera with me in my briefcase and intend to hear the other opera,[228] I'll be seeing individuals close to my heart—but I cannot think without sorrow of that young girl whom I met here who deserves sympathy, and who is wallowing in a morass of debauchery, and whom I don't have the slightest prospect of rescuing—which I bitterly regret![229] Something else is also bothering me; I'm afraid I don't have enough money to get to Berlin! It's so long since I've been in such a situation!

For the first time in my life I've been reading *Les Confessions* of Rousseau.[230]

My! What an incomparable work! There are passages which positively astound me. He says things which are incredibly familiar to me, and which I have never talked about with anyone because I was incapable of expressing them, and here I find Rousseau expressing them perfectly!!

When I get to Berlin, I'll send you a telegram with the time and date when I'll be leaving there for St. Petersburg. Kisses, my dear. P.T.[chaikovsky]

✦✦✦

34. TO PYOTR IVANOVICH JURGENSON

Simaki [25 August 1879][231]

Merci! Very grateful to you for kindly agreeing to accept the new movement. You write that the *Marche Miniature* should be left as it is.[232] Well, my dear fellow, for some time now I have been feeling that this miniature march is just a miniature piece of shit.

To be frank, I would like to discard this garbage altogether. In any case, I think six movements is too many. The best thing would be if you were to agree to what I suggested in my letter yesterday and simply leave the Miniature out. That would leave:

1) Intro[duction] and Fugue
2) Divertimento (incidentally, it seems that I forgot to put in the title, i.e. the new movement)
3) Andante
4) Scherzo (formerly No.2)
5) Gavotte

The thing is that I am a poor judge of my own work until it has been played.

I believe *Taneyev* knows the Suite. I have *complete* faith in his judgment. Please send him a note and ask him for his *honest* opinion. If he can put his hand on his heart and say that it would be a pity to leave out the *Miniature,* then keep all six parts. If not, get rid of it! I'll bear the cost (no need to be noble about it), it would only be fair.

If, however, Taneyev tells you to include the little piece of shit, then the order would be as follows:

1) Intro[duction] and F[ugue]
2) Divertimento
3) Scherzo
4) Little Piece of shit
5) Gavotte[233]

I'll be seeing you quite soon. I would ask you to write just for once to the address I gave yesterday. I'll be going there in a few days.
Yours P. Tchaikovsky
(Begetter of the little piece of shit)

✦ ✦ ✦

35. TO MODEST ILYICH TCHAIKOVSKY

Berlin, 5/17 M[arch] 1880.[234]

The day I have just spent had its pleasant moments interspersed with some dull ones. I spent the morning in the Aquarium[235] and was absolutely delighted with the *chimpanzee,* which lives on extraordinarily friendly terms with a small dog. It was delightful to watch their antics and their play; they were constantly in movement; the chimpanzee made astonishing leaps, smiling delightful as he did so when he wanted to get away from the little dog to a place which the dog could not get to! His intelligence was remarkable; with his keeper he behaved exactly like a child with a nanny. It was a real pleasure to see. At twelve noon I had some coffee and pastries. Then I went to the Museum.[236] You wouldn't recognize it now. Do you remember the tremendous disorder and the way the pictures were hung according to no discernible system? Now everything is beautifully and systematically organized. I can see that I have made great progress in terms of my understanding of the art of painting. It gave me real pleasure to see the paintings on view, especially the Flemish School, not to mention Tenier, Wuwerman, and Ruisdael, whose work I enjoy better than the much vaunted Rubens even, whose Christ has fat, pink haunches and unnaturally rosy cheeks. There was one thing that even began to make me see myself as some kind of *great expert. I recognized Correggio's brush work from his style even before I saw his name in the catalogue!!!* Wow!!! Of course, Correggio must have been an *idiosyncratic* artist because all his male faces and figures bore a resemblance to the Christ in the Vatican, and the female ones to Danae in the Villa Borghese.[237] I didn't see the sculpture—I'll go today. At four o'clock I had the usual dinner, exactly the same as always; I was put out because some gentlemen sitting opposite me kept on staring at me, and I found this embarrassing and put me in a bad mood. I spent the time between dinner and the theatre walking around and met a youth of *stunning beauty* although of a purely German kind. After our walk, I offered him some *money,* which was refused. He does it for the love of art and adores *men with beards.* I had to arrange a rendezvous, but I'll have to stand him up because it is for tomorrow, and I am leaving today. The "Dutchman" I found frightfully noisy and boring.[238] The singers were bad, the prima donna [Mallinger] had no voice and was worse than mediocre. I left before the end; I went to see Bilse,[239] and then went for a walk and made another acquaintance, had supper and drank some beer. Kisses and hugs to you, Kolya and Aleksey.

Yours, P. Tchaikovsky

✦✦✦

36. TO PYOTR IVANOVICH JURGENSON

3 May 1880, Kamenka.[240]

I received the proofs and I'm working hard on them. There will be a host of errors, i.e. my own amendments, but it's not the fault of the typesetters, it's that Messer[241] who is to blame. I keep on having to correct his crappy work. However, I can tell you right now there'll be less trouble with the third and fourth acts. I don't know what you will be sending me, the second or the third set of proofs, but in any case, I should warn you that I'll be needing one further, final set. Best of all, if you were to send me all four acts together, after my current set of amendments has been corrected. *I am dead against having French titles for the separate numbers,* and urge you to get rid of them and have Russian titles put in in the middle.[242] What for? Well, there's no French text to begin with, is there? Some of the titles are wonderfully translated.

For example, *Choeur des filles!!!*—which sounds just like "Chorus of whores"!!!

To hell with it, anyway, dear fellow.

If it's not too much trouble, please send me a *metronome;* I really need one, I keep meaning to get one, but keep on forgetting. For example, the *Italian Fantasy* (which I'm orchestrating), which will be impossible to issue without metronome markings.

Please give Tolya[243] all possible loving care.

Yours. P. Tchaikovsky

✦✦✦

37. TO PYOTR IVANOVICH JURGENSON

[Kamenka] 16 May 1880[244]

Many thanks for the metronome. The score and piano reduction of the Italian Capriccio (not Fantasia)[245] are ready, but both will need some reviewing and playing through. The corrected proofs of Act 1 are also ready, but when Act 2 has been proof-read, I want to play through them both again. So in three days or so, I'll most likely be sending you everything at once, i.e. both the score and piano reduction of the Capriccio and the corrected proofs of both acts. The innumerable mistakes are not the fault of the typesetters, but of that Mr. Messer who, in spite of my earnest requests, could not be bothered to put in the correct markings that were in the score, and has left in a multitude of mistakes which were probably already in his lousy manuscript. What a weird character. There are whole lines *without a text* which he never even noticed. And in one place there is a syllable missing, and the spot has been embellished with a blue cross together with the words *Text fehlt* [German: missing text] in huge letters. And there are quite a few examples of this kind of tomfoolery!

In Russian, if you write *хор девок* [chorus of girls] without a qualifier such as *"of chambermaids," "housemaids"* or *"peasants"* etc., everyone will think that by *девка* [girl] you mean whore. For example, when Laroche says: *"Today I met a девка on the Kuznetsky Bridge,* everyone will think that he meant a whore. It's the same with the French *"filles,"* if there's no word like *jeunes* or *vieilles* etc. in front of it, then people will take *fille* to mean whore. For example, when someone says: "I screwed a девка," that doesn't mean "I had sex with a young girl," but "with a whore"; otherwise the words *"une jeune fille"* would have been written.

So, you're beaten.

Let me know, old man, when I can expect to receive the third act.
Yours, P. Tchaikovsky

♦♦♦

38. TO MODEST ILYICH TCHAIKOVSKY

7 August 1880[246]

You will be very surprised to learn, Modichka, that I have just returned from Kiev. I went there to get the money that Jurgenson sent me, as well as to run a thousand errands for all our friends and relations, and to buy a lot of supplies for the next few months when I don't intend to go anywhere. Although it was extremely tedious to go around buying wool, silk, thermometers, sticks, perfume, toiletries, and everything that people wanted me to get for them, nevertheless I had a very good time throwing money around like a nabob, and for my dinner I ordered chilled champagne. For myself I bought anything that happened to catch my fancy and occasionally taking the time to pop in to the Imperial Garden to admire the views and looking for adventures—*and not entirely without success.* I spent two successive evenings in the Chateau[247] and enjoyed myself like a small child watching the acrobatics of the Bratz family or the four Viennese Jews, you remember, the ones who sang:

Their repertoire had been enriched by various delightful numbers. Half of the next day of my stay in Kiev was ruined by running into Zhenya Kondratiev[248] (but there is worse to come!) from whom I learned that Donaurov[249] is here with him in Kiev and suffering from one of his migraine attacks. Reluctantly I stopped by his place and we had to spend the evening together. Suddenly I realized for the first time that I had never liked Donaurov. It was *unpleasant* to see him. Physically, he hasn't changed in the slightest and is exactly the same as ever, only he lies an awful lot and boasts about his conquests; to hear him tell it, practically the whole army that fought in the last war has spent the night with him. Everyone is in awe of his intelligence and his talents and everyone knows about his songs, something he affects to be surprised at but in actual fact makes him as pleased as punch.

I arrived yesterday evening and found Tolya already here; he had arrived from Kolya's[250] via Znamenka. I found Tolya looking extremely well, suntanned, cheerful and in excellent spirit. It appears that he has now become a true Moscovite and never had a dull moment while he was there, and that he doesn't miss St. Petersburg in the least and is really looking forward to his future life in Moscow.[251] I am very pleased for him. He told me the whole story of what has been happening to Laroche recently. It was all immensely interesting, and my God, I can't think of a more rewarding subject for depicting in some literary form! It is a sorry tale of the most shameless despicable and shabby behavior and dithering between Kat[erina] Iv[anovna][252] and his personal freedom. It ended when he got 5,000 rubles in silver from Kat[erina]

Iv[anovna]'s mother and stopped visiting Rubinstein and Tolya and left by *ship for Paris with Kat[erina] Iv[anovna]*. I am terribly curious to know whether they made it to Paris and what they are going to do there. Of course, it is quite possible that this may turn out to be Laroche's salvation and that in Paris he will get a new lease on life. Before he left, he drove around at breakneck speed and dressed to kill, but studiously avoided Tolya.

I still like Kamenka; and it still gives me a pang when I think of Simaki.[253]

Modya, which do you prefer? To live in Pelazia's[254] room or in a wing of the main house? These two options are both open. Let me know.

Merci for the letters. Kisses. Hugs from Tolya.

P. *Tchaikovsky*

♦ ♦ ♦

39. TO MODEST ILYICH TCHAIKOVSKY

Saturday, 9 Aug[ust 1880, Kamenka][255]

Dear Modosha! I just remembered that for you to get our latest news by Thursday, I have to write today—so here I am sitting down right away to write this. Everything is more or less all right here; a lot of people are sick: *Miss Eastwood*[256] (*disenteria sanguinensis*), *Flegont*[257] (*febris gastrica*), *Tanya* (*migrainia obstinatis*), *Tolya* (as usual 15 ailments a day for which there is no name), *Pelazia* (also some kind of *febris*),[258]—but there is nothing serious about any of these ailments. As to the show,[259] everyone seems to be losing interest and are taking part in it only with reluctance. It is Mitya's[260] birthday today; I presented him with a watch (and also one to Bob). Tremendous, almost frenzied rejoicing. Vera Butakova[261] from Verbovka came to dinner and cheered us all up a little. I went to see Aleks[andra] Iv[anovna][262] today; she, bless her, was much better; and even talked just the way she always does, about how our children are not brought up as well today as they used to be. Aunt Liza[263] is having trouble with her nerves; she spoke to me about Tanya's illness and how troubled and upset she is about her constant ill health, and suddenly burst into tears. Tolya is living in the main house in that wing, although he spends the whole day here, i.e. in my room. I am doing the corrections of the concerto and the Capriccio.[264] I paid my debts to Alyosha and Evstafy with whom I am more in love than ever. My God, what an angelic creature and how I long to be his slave, his plaything, his property! When I read in your letter about the episode with Vanya, a passing spasm of desire for him suddenly flared up. Everything is ephemeral, everything is transitory and the beauty of Ostapka[265] is the only *constant,* before which I will grovel in the dust for as long as I live.

Modya, write and tell me roughly when you think you might come here. Apologize to Kolya for me; I'll have his letter ready for the next post. Kisses and hugs to you both.

P. Tchaikovsky

♦ ♦ ♦

40. TO MODEST ILYICH TCHAIKOVSKY

Moscow, 8 Dec[ember] 1880[266]

I arrived in Moscow yesterday evening. You remember the bath attendant who washed us (you, Kolya, Anatoly, and me) at the Chelyshev baths? Anatoly wrote to me in Kamenka to tell me that he had seen him at other bath houses and was even the target of advances from that attendant. This made me spend the whole journey thinking about him. Since Anatoly was only expecting me today and not yesterday, I couldn't spend the evening with him, so I took the opportunity to visit the baths. Too bad, it was someone else who washed me! But I spotted him on the way out and was invited to come the same evening—which I did. I spent about three hours at the baths *a la Volodya Shilovsky,* i.e. I drank, ate, treated all the staff beginning with the steward, and finally found myself alone with Vasya. What a delight! Nothing, nothing, silence . . .

I was hoping to find a letter here from you. I'm terribly curious about the fate of the comedy.[267] I was excited and absolutely overjoyed to hear that Savina[268] had chosen it for her benefit performance. I'm waiting for news.

Today, there's a rehearsal of *Onegin.*[269] Will you be coming? If the comedy is performed, I don't think you'll have time to come.

I'll be seeing Begichev[270] at the rehearsal, and I'll talk to him about *The Benefactor,* and let you know right away. I was left with the gloomiest memories of Kamenka. Nevertheless, I do feel that it was a very good thing that I went there. Now I'm off to the rehearsal.

Big kiss. Yours P. Tchaikovsky.

✦ ✦ ✦

41. TO ALEKSEY IVANOVICH SOFRONOV

[Kamenka], 24 June 1881.[271]

Dear, dear Lyonya!

I finally received a letter from you and was overjoyed, since for some reason I had gotten very worried and found myself missing you, and every night I seemed to dream that you were sick and somehow unhappy and moping.

Today, my sister[272] and Nataliya Andreevna[273] are going abroad. For the moment I'm staying here, but perhaps in July I'll take a trip to Kiev or even Moscow. Nadezhda Filar[etovna] has been urging me to come to Simaki, but I have categorically refused because without you I will simply find it unbearable. Being there would make me feel even more keenly and strongly that I was undergoing a forced separation from you. But you know what occurred to me? What about us both going there in September when you'll be free. I think that you will have to spend a few days with your mother in Tiliktino;[274] it will be a solace to her. Then you could come to Kamenka and stay here for a week or so and then we could go to Simaki for ten days or a couple of weeks. Let me know what you think about that.

Please don't think you have to limit yourself to spending ten rubles a month. Spend as much as you want. Do you really think, Lyonya, that I begrudge you money? I want you to be properly fed and content, and don't worry about money! I will be only too happy to give you whatever you need. While we're on the subject, let me know if I should use the money you left with me to buy you some paper.

I know nothing about Ev[s]tafy,[275] he doesn't write to anyone. Stepan[276] isn't here yet. We had a big fire here the other night. I was really scared. The fire broke out very near here next door to the chemist's shop. It's been a very good harvest here for wheat and beetroot. Lev Vas[ilievich][277] will make a handsome sum.

Goodbye, my precious. Perhaps I'll be with you in July—although it's not certain. Big kiss.

Yours P. Tchaikovsky.

✦ ✦ ✦

42. TO MODEST ILYICH TCHAIKOVSKY

26 July [1881, Kamenka][278]

Modya! Today, I only have very little time write to you about myself. I spent four whole days in Kiev, because by the second day I had spent all the money I had with me and had to wait for help from Kamenka. I got terribly bored. I went looking for *girls*—not without success. I met a very nice one who was ready for anything, but, strange as it may seem, it didn't give me any pleasure. I've been spending all my evenings at the *Chateau* and I know all their cabaret songs by heart now. I've spent untold sums of money and am tortured with remorse. I've bought 80 silver rubles!!! worth of books. And for what? Finally, I had to put up with a dreadful journey from Kiev to Fastov (God! How I hate travelling by train), and was *so* happy to get back to Kamenka, the same Kamenka which I actually hate and gives me practically no satisfaction. I'm terribly touched by how happy Lyova[279] was to see me when I arrived back. You know, there's no one (not Sasha, not Tanya) I'm sorrier for than him in the midst of all the bickering and disorder of that household. He suffers more than any of them, although he never complains, and just keeps it to himself. I found Tanya with a new boil which had just developed from the morphine.[280] She looked as if she might be a little more cheerful than usual. But, again, another sleepless night and a headache, and, of course, she's lying down. In a word—things are bad. Some encouraging news from Sasha. She's found a lot of friends and acquaintances there,[281] and is having a nice time. But alas! She believes all the lies she's been told in the letters she's been receiving about Tanya, so she's going to get even more of a shock when she gets back. Kisses to you and Kolya

P. Tchaikovsky

✦ ✦ ✦

43. TO MODEST ILYICH TCHAIKOVSKY

Moscow, 28 March [1882][282]

Will this letter reach you? Will you wait until it comes? Briefly, this is what has happened so far. Traveling from Warsaw I had the usual trouble sleeping—but it was quiet and there were moments when it was even comfortable and cozy. Tolya and Jurgenson met me.[283] Tolya was in good spirits and apparently perfectly happy. But after only about an hour, a fly appeared in the ointment. He told me about the suspicions he had had that he was showing signs of syphilis. But of course I could see right away that that was nonsense. On the same day I met Parasha[284] and her father and brother[285] and immediately felt on terms of easy familiarity with them. Parasha is very likable, a nice girl, simple and natural and totally without affectation. In the course of the day several times Tolya had problems with his throat, or his lips or his nose and thought he saw signs of syphilis in all this. But I tried to put his mind at rest, and he was on the way to acknowledging that it was an obsession. Yesterday he gradually became quite convinced that not only did he have syphilis, but that Parasha had also already been *infected* and that her lips were already swollen. He had been to the doctor, who, although he had told him that he did not have syphilis, Tolya thought he could tell from his tone that he was trying to hide the truth. By the evening he was in deep despair and finally I yielded to his fear and could no longer do anything to set his mind at rest. It was an unbelievably painful evening. He had to make a show of being happy and cheerful from dinner time until three o'clock in the morning, since we had spent the whole evening with Parasha, had been to the Kremlin and then attended matins and the ending of the fast. Both of us felt all the more distressed since we were never alone and couldn't even talk. The whole night he lay awake fussing with all the places where he imagined he was infected. By this morning he was hysterical—just at the time when people came to offer their Easter greetings! You can't imagine what I was going through! My mind was telling me that the whole thing was an obsession on the part of Tolya, but my feelings were vibrating with his fears and I was beginning to believe that he was infected.

I hope, indeed I am confident that this whole nightmare will vanish like a puff of smoke, and that by tomorrow we will be laughing about it. I got your letter. Modichka, how can you say that *you have been a drain on me,* you should be ashamed![286] Just think for a moment what I would have done, if it hadn't been for you and Kolya! It was you two who saved me! Without both of you I would have spent the whole winter tormented and depressed. When I think of you, tears come to my eyes and it is only now that I realize what I was losing when I said goodbye to you and Kolya!

Big hug
Yours P. Tchaikovsky
I'll write again tomorrow.

✦ ✦ ✦

44. TO MODEST ILYICH TCHAIKOVSKY

[Moscow, 29 March 1882][287]

Modichka! Yesterday I wrote you a letter which reflected my painfully disturbed state of mind. Today I want to give you some more cheerful news. Tolya has stopped imagining he has syphilis, he has cheered up and is in much better spirits. How long this will last is impossible to predict. Nearest and dearest will soon be descending on us from all over, and I hope that the task of taking care of his guests will take his mind off this *idee fixe*. Every day I go and spend time with the Konshin family and have been able quickly to get on a familiar footing with them. It would be interesting to describe them all to you—but there is no time. Life is hectic here. Our life in Italy now seems to be strangely remote. It's like a sweet dream.

I am writing to you from Jurgenson's and I'm rushing off to Albrecht's for dinner.

Big kiss
Yours, P. Tchaikovsky
Your letter arrived yesterday

✦ ✦ ✦

45. TO PYOTR IVANOVICH JURGENSON

Kamenka, 15 September, 1882.[288]

My dear fellow,

I got your letter in which you shed tears over the publishing house. Well, I think that with all the unfavorable circumstances of which you complain, i.e. the lack of assistants, proof readers, etc. you should moderate your publishing zeal. There are things in your business that

I know absolutely nothing about. It's hard to believe that apart from your mad passion and hunger for every kind of printing plates, there are still other motives driving you to spend a thousand rubles for the manure you've been telling me about.[289] And by the way, your analogy with manure doesn't work in this case. If you're running a farm, the manure is a valuable asset and improves the quality and quantity of the crops which it helps to grow. But what fruit can the musical manure you've been acquiring possibly bear? Just a few more hundredweight of scrap metal where you store your plates—and music doesn't skim off any cream from that shit. I just don't understand! Of course, I don't mean to say by this that you should simply confine yourself to the creations of P. I. Tchaikovsky, and try to spread as many as possible of the scribblings of that hack around the world. Quite the contrary, it's always seemed to me that the market value of my stuff is something different, something artificial, and that's why I'm embarrassed to keep on sending it to you. Nevertheless, you can expect a surprise in a few days, consisting of six piano pieces[290] to which I've just given birth. I wouldn't have dreamed of writing to you if it hadn't been for Osip Ivanovich encouraging me to do so. I have to confess that financial considerations weren't entirely absent from the pianistic inspiration that suddenly descended upon me. You can blame Osip Ivanovich if you have to cough up.[291]

Fitzenhagen has given me a big fright with his fifth set of corrections.[292] I have every reason to fear that he will find even more problems to dig up and I'm practically getting ready to ask him for *a sixth set*. Why on earth did you take it into your head to give him the trio to proofread? For God's sake send all my stuff to me—and only to me! Believe me. You will never find a better proofreader for it than me. Well, let's hope it will all work out successfully, and after all Fitzenhagen's fussing, just go ahead, and publish the trio—and the best of luck to you!—send me a copy (one).

I've finished work on the opera[293] and I'm starting work on the orchestration. I think the opera is going to be a good one. I think this time you won't lose money on it because of me; I think everyone's going to be pleased, the audience, the singers, me, and Jurgenson. But who the hell knows!

Goodbye for now, dear fellow, and thanks for the letters.
Yours P. Tchaikovsky

✦✦✦

46. TO MODEST ILYICH TCHAIKOVSKY

Moscow, 8 Dec[ember 1882][294]

Dear Modichka!

I think you will be angry with me because I still haven't left. There are many reasons why I had to stay here for another week: 1) unfinished work,[295] 2) on Friday I want to go to a concert of sacred music where part of my *vespers* is being sung,[296] 3) I want to hear Taneyev's Overture[297] at the Symphony Concert, 4) a lot of people have been asking me to stay a little longer, etc, etc. Tolya also bears some of the responsibility for keeping me here. Today Tanya is passing through on her way to St. Petersburg; happily, she won't be staying. Tolya was horrified at the thought that she might be staying. I don't think you are too keen on seeing her either.[298] In any case, I'll be leaving on Sunday, probably on the express and will send you a telegram the day I leave. Among the interesting details of my stay here I can tell you that I patched things up with Volodya Shilovsky and I have already been out drinking with him twice. Golitsyn[299] and three Italian *molto belli cocchieri* [Italian: very beautiful coachmen] in Saratov.[300] *Uno di questi tre mi piace multissimo e sono un poco inamorato* [Italian: I found one of them extremely attractive and am a little bit in love]. But all this kind of life, in which there are many pleasant hours—but even more tedious ones—absolutely wears me out *et je soupire après ma liberte.* [French: I long for my freedom] And what's more, so much time is wasted. Not to mention money. Goodbye for now, my dear.

Bear in mind that, at the very least, I'll be spending three days or so with you *incognito*. Kisses.

P. *Tchaikovsky*

✦✦✦

47. TO MODEST ILYICH TCHAIKOVSKY

Par[is], 22 Apr[il]/4 May 18[83][301]

Modinka! Please don't worry about me. There's nothing wrong with my nerves and I'm altogether in excellent health. Of course, if it was possible, I wouldn't be staying in Paris—but since I have to, it can't be helped. But the main thing is, please don't think you have anything to reproach yourself for. You've done *everything and exactly* what you should have done. As to the idea that you should have left me out of all this—well, that's just ridiculous. What do you think is better for me: to have shared with you this misfortune which has been visited upon us, or to have just gone cheerfully about my business somewhere in Rome, knowing that you were having to cope with the ordeal all by yourself.[302] It's not even worth talking about. We're both victims of an unfortunate set of circumstances.

Yesterday was a holiday here, and everything was closed.[303] A bitter north wind was blowing, and I went out with a warm overcoat. Tanya was asleep when I got back; I sat with Liz[aveta] Mik[hailovna][304] for an hour, but seeing that Tanya was still sleeping, I left. Just imagine! Yesterday evening after dinner, all three of them[305] went to the Hippodrome and sat through the whole performance, which they really enjoyed. Could we have imagined such a thing just a month ago? When they told me today, you could have knocked me down with a feather.

Yesterday again, I didn't have dinner until awfully late, and then went for a walk in the Champs Elysees. The *club* is a club indeed! I took a long hard look at that whole crowd of Rivol[i]s and Rabuses engaged in their idle revelry.[306] They were squealing and shrieking, running around, and sometimes joining hands to sing and dance in a circle in their high-pitched voices. You could hear them exclaiming: *"Que cherches tu donc, Suzanne?"* [French: What are you looking for, Suzanne?], or *"Je ne sais ce que j'ai, je crois que je suis enceinte"* [I don't know what's wrong with me, I think I must be pregnant], or *"Ah, mesdames, nous aurons chacune un homme ce soir"* [Ladies, we'll all have a man tonight] etc. etc. Later on, I witnessed a weirdly dramatic event—remind me to tell you about it when we meet. Slept well. Worked hard.[307] Today, Tanya stayed in bed to entertain her guests. She was feeling great and was in excellent spirits. I've even stopped expecting that what we thought would happen will ever actually happen. There's no sign of it, and you've already been gone over two weeks.

Lyova has sent 600 rubles. The cold is awful today; a lot of people are going around in their furs.

Just imagine; it looks as if I'm going to finish my opera before Tanya finishes hers.[308] I'm delighted to have lifted that burden from my shoulders, but I fear that without any work on hand the waiting is going to be even more difficult; but who knows, maybe the whole thing will be over soon and will end well. Modya, I really mean it—you shouldn't worry about me.

Yours P. Tchaikovsky

✦ ✦ ✦

48. TO SOFIA IVANOVNA JURGENSON

[Maidanovo, Before 13 June 1885][309]

I am sending you Pchelnikov's receipt.[310]
My dear Sofia Ivanovna!

The score of *Cherevichki,*[311] copied by Langer[312] was delivered by me to Pavel Mikhailovich Pchelnikov and I have been keeping the receipt. Neither you nor Pyotr I[vanovich][313] need worry about the copying of the orchestral parts—that's their business.[314]

I don't have Taneyev's[315] address, since he and I have agreed that, once he has settled in, he will write first. Anyway, you can send mail to Essentuki marked *poste restante.*

I'll be delighted to see you here with us in Maidanovo. If you come, you could bring Borka[316] with you.

I kiss your hands. P. Tchaikovsky

✦ ✦ ✦

49. TO ZINAIDA GERMANOVNA LAROCHE

[Maidanovo, 11/23 October 1886][317]

To Zinaida Germanovna *Laroche*
Although you have my photograph, it might interest you to know that I sometimes look like a General or a Minister.

✦ ✦ ✦

50. TO KARL EDUARDOVICH VEBER

Klin, Maidanovo [29 January 1887][318]

Karl Eduardovich, my deepest respects!

Forgive me for taking so long to write and not having yet replied to your question about the libretto for "The Last Day of Pompeii." After reading it, I have come to the conclusion that, however much I would like to be of service to Madam Gravert, I cannot use it. The libretto reveals an amateurish and inexperienced hand, and I very much doubt that there will be anyone who would be keen to use it for an opera. What should I do with it? Return it to you, or send it to *V. P. Prokunin?* In the hope that your wish to join the teaching staff of the Moscow Conservatory (if not now, then later on) is granted, I remain your obedient servant,

P. Tchaikovsky.

✦✦✦

51. TO ANNA YAKOVLEVNA ALEKSANDROVA-LEVENSON

Borzhomi, [June–July 1887][319]

[*missing text*] days, and I was so busy with matters I had to attend to, that except for going to the Conservatory on business, I never visited anyone. But as they say, if the mountain won't go to Mahomet, then Mahomet must go to the mountain. If only you had called on me in the morning or sent a message to say that you would like to see me at a certain time, I would have found a way of seeing you. I am always pleased to see you, but I have such a vast crowd of friends and acquaintances in Moscow that it's physically impossible to see any of them who, like Mahomet, don't want to go to the mountain.

I am now in Borzhomi at Praskoviya Vladimirovna's;[320] she sends you her regards. I am taking the waters, going for walks, and doing absolutely nothing. Did you know that the wonderful N. D. Kondratiev[321] is dying? His days are numbered. He's suffering from dropsy, the result of a kidney infection, and quite incurable. You wouldn't believe how beautiful the *Caucasus* is! Impossible to imagine anything more enchanting than Borzhom [*sic*]!

Keep well, dear Anna Yakovlevna.

Yours P. Tchaikovsky

✦✦✦

52. TO VYACHESLAV OSIPOVICH KOTEK

[21 September] 1888, Klin, Frolovskoye.[322]

Vyacheslav Osipovich! Take the trouble to visit Koreivo's music store once a month, and he should pay you [25 rubles]. [*Part of the text missing*]

Tchaiko[vsky]

✦ ✦ ✦

53. TO SERGEY MIKHAILOVICH TRETYAKOV

[Moscow, January 1890 (?)][323]

Paris Grand Hotel Tretiakoff

Reunis tous apres concert gaite complete generale rien ne manque a notre felicite Jurgenson dit billets vendus. [We all got together after the concert. Everyone delighted, our happiness complete Jurgenson says tickets sold.]

Rubinstein, Tschaikovsky, Safonoff, Mamontoff, Roukavischnikoff, Siloti, Jurgenson, Jakowleff, Kaschkine, Serge Anne Rebesoff.

✦ ✦ ✦

54. TO MODEST ILYICH TCHAIKOVSKY

2/14 March 18[90], Florence[324]

You've probably received my short letter, so I don't need to repeat that I am enormously pleased with the seventh scene, just as I was with *all the others*.[325] The Brindisi[326] must have a second couplet; I didn't send you a telegram because that detail won't hold me up at all. The second couplet must have the same rhythm as the first, and therefore, beginning with "today you, *tomorrow me*," the words must stay. I couldn't make out one of the gambling terms because it wasn't clearly written. It's where *Surin* says: "I'll bet on the 'ruzhe.'" What's the meaning of "ruzhe"?[327]

We need to find the beginning of the gamblers' song, but I don't know where. No doubt Apukhtin knows it by heart. I remember the first three lines:

"Ah, where are those islands.
Where the happy grass grows.
Brattsy (Fellows)
. . . .
. . . .
Svyattsy"[328]

Anyway, it doesn't matter.

Oh yes, I forgot to tell you before: I want you to find words for the chorus "Glory to thee, Ekaterina"[329] to follow "our loving mother."

I need another two lines. I don't know what makes you think that I would include women in the last scene.[330] That's out of the question, it would be an outrageous stretch! In any case, apart from tarts, there shouldn't be any women in a gambling den, and certainly not a whole chorus of whores—that would really be too much . . .

What made you think I'd be changing the words of the chorus? I've just added a couple of words in two places for musical reasons—by no means.

By the time you get this letter, I'll be in Rome. I've decided to write the piano reduction there. I'll send you a telegram with the address. Yesterday morning I received 810 francs [by order of M. Konradi]. I'm waiting for some explanation for this delivery, but my guess is that it is the allowance that Kolya has been paying me. The summery weather is continuing. I find Florence just as unappealing as ever, and except for my rooms, and a few places in Cascino, I find everything about the place positively unpleasant. Most recently, I've also acquired an aversion to the hotel food—I just can't take the same old food all the time. Hugs to you and Kolya—and a thank you to him. Next time I'll write to *Kolya*.[331]

Nazar[332] sends his regards.

♦ ♦ ♦

55. TO IVAN ALEXANDROVICH VSEVOLOZHSKY

[Paris] 6 Apr[il] [18]91[333]

Ivan Alexandrovich, deepest respects!

Allow me to introduce *A. M. Markova*,[334] an excellent young singer, who, in my opinion, is sure to be a valuable asset to any opera house where she may perform.

Yours most sincerely, P. Tchaikovsky.

♦ ♦ ♦

56. TO PAVEL LEONTIEVICH PETERSSEN

25 Sept[ember] 18[91].[335]

Dear Pavel Leontievich!

I will choose the 23rd of November. I'll be very grateful to Auer if he will conduct the soloist.

I don't yet know when I will be in St. Petersburg; it depends on a number of as yet undetermined factors. In any case, on 23 November, I'll be visiting Northern Palmyra again and will be sure to call on you.

A warm handshake
P. Tchaikovsky

✦✦✦

57. TO OSIP IVANOVICH JURGENSON

Paris, 10/22 January [18]92.[336]

Dear Osip Ivanovich!

Could I trouble you to give the bearer of this 200 (two hundred) rubles in silver. Since you are no longer holding any cash of mine, could you take it from the Theatre, or perhaps give it in the form of a loan and return it from my total which you will be getting for the second half of the season?

I apologize for putting you to this trouble.

Yours P. Tchaikovsky.

✦✦✦

58. TO KONSTANTIN STEPANOVICH SHILOVSKY

[Moscow] *26 Apr[il]* [1892][337]

Dear Kostya!

Please come and see me tomorrow at about five o'clock before dinner. At your request, I gave the porter a note indicating the time of our meeting. I don't know why he never gave it to you. In any case, come at that time tomorrow, and please be *exact* [French: on time]; there'll be a whole lot of stuff to get through.

Yours P. Tchaikovsky.

The autograph of Tchaikovsky's musical letter to Bob Davydov

4 Musical Souvenirs

TCHAIKOVSKY'S MUSICAL JOKES and souvenirs published in this chapter serve as a gentle reminder that the creator of the *Pathétique* Symphony and the *Romeo and Juliet* Overture was also the author of a comic opera, *Cherevichki* [The Tsarina's Slippers] and Monsieur Triquet's humorously dignified couplets in *Eugene Onegin*.

The composer penned these little musical pieces either as mementos in the album-writing tradition or as funny musical messages stylistically on par with some of the jocular passages in his letters to his brothers and friends.

The majority of the material presented here has not been published until the Russian edition of this book.

"ANASTASIA WALTZ" FOR SOLO PIANO

Dedicated to A. P. Petrova, 1854[1]

Cet accord ne
doit pas être touche
[Этот аккорд брать
не следует].

Pas jouer
[не играть]

Pas jouer
[не играть]

Pas jouer
[не играть]

Pas jouer
[не играть]

Pas jouer
[не играть]

Pas jouer
[не играть]

Le fine couronne l'oeuvre (Proverbe française)
[Конец венчает дело (по французской поговорке)]
Pierre Tschaikovsky.

"MAZURKA" FOR A. N. OSTROVSKY'S DRAMA
THE FALSE DMITRY AND VASILY SHUISKY

Transcription for piano solo by the composer

Dedicated to V. V. Davydova, 1867[2]

"A VILE DOG . . ."

A musical joke written by the composer for an album of M. A. Golovina, 1875–76[3]

Собака низкая, бессовестная Бишка,
ты изменила мне, оставила меня!
Ты видишь, болен я, чахотка и одышка
теснят младую грудь,
теснят младую грудь,
умру я, жизнь кляня!

A vile dog, oh shameless Bishka,
The one who betrayed, abandoned me!
Consumption and fatigue—you see—
compress my chest, my youthful chest.
I'll die, goodbye, I damn my life!

Sobaka nizkaya, bessovestnaya Bishka,
ty izmenila mne, ostavila menya!
Ty vidish' bolen ya, chakhotka i odyshka
tesnyat mladuyu grud',
tesnyat mladuyu grud',
umru ya, zhizn' klyanya!

"CHIZHIK, CHIZHIK . . ."

September 22, 1876[4]

П. Чайковский.
22 сент[ября] 1876 г.
Москва.

Чижик, чижик, где ты был,
на Фонтанке водку пил!
Выпил рюмку, выпил две,
Зашумело в голове!

Chizhik-chizhik, where've you been?
Drinking vodka on the Fontanka.
Took a shot, took another—
And my head begins to spin!

Chizhik-chizhik, gde ty byl?
Na Fontanke vodku pil.
Vypil ryumku, vypil dve—
Zashumelo v golove.

MUSICAL LETTER TO A. N. LITKE

July 22, 1891, Maidanovo[5]

Не знаю! Позвольте и нам получать письма от Бобика! Да!
Мы получили их целых три, да еще каких милых! Не знаю!
Прежде вы находили удовольствие в посещении
Зоологического Сада!
Вы тогда не называли себя идиотом! Обнимаю Вас.
П. Чайковский

I don't know! Please allow us also to receive letters from Bob! Yes!
You've already received three letters from him, and such nice letters!
I don't know!
Before, you used to enjoy visiting the Zoo Garden!
Back then, you didn't call yourself "an idiot"! Big hugs.
P. Tchaikovsky

Ne znayu! Pozvol'te i nam poluchat' pis'ma ot Bobika! Da!
Vy poluchili ikh tselykh tri, da eshchye kakikh milykh! Ne znayu!
Prezhde vy nakhodili udovol'stvie v poseshchenii Zoologicheskogo
Sada!
Vy togda ne nazyvali sebya idiotom! Obnimayu Vas.
P. Tchaikovsky

MUSICAL LETTER TO V. L. DAVYDOV

1893[6]

_вы, би_ _би,_ га _ га!!!_   И   ку _ шать мне   о.

_хо_ _ты нет_ ни   щей,   ни   пи _ ро_ _га!_

От милого нету вести,
уж стало невмочь мне ждать!
Хоть маленькую писульку
ему бы ко мне написать!
А как бы знать хотелось,
что делает миленький мой!
И грустно мне, и скучно мне,
увы, биби, гага!!!
И кушать мне охоты нет
ни щей, ни пирога!

There's no news from my darling,
I simply can't wait anymore!
He could have written at least
a tiny little letter to me!
Yet, I am so eager to know
how my darling is doing!
I am so sad, I am so bored,
alas, bi-bi, ga-ga!!!
I've even lost my appetite
for shchi and pirogi!

Ot milogo netu vesti,
uzh stalo nevmoch' mne zhdat'!

Khot' malen'kuyu pisul'ku
emu by mne napisat'!
A kak by znat' khotelos',
chto delaet milen'kii moi!
I grustno mne, i skuchno mne.
Uvy, bibi, gaga!!!
I kushat' mne okhoty net
Ni shchei, ni piroga!

Pyotr Ilyich Tchaikovsky receiving an honorary Doctorate of Music at
Cambridge University, 1/13 June 1893

5 Key Documents

WHEREAS THE PRECEDING papers from the Tchaikovsky archive reveal some of the most private aspects of the composer's life, the documents in this chapter outline his official record. These important documents help us to see events of Tchaikovsky's personal and professional life in the administrative, economic, and political context of the time. They also shed new light on the composer's public image and social status in Imperial Russia.

◆◆◆

1. BIRTH CERTIFICATE OF PYOTR
ILYICH TCHAIKOVSKY[1]

Birth Certificate.
Pursuant to the decree of His Imperial Majesty, the Vyatsk Ecclesiastical Consistory hereby issues this certificate attesting that the register of the Cathedral of the Annunciation of the Votkinsk factory, Sarapulsk region, contains the following document dated 1840 and bearing the number 187: at the Kamsk-Votkinsk factory on the twenty-fifth of April, a son, Pyotr, was born to mining director Lieutenant Colonel, Cavalier Ilya Petrovich Tchaikovsky and his lawful wife, Aleksandra Andreevna. The infant was christened on the fifth of May in the year eighteen forty; the godparents were Archpriest Vasily Blinov

of Kamsk-Votkinsk, and Nadezhda Timofeevna, wife of Chief of the Mine Police Department, Collegiate Secretary Aleksey Valtsov. February 1846.

♦ ♦ ♦

2. APPLICATION BY ALEKSANDRA ANDREEVNA TCHAIKOVSKAYA FOR THE ADMISSION OF HER SON PYOTR TO THE PREPARATORY CLASS OF THE IMPERIAL SCHOOL OF JURISPRUDENCE[2]

To the Board of the Imperial School of Jurisprudence.
From Aleksandra Andreevna, wife of Major General Tchaikovsky Retd.
Application.
I hereby apply for the admission of my son Pyotr to the Preparatory Class of the Imperial School of Jurisprudence. In support of which I certify that he has reached the required age and that he will be financially fully self-supporting. I enclose the following supporting documents: 1) Birth and Baptismal Certificate. 2) Certificate of Noble Descent. 3) Certificate of Smallpox vaccination and state of health.

I respectfully request that he be granted admission to the class in question.

Aleksandra Tchaikovskaya, wife of Engineer Major General Retd.
11 September 1850.
Permanent Address: 1st. Admiralty District, 1st Quarter, c/o Peters, Millionaya St.

♦ ♦ ♦

3. COMMITMENTS ENTERED INTO BY ILYA PETROVICH TCHAIKOVSKY IN CONNECTION WITH THE ENROLLMENT OF PYOTR ILYICH TCHAIKOVSKY IN THE IMPERIAL SCHOOL OF JURISPRUDENCE[3]

Undertakings:
I the undersigned, Ilya Petrovich Tchaikovsky, Major General of the Corps of Mining Engineers, Retd., permanently resident in St. Petersburg, Liteinaya District, 4th Quarter, Sergievskaya St. care of Major General Nikolaev, hereby undertake to pay annually, and not later than August 1st, the sum of 450 rubles silver to cover the entire cost of

the maintenance of my son Pyotr upon his admission to the Imperial School of Jurisprudence for the duration of his attendance threat; in the event of his expulsion therefrom, I undertake to assume full financial responsibility for him thereafter.

24 August, 1852.
Major-General Ilya Tchaikovsky.

✦ ✦ ✦

4. CERTIFICATE OF GRADUATION OF PYOTR ILYICH TCHAIKOVSKY FROM THE IMPERIAL SCHOOL OF JURISPRUDENCE[4]

THE BOARD OF THE IMPERIAL SCHOOL OF JURISPRUDENCE hereby certify that student of this School, P. I. Tchaikovsky, has

The Imperial School of Jurisprudence graduating class of 1859. Tchaikovsky is the sixth from right on the front row. St. Petersburg, 29 May/10 June 1859.

demonstrated good behavior and met the requirements in the following subjects with the following grades:

Divine Law: Very Good. Canon Law: Excellent. State Law: Very Good. Civil Law: Excellent. Criminal Law: Excellent. Civil Proceedings: Excellent. Criminal Proceedings: Excellent. Surveying Law and Land Surveying: Very Good. Local Regulations: Excellent. Roman Law: Excellent. Encyclopedia of Jurisprudence: Excellent. History of Russian Law: Excellent. Financial Law: Excellent. Forensic Medicine: Excellent. Logic: Very Good. Psychology: Very Good. Russian Literature: Excellent. Latin: Very Good. German: Very Good. French: Excellent. World and National History: Very Good. World and National Geography: Very Good. World and National Statistics: Very Good. Mathematics: Good. Natural History and Physics: Good.

Therefore, in accordance with the Imperial Charter of this Institution the rank of Ninth Class is hereby conferred.

In witness thereof he is awarded this certificate duly signed and sealed with the Great Seal of this Institution.

Saint Petersburg. This day, the 29th of May, 1859. No. 593

♦ ♦ ♦

5. APPLICATION OF PYOTR ILYICH TCHAIKOVSKY TO THE RMO SCHOOL

22 August 1862[5]

To the Directorate of the Russian Musical Society.
Pyotr *Tchaikovsky*, Nobleman
Application

I am interested in studying music, particularly musical theory at the School recently Founded by the Russian Musical Society, and it is my honor respectfully to request the Directorate of the Society for admission to this institution as a student. In support of this application I hereby submit the Certificate of Graduation issued to me by the Imperial School of Jurisprudence on May the 29th 1859. I enclose 50 rubles silver.

P. I. Tchaikovsky, Nobleman

✦✦✦

6. MINUTES OF THE BOARD OF PROFESSORS OF THE SAINT PETERSBURG CONSERVATORY[6]

No. 17

Minutes of the twenty-second *Meeting of the Board of Professors.*
12 October 1865
Attending:
A. G. Rubinstein: *Director of the Conservatory*
Professors: Venyavsky, Gerke, Dreishok, Zaremba, Leshetitsky and Repetto.

The Board of Professors decided to instruct the students Tchaikovsky and Rybasov of senior theory class to set to music in the form of a cantata with orchestral accompaniment, Schiller's Ode To Joy (An die Freude) in a Russian translation, for performance at their 1865 public diploma examination.

✦✦✦

7. MINUTES OF MEETING OF THE BOARD OF PROFESSORS OF THE ST. PETERSBURG CONSERVATORY TO CONFER THE STATUS OF "FREE ARTIST" TO GRADUATES OF THE CONSERVATORY[7]

No. 19

Minutes of the twenty-sixth meeting of the Board of Professors on 29 December 1865.

The Board of Professors of the Conservatory, having reviewed the results of the annual Examinations, and in accordance with Article 18 of the Imperial Statutes of the Conservatory, have found the following students worthy of the status of "Free Artist," and have decided to confer said status upon: Messrs. Albrecht, Bessel, Gomillius, Rybasov, Kross, Reichardt, and Tchaikovsky.

A. G. Rubinstein.

Brothers Nikolay (left) and Anton (right) Rubinstein, 1862. In the same year as this photo, Anton Rubinstein founded the St. Petersburg Conservatory, from which Tchaikovsky graduated in 1865. In 1866, Nikolay Rubinstein founded the Moscow Conservatory and hired a newly graduated Tchaikovsky as a professor of music theory and harmony.

✦✦✦

8. GRADUATION DIPLOMA FROM THE ST. PETERSBURG CONSERVATORY OF PYOTR ILYICH TCHAIKOVSKY[8]

The Imperial St. Petersburg Conservatory of the Russian Musical Society.

Diploma.

The Board of the Conservatory hereby certifies that Court Counselor Pyotr Ilyich Tchaikovsky, of the Orthodox faith, 29 years of age, son of Engineer Major-General Tchaikovsky, graduated from the Conservatory in December 1865, having completed the course of musical studies, achieved the following grades in the examinations in the following major subjects: composition theory (class of Professor Zaremba) and instrumentation (class of Professor A. Rubinstein)—excellent; organ performance (class of Professor Shtil)—good; in (mandatory) minor subjects: piano performance—extremely good, and conducting—satisfactory.

As a consequence whereof, and in accordance with article 19 of the Statutes granted by His Imperial Majesty, the Board of the Conservatory with the concordance of the President of the Russian Musical Society on 31 December 1865 confers upon Pyotr Tchaikovsky, the status of Free Artist with all the rights and privileges attaching thereto; in consideration of his outstanding abilities, Pyotr Tchaikovsky is awarded the silver medal. In certification thereof, Tchaikovsky is awarded this diploma bearing the seal of the Conservatory and dated the 30th day of March 1870. No. 28.

[Grand Princess] Yelena. President.

N. Zaremba. Director of the Conservatory.

✦✦✦

9. AGREEMENT BETWEEN PYOTR ILYICH TCHAIKOVSKY AND THE DIRECTORATE OF THE MOSCOW BRANCH OF THE RUSSIAN MUSICAL SOCIETY[9]

On the 1st of May 1866, I, the undersigned, Collegiate Assessor Pyotr Ilyich *Tchaikovsky* concluded this agreement with the Directorate of the Russian Musical Society in Moscow for a period of three years with effect from the 1st of September 1866 through the 1st of September 1869 with the following terms and conditions:

1) I, Tchaikovsky, undertake to give instruction in the Conservatory in classes of musical theory as an acting Professor for not less than ten

hours per week without reservation, if there are a sufficient number of students to warrant that number of hours.

2) I, Tchaikovsky, undertake to report to the Conservatory ten minutes before the commencement of classes; if I fail to report within fifteen minutes of the commencement of the class, I shall be deemed to have missed the entire one-hour class. In such a case, I shall be obliged to offer the Director of the Conservatory an explanation for my lateness. The missed hour may at the discretion of the Director be made up at some other time, otherwise, for every hour of lessons missed 5 rubles silver will be deducted from my earnings.

3) In the event of illness, after one class has been missed, my classes will be taken, at the discretion of the Director, by another Professor, or the Adjunct. If I am replaced by the Adjunct, and I am on sick leave for no longer than one month, I shall receive only one third of my salary, and the Adjunct who has replaced me will receive the other two thirds. If my sick leave extends beyond one month, I shall receive no payment, and I shall be replaced by another Professor until I have recovered from my illness. Upon my replacement by another Professor, and not by the Adjunct, all payment to me ceases. The first of my classes missed through illness may be replaced by another lesson, or will be deducted from my salary on a pro rata basis.

4) I, Tchaikovsky, shall be paid at the rate of seventy-five rubles silver per year for my weekly teaching hours, this sum to be paid over the course of nine months, that is by the beginning of the vacation. In the event of any increase or reduction in the number of my teaching hours my salary will be adjusted accordingly at the rate of one and one third month's salary in each month of the academic year for each extra teaching hour.

5) I pledge to treat my students with respect and to refrain from any inappropriate behavior with regard to my students, both male and female.

6) I undertake not to teach classes anywhere other than at the Conservatory, although I may give private lessons at home on the following conditions: a) not to advertise for private lessons; b) to charge no less than five rubles silver for each hour of lessons.

7) I, Tchaikovsky, may not take part in any concerts outside the Russian Musical Society without the consent thereto of the Board of the Conservatory and the Directorate of the Russian Musical Society.

8) I am bound to observe all the rules laid down by the Directorate of the Society and approved by the President of the Society and to do so unswervingly. Breach of contract is subject to penalty.

9) In the case of breach of contract by either party, the guilty party shall be subject to a fine of five hundred rubles silver.

10) In the case of any conduct on the part of myself, Tchaikovsky, which would make me liable to dismissal by a decision of the Board of the Conservatory and definitively endorsed by the Directorate of the Society, the Directorate will be entitled to dismiss me without payment of the penalty stated in clauses 9 and 11 above, this Condition to be honored by both parties as sacred and inviolable.

The original of this document is to be kept in the possession of the Directorate of the Society, and I, Tchaikovsky, am to receive a copy duly certified by the Directorate.

To this condition Collegiate Assessor, Pyotr Tchaikovsky, has set his hand. To this Condition the following Directors of the Russian Musical Society in Moscow have set their hands: Provincial Secretary Nikolay Grigoriev Rubinstein, Hereditary, Honorary Citizen Aleksandr Aleksandrovich Torletsky, Prince Nikolay Petrovich Trubetskoy.

✦ ✦ ✦

10. LETTER FROM N. P. TRUBETSKOY, MEMBER OF THE DIRECTORATE OF THE MOSCOW BRANCH OF THE RUSSIAN MUSICAL SOCIETY, TO D. A. OBOLENSKY, VICE PRESIDENT OF THE RUSSIAN MUSICAL SOCIETY, REGARDING THE OVERTURE ON THE RUSSIAN AND DANISH NATIONAL ANTHEMS BY P. I. TCHAIKOVSKY ON THE OCCASION OF THE WEDDING OF THE DANISH PRINCESS DAGMAR TO THE HEIR TO THE THRONE OF RUSSIA[10]

Sir,
Prince Dmitry Aleksandrovich.

In consequence of your highly esteemed letter addressed to me (No. 57) in which you inform me that Their Imperial Majesties, His Highness, the Heir to the Throne, Her Highness, Grand Princess, the Tsesarevna have given their gracious consent to the dedication to Their Imperial Majesties of the ceremonial overture on the Russian and

Danish national anthems composed by Mr. Tchaikovsky, Professor of
the Moscow Conservatory, I have hastened to convey to Mr. Tchaikovsky the gracious attention granted to his work by Their Imperial
Majesties. I have also given to Mr. Tchaikovsky the gift of pearl cuff-
links presented to him by Their Majesties enclosed in your letter to
me: in conveying this information to you with my deepest respect and
devotion, I have the honor to remain

Your most humble servant
Prince Nikolay Trubetskoy.
The 29th day of January, 1868
Moscow

♦ ♦ ♦

11. APPLICATION OF PYOTR ILYICH TCHAIKOV-
SKY TO THE BOARD OF THE AUXILIARY FUND OF
MUSICAL ARTISTS AND MEMBERS OF THE STAFF
OF THE IMPERIAL RUSSIAN MUSICAL SOCIETY[11]

Application of Free Artist Pyotr Ilyich Tchaikovsky to the Board of the
Auxiliary Fund of musical artists and staff members of The Imperial
Russian Musical Society in St. Petersburg.
Application.

I wish to join the Auxiliary Fund, and hereby request the Board in
accordance with article 12 of the Fund to convey this request to the
Council of the Fund and to inform me of the outcome. In this connection it is my duty to add that I undertake to pay the membership fee of
twenty-four rubles silver per annum as provided in article 13 of the Statutes, and to obey all the rules of the Statutes of the Auxiliary Fund.

Pyotr Ilyich Tchaikovsky.

Required Information:
1) Date of birth . . . . 25 April 1840
2) Citizenship . . . . Russian
3) Marital Status. . . . . Married
4) If married, name and date of birth of wife . . . .
. . . . Antonina Ivanovna. 1848
5) Name and Date of birth of each child. . . . .
6) Place of employment and occupation . . . . Composer

Address in St. Petersburg (c/o my brother Anatoly Ilyich Tchaikovsky)
nr. Nevsky Prospekt, Novaya St. No. 2

✦✦✦

12. APPLICATION TO THE BOARD OF THE AUXILIARY
FUND OF THE ST. PETERSBURG BRANCH OF THE RMO[12]

Application to the Auxiliary Fund of the St. Petersburg Branch of the Imperial Russian Musical Society from Pyotr Ilyich Tchaikovsky, member of the Fund.
Application.

I hereby request the Board to grant me a loan of four hundred rubles silver which I undertake to repay in six months out of my salary.[13]

Pyotr Tchaikovsky
5 November 1879

✦✦✦

13. APPLICATION TO THE BOARD OF THE AUXILIARY
FUND OF THE ST. PETERSBURG BRANCH OF THE RMO[14]

Application to the Board of the Auxiliary Fund of the St. Petersburg Branch of the Imperial Russian Musical Society from Pyotr Ilyich Tchaikovsky, member of the Fund.
Application.

I hereby request the Board to grant me a loan of two hundred rubles silver which I undertake to repay in twelve months out of my salary.[15]

Pyotr Tchaikovsky
5 February 1881

✦✦✦

14. DECREE AWARDING PYOTR ILYICH
TCHAIKOVSKY THE ORDER OF ST. VLADIMIR,
EQUAL-TO-THE-APOSTLES, FOURTH DEGREE[16]

By the grace of God
We, Alexander the Third,
Emperor and Autocrat
Of All the Russias,
Czar of Poland
Grand Prince of Finland
Etc., etc., etc.
To Our Retired Court Counselor, Composer Pyotr Tchaikovsky.

As an expression of Our especial favor, by the decree of the 23rd day of February issued to the Chapter, We have most graciously conferred

upon you the title of Cavalier of the Imperial Order of Our St. Vladimir Equal-to-the-Apostles Fourth Degree.

In witness thereof, We have ordered the Chapter of the Russian Im-
perial and Czarist Orders to sign this citation, to stamp it with the seal
of the Order, and to present you with the insignia of the Order.
Done at St. Petersburg on the 28th day of February 1884.
Head of the Chapter of Orders, Capitular of the Chancellery of orders
No. 239

✦✦✦

15. DOCUMENT CONCERNING THE ELECTION OF PYOTR ILYICH TCHAIKOVSKY AS A DIRECTOR OF THE MOSCOW BRANCH OF THE IMPERIAL RUSSIAN MUSICAL SOCIETY

10 February 1885[17]

At the general meeting of the members of the Moscow Branch of the
Society held on the 10th of February inst. In accordance with articles 47 and 48 of the Imperial Charter of the Society the composer
Pyotr Ilyich Tchaikovsky was elected unanimously as a Director of the
Moscow branch for the next three-year term of office to replace the
outgoing Director, V. P. Zubov. The undersigned have the honor most
respectfully to convey this information to the Governing Directorate
on behalf of the Directorate of the Moscow Branch in accordance with
article 48 of the Statutes, and humbly request confirmation of the elec-
tion of P. I. Tchaikovsky as a Director of the Moscow Branch of the
Society.
Sergey Tretyakov, Director
Pyotr Jurgenson, Director
Nikolay Alekseev, Director
Aleksandr Baranovsky, Director

✦✦✦

16. DIRECTIVE OF THE MINISTRY OF THE IMPERIAL COURT ON THE AWARD OF A PENSION TO PYOTR ILYICH TCHAIKOVSKY[18]

To the Cabinet of His Majesty.

His Imperial Majesty is pleased to order the Cabinet of His Imperial
Majesty to arrange the award of a Pension of *three thousand rubles*

a year to the composer Pyotr Ilyich Tchaikovsky in recognition of his outstanding services to Russian music.

By the supreme authority of His Majesty, I hereby present the following order to His Cabinet for implementation.

Minister of the Imperial Court, Count Vorontsov-Dashkov.

Your Excellency's permission is requested to include the following item of expenditure in the budget for the current year in compliance with the order from the Highest Authorities dated 31 December 1887: that with effect from 1 January 1888 an annual pension of 3,000 rubles be awarded to the composer Pyotr Ilyich Tchaikovsky.

Assistant Cabinet Administrator.

✦ ✦ ✦

17. DOCUMENT CERTIFYING THE ELECTION OF
PYOTR ILYICH TCHAIKOVSKY AS A DIRECTOR
OF THE MOSCOW BRANCH OF THE RMO

22 February 1888[19]

To the Directorate of the Imperial Russian Musical Society.

At the General Meeting of Honorary and Full members of the Moscow Branch of the Society held on the 7th of February this year, pursuant to article 48 of the Society's Charter bearing the seal of the Highest Authority, the following were unanimously elected Directors of this branch for the next triennium: Konstantin Vasilievich *Rukavishnikov* (to occupy the seat on the Board voluntarily vacated by K. S. Alekseev), Pavel Ivanovich *Khoritonenko* (to fill an existing vacancy), and Pyotr Ilyich *Tchaikovsky* (pursuant to article 48 of the Charter, to fill the vacancy left by an outgoing member whose term of office has expired). Whereof the Board of Directors of the Branch has the honor to inform the Directorate, and humbly requests confirmation of the persons elected as members of Board of Directors of the Moscow Branch of the Society.

S. Taneyev, Director
N. Sitovsky, Manager

✦ ✦ ✦

18. CERTIFICATE OF SERVICE OF PYOTR ILYICH TCHAIKOVSKY IN THE MINISTRY OF JUSTICE [20]

The record of the Applicant, Pyotr Ilyich Tchaikovsky, Court Counselor, employed in the Department of the Ministry of Justice, can be found in his service dossier, 27 years of age, of the Orthodox confession, hereditary member of the nobility, bachelor, not in possession of a hereditary or acquired estate, or in receipt of allowance.

Upon completion of his studies at the IMPERIAL School of Jurisprudence, by an Order (no. 7) within the jurisdiction of the Ministry of Justice on the 23rd of May 1859, was assigned to the Department of the Ministry of Justice with the rank of Titular Counselor with effect from the 13th of May, eighteen hundred and fifty nine. Assigned to the first division of the Department of the Ministry of Justice on the 3rd of June of the same year. Appointed Junior Assistant to the Chief of Bureau on the 9th of December. Appointed Senior Assistant to the Bureau chief on the 9th of February, 1860.

The Chief of Bureau 2 of the first division having been granted leave of absence for 28 days, he performed his Chief's functions during that time. By a decision of the Governing Senate dated the 12th of July 1862 was promoted on grounds of seniority to the rank of Collegiate Assessor with effect from the 13th of May, 1862. Was MOST GRACIOUSLY awarded the sum of 150 rubles silver on 23 December 1862. At his own request, he was seconded from his post of Senior Assistant to the Bureau Chief to the department of the Ministry of Justice on the 1st of May 1863. By a decision of the Governing Senate dated the 20th of October 1866, he was promoted on grounds of seniority to the rank of Court Counselor with effect from the 10th of May, 1866. By order of the Director of the Department of the Ministry of Justice, he was reassigned to the office of the Officer in Charge of Special Assignments at the Ministry of Justice, Counselor of State Repinsky on the 7th of January 1867. By order of the relevant department of the Ministry of Justice (No. 77), dated the 19th of September 1867, he was discharged from the service at his own request. He took leave at the following times: 1860, 15 days; returned in time. 1861, abroad from 24 June for 28 days; returned only on 18 September of the same year because of illness for which he produced a medical certificate which the authorities deemed acceptable. 1863, from 1 June for 3 months. 1864, from 4 July for 3 months, and in 1865, from 10 May for 3 months. No resignations, no military service, no criminal convictions or prosecutions, and no cases where he lost eligibility for the rating of "excellent" for his work. In witness thereof Court Counselor Tchaikovsky is hereby granted this certificate with the seal of the Department of the Ministry of Justice.

23 May 1868.

Signed: Counselor of State with the rank of General of HIS IMPERIAL MAJESTY, MY MOST GRACIOUS SOVEREIGN, Director of the Department of the Ministry of Justice, with the following decorations: Order of St. Anna, first degree; Order of St. Stanislav, first degree; Cavalier 3rd degree of the Order of St. Vladimir, Prince, Equal-to-the Apostles; holder of the bronze medal with the Andreev ribbon for service in the war of 1853–1856.

Essen.

Sealed: Head of Chancellery at the Ministry of Justice.

V. Adamov.

The subject of this certificate, Court Counselor Pyotr Ilyich Tchaikovsky, on the 6th day of July, 1877 was joined for the first time in lawful matrimony to Antonina Ivanovna Milyukova, spinster, of noble birth, at St. George's church on Vspolie St. near Kudrin. In witness thereof, we, Archpriest Dmitry Razumovsky and Deacon Aleksandr Krylov, affixed the church seal of the aforementioned St. George's church on Vspolie St., near Kudrin.

The 6th day of July 1877. No. 76.

This decree, transmitted at the behest of the Supreme Authority

In document No. 1328, dated 31 December 1887 to the Minister of the IMPERIAL Court, and Director of the IMPERIAL Theatres, directs him to provide from the Cabinet of HIS MAJESTY an annual pension of 3,000 rubles in recognition of his outstanding services to the cause of music in Russia, to Court Counselor Pyotr Ilyich Tchaikovsky. In witness whereof is affixed the letterhead of the St. Petersburg Office of the IMPERIAL Theatres duly signed and sealed. St. Petersburg, the 4th day of May 1888.

Signed: For the head of the Office of the IMPERIAL Theatres P. Domershchikov.

Sealed: Office Manager Krashevsky.

This copy from the Chancellery of the Ministry of Justice has been issued to retired Court Counselor Tchaikovsky on the understanding that the original of his certificate of Retirement has been rendered unusable and needs to be replaced.

Stamp Duty has been paid. St. Petersburg, 16 December 1889.
Manager, Chancellery of the Ministry of Justice
Member of the Consultative Committee [signature]
For the Editor [signature]

✦ ✦ ✦

19. TRIBUTE TO PYOTR ILYICH TCHAIKOVSKY FROM THE ST. PETERSBURG BRANCH OF THE RMO

3 December 1890[21]

Esteemed Pyotr Ilyich!

It was twenty-five years ago that you embarked on your musical career, and since that time your contribution to art has been an uninterrupted stream of true creative endeavor of the highest level, which has inscribed your name among those of the greatest composers. Pure inspiration, unremitting and high-minded drive, strict attention to the highest artistic standards in musical composition, single-minded devotion to the cause, have all been the distinguishing features of your work, to which Russian society is indebted for so many hours of profound beauty and uplifting enjoyment, and Russian music for so many brilliant and rapid steps forward.

The St. Petersburg Branch of the IMPERIAL Russian Music Society, to whose members your music and your fame means more than to any other, is delighted to proclaim all this today when congratulations and tributes to you, so supremely well-deserved, are streaming in from everywhere—an outpouring of gratitude for all that you have done. Along with all those who understand your significance and your unique talents, we have no doubt that what you have achieved so far is but a part of the ever greater success it remains for you to achieve in the future—and it is from this conviction that we derive the comfort of knowing that the future of our art is secure.

✦✦✦

20. TRIBUTE TO PYOTR ILYICH TCHAIKOVSKY FROM THE ST. PETERSBURG CONSERVATORY

3 December 1890[22]

Esteemed Pyotr Ilyich!

The St. Petersburg Conservatory, in addressing to you this tribute to mark the twenty-fifth anniversary of your outstanding contribution, shares with all friends of art our feelings of sincere, unreserved joy and exaltation on such an important day in the chronicles of Russian music.

But to these feelings, we add another of particular relevance on this occasion, that of justifiable and legitimate pride in the fact that it was within these walls that those talents, with which nature has so generously endowed you, took root and flourished, and that it was from here that you emerged to make such swift and independent progress along that path towards which your creative spirit beckoned and opened for you.

The name of Tchaikovsky, and everything created by your inspiration and talent, your sacred love for art and the steadfastness of a true artist in the pursuit of your goals—all this has been indelibly inscribed within the pages of the history of our institution. Animated as we are by all these feelings, we extend our heartfelt congratulations to you, and earnestly hope and believe that you will bestow upon your *alma mater,* and indeed upon all those who hold dear the future of our art, many more glorious hours.

✦✦✦

21. TRIBUTE TO PYOTR ILYICH TCHAIKOVSKY FROM THE STUDENTS OF THE ST. PETERSBURG CONSERVATORY

3 December 1890[23]

Esteemed Pyotr Ilyich!

We, the students of the St. Petersburg Conservatory, in the very institution where you yourself received your musical education, which, together with your great talent, enabled you to render your invaluable services to art and to make your name illustrious, extend to you this day our warmest greetings and congratulations. It is this circumstance which strengthens our own motivation, determination, and energies, as we embark, within the very same walls, on the same path that you have trodden. And while, of course, none of us even dares to dream of a future which would approximate your own, nevertheless we do, and will always see you as a brilliant and precious model worthy of our unflagging and zealous emulation.

May God grant you many more years to complete your heroic journey, which will serve as a lodestar for all those young people who are unsparing in their efforts, who understand the great importance of art, and are resolved to commit all our energies and resources to its service.

+ + +

22. LAST WILL AND TESTAMENT OF PYOTR ILYICH TCHAIKOVSKY

30 September 1891[24]

In the name of the Father, the Son, and the Holy Spirit, I, retired Court Counselor Pyotr Ilyich Tchaikovsky, being of sound mind and memory, in the exercise of my right under the law (addendum to article 118, Vol. X, pt. 1, vide Annexe 1863).

My immovable property, if there be any such, wherever it may be located, in my possession after my death, I leave in its entirety to my nephew (adopted son of my brother, Nikolay Ilyich Tchaikovsky) Georgy Nikolaevich Tchaikovsky, that is to say the whole of my estate complete with its buildings, structures, and facilities, and all their contents, namely furniture, fittings, fixtures, cattle, crops, and with all the rights and obligations attaching thereto.

All the capital I have acquired in my own lifetime which remains after my death I also leave in its entirety to Georgy Nikolaevich Tchaikovsky with the proviso that he give one seventh of that sum to my servant, reserve corporal Aleksey Sofronov.

The performance fees due to me during my lifetime, and to my heirs after my passing, for performances of operas I have composed, as well as those which I may compose in the future, whether in the Imperial theatres, or in any foreign capitals or on any provincial stages,

Tchaikovsky with his nephew Vladimir Davydov; Paris, June 1892

I leave in their entirety to my nephew Vladimir Lvovich Davydov, currently a student at the Imperial School of Jurisprudence, on condition that from these funds he pay annually 1) To my brother Modest Ilyich Tchaikovsky one fifth of the proceeds from performances of the operas "The Queen of Spades" and "Iolanta," as well as others whose libretti were composed by him; however, if the total of such sums accruing to my brother should fall short of 1,800 rubles silver, then my nephew Vladimir Davydov shall make up the difference from the proceeds from performances of my other operas. 2) To my lawful wife, Antonina Ivanovna Tchaikovskaya, 1,200 rubles silver. 3) To the above-mentioned Georgy Nikolayevich Tchaikovsky 1,200 rubles. 4) To my servant, reserve corporal Aleksey Sofronov, 600 rubles silver. In the event that the total sum collected from theatrical performances in a given year should fall short of the 4,800 rubles silver to be divided on the foregoing basis to my brother, my wife Antonina, my nephew Georgy, and my servant Sofronov then the entire sum should be divided into five parts as follows: two and a half parts to Modest Ilyich Tchaikovsky, one part each to Antonina Tchaikovskaya and Georgy Tchaikovsky, and half of one part to Aleksey Sofronov. Those portions of the proceeds from performances, which would have been assigned to the above-mentioned persons, I leave in their entirety, in the event of their deaths, to Vladimir Lvovich Davydov. Should Vladimir Davydov predecease me, I leave all the theatrical performance proceeds to my nephew Georgy Nikolaevich Tchaikovsky on condition that he or his guardians observe the above-mentioned conditions regarding the amounts to be paid annually to the legatees in question. All the author's fees accruing to me and my heirs, as well as all the royalties accruing from my musical works, I leave to my nephew Vladimir Lvovich Davydov, and, if he should predecease me, to Georgy Nikolaevich Tchaikovsky. From my goods and chattels, the gold, black enamel watch inlaid with little stars and the gold figures of Joan of Arc, Apollo, and two of the Muses, which has been stolen, in the event of its being found together with the watch chain and returned to me, I leave to my nephew Vladimir Lvovich Davydov and, in the event of his death, to my nephew Yury Lvovich. The rest of my goods and chattels, i.e. everything in my permanent apartment in the country or in town, such as furniture, clothing, footwear, linen, instruments, books, metal garlands, various gifts from members of the public, in brief, everything without exception, I leave in their entirety to my servant, reserve corporal Aleksey Ivanovich Sofronov. This will and testament to remain in full force and effect after my death. I appoint as my executors Pyotr Ivanovich Jurgenson and Boris Petrovich Jurgenson. Amen.

To this, my last will and testament, written by my own hand, I, retired Court Counselor Pyotr Ilyich Tchaikovsky, hereby set my hand.

That this last will and testament was written by the testator himself, retired Court Counselor Pyotr Ilyich Tchaikovsky, and signed by his own hand, and that the testator, in the course of making this will in my presence was of sound mind and memory, I hereby bear witness and sign my name; merchant of the First Moscow Guild, hereditary citizen in good standing, Pyotr Ivanovich Jurgenson. That this last will and testament was written by the testator himself, retired Court Counselor Pyotr Ilyich Tchaikovsky, and signed by his own hand, and that the testator in making this will in my presence, I found to be of sound mind and memory, I hereby bear witness and sign my name; Moscow Tradesman, Pavel Ivanovich Yurasov.

On the 19th day of November 1893, pursuant to the Decree of His Imperial majesty, the St. Petersburg District Court of the 7th Division, having heard the application for probate of the last will and testament of retired Court Counselor Pyotr Ilyich Tchaikovsky, issued the following ruling: the privately drafted last will and testament of retired Court Counselor Pyotr Ilyich Tchaikovsky, who died on the 23rd of October 1893, made on the 30th of September 1891 is hereby granted probate and shall be duly registered and published in the Proceedings of the Senate. The following charges are payable: a fee of 3 rubles for publication of probate, registry charges, 3 rubles. 60 kopeks, stamp duty, 80 kopeks, and death duties, 960 rubles. The application of Hereditary Citizen In Good Standing, Pyotr Ivanovich Jurgenson, submitted on 6 November 1893 to be released from his duties as executor of the Tchaikovsky estate is duly noted.

On 22 November 1893 the Court issued a ruling on this same case: the payment of death duties of 960 rubles owed by Collegiate Assessor, Vladimir Lvovich Davydov, by a ruling of the Court on this matter is deferred for one year. The Court, in order to recover the debt owed to the treasury, orders the performance proceeds from the Management of the Imperial Theatres accruing to Tchaikovsky's heirs to be placed under sequestration. The registry charges mentioned above for attaching the seal and stamp duty, a total of 7 rubles, 40 kopeks, were forwarded to the department of the St. Petersburg Provincial Treasury, and credited to its account. A receipt for this sum was issued on 25 November 1893 and entered as Item No. 10.060.

This last will and testament was released to Collegiate Secretary Vladimir Lvovich Davydov.

Stamp duty was paid on the 25th day of November, 1893.
Deputy Chairman
Secretary Vishnevsky.

+ + +

23. GRANTING OF POWER OF ATTORNEY BY PYOTR ILYICH TCHAIKOVSKY TO HIS SERVANT ALEKSEY IVANOVICH SOFRONOV[25]

Dear Mr. Aleksey Ivanovich,

By this power of attorney I grant you the right to act for me in all current matters as well as in all other matters which may arise in the future, in all courts and administrative institutions, in all dealings with officials of all departments in connection with all civil and criminal proceedings, where you may submit requests, make statements, respond to written decisions and other communications, lodge complaints, receive documents and money to be transmitted to me, file appeals to courts at all levels, and settle litigation out of court. I shall refrain from criticizing or finding fault with any action you may take under this power of attorney. This power of attorney belongs to reserve corporal Aleksey Ivanovich Sofronov, peasant, district of Klin, Moscow Province.

Pyotr Ilyich Tchaikovsky. The 12th day of December 1891. Maidanovo Village.

✦ ✦ ✦

MESSAGES IN RESPONSE TO THE ILLNESS AND
DEATH OF PYOTR ILYICH TCHAIKOVSKY

24. TELEGRAMS FROM GRAND DUKE KONSTANTIN
KONSTANTINOVICH TO MODEST ILYICH TCHAIKOVSKY

From Strelnya 24 October/5 November 1893[26]

The Grand Duchess and I are deeply concerned for Pyotr Ilyich. Would
be sincerely grateful to you for news of his health.
Forgive this indiscreet inquiry
Konstantin.

From Strelnya 25 October/6 November 1893[27]

A great shock, we deeply mourn the loss of Pyotr Ilyich.
We have grown to love him dearly over the years. May the Lord rest
his soul in peace and grant you comfort.
Konstantin, Elizaveta.

✦ ✦ ✦

25. TELEGRAM FROM THE ACTRESS MARIA
NIKOLAEVNA ERMOLOVA AND HER HUSBAND
THE LAWYER NIKOLAY PETROVICH SHUBINSKY
TO MODEST ILYICH TCHAIKOVSKY

From Moscow 26 October/7 November 1893[28]

Dear Modest Ilyich,
Our heartfelt condolences in your grief; the one consolation, the
whole of Russia shares it with you.
Ermolova, Shubinsky.

✦ ✦ ✦

26. TELEGRAM FROM THE CITIZENS OF MOSCOW
TO ANATOLY ILYICH TCHAIKOVSKY

From Moscow, 27 October/8 November 1893[29]

We feel duty bound to convey to you the wishes of your late brother
Pyotr Ilyich to be buried in Moscow, the heart of Russia, beside the

tomb of Nikolay Grigorievich Rubinstein, or in the town of Klin. As Muscovites, we in turn urge you to grant the wishes of the departed, and the sincere desire of Muscovites to see the ashes of the unforgettable composer finding their last resting place within the walls of our city.

Citizens of Moscow, signatures supplied on request.
Reply to Blok.[30] Moscow.

✦✦✦

27. PETITION OF CITIZENS OF MOSCOW FOR THE BURIAL OF PYOTR ILYICH TCHAIKOVSKY IN MOSCOW[31]

The undersigned citizens of Moscow, having followed for many years the contribution of Pyotr Ilyich to the musical life of the original capital city of our country, and his zealous concern for its artistic interests, express the wish to see the ashes of our Great composer buried in Moscow.

✦✦✦

28. TELEGRAM FROM THE MARSHAL OF THE NOBILITY FOR THE PROVINCE OF SMOLENSK TO MODEST ILYICH TCHAIKOVSKY[32]

From Dugino 28 October/9 November 1893.

Please accept the condolences of the fellow townsmen of the great Glinka. The Lord has put an end to the service of your brother to the art of our nation. May his sensitive soul rest in peace, and may the memory of the man who has bequeathed his enchanting songs to the delight of our nation be everlasting.

Marshal of the Nobility of the Province of Smolensk.

✦✦✦

DOCUMENTS RELATING TO THE PERPETUATION OF THE MEMORY OF PYOTR ILYICH TCHAIKOVSKY

29. REQUEST OF THE NORTH AMERICAN ENVOY TO THE COMMITTEE ON THE COLLECTION OF CONTRIBUTIONS FOR PERPETUATING THE MEMORY OF PYOTR ILYICH TCHAIKOVSKY

12 May 1895[33]

To the Imperial Committee on the Collection of Contributions to perpetuate the memory of Pyotr Ilyich Tchaikovsky.

The North American Envoy in St. Petersburg has informed the Ministry of Foreign Affairs that the Carnegie Music Hall in New York proposes to erect a statue of the composer Tchaikovsky which would be a reproduction of the statue commissioned by the late EMPEROR ALEXANDER III for the new Moscow Conservatory.[34] In this connection, Envoy Breckenridge ventures to inquire whether the IMPERIAL Government would feel it possible to have the sculptor who created the statue referred to above, make a copy of it for the musical institution in New York referred to above, and if so, what would be the cost. Otherwise, the Envoy asks to be informed of the name and address of the sculptor.

The Cabinet of HIS IMPERIAL MAJESTY on instructions from the Head of the Ministry of the IMPERIAL Court accompanies this report with the original American note on the subject, and has the honor most humbly to request the Committee to inform directly the Department of Internal Relations of the Ministry of Foreign Affairs of the action to be taken, including the return of the note attached.

Acting Administrator of the Cabinet His Majesty.
Office Manager

Chronology

20 July/2 August **1795** — Birth of Ilya Petrovich Tchaikovsky, the composer's father.

30 July/11 August **1812** — Birth of Aleksandra Andreevna Tchaikovskaya (née d'Assier), the composer's mother.

9/21 May **1838** — Birth of Nikolay Ilyich Tchaikovsky, the composer's older brother.

25 April/7 May **1840** — Birth of Pyotr Ilyich Tchaikovsky in Votkinsk.

28 December **1841**/9 January **1842** — Birth of Aleksandra Ilyinichna Tchaikovskaya, the composer's sister.

10/22 April **1843** — Birth of Ippolit Ilyich Tchaikovsky, the composer's brother.

November **1844** — Fanny Dürbach becomes governess to the Tchaikovsky family.

1845 — Pyotr Tchaikovsky begins piano lessons.

September **1848** — Fanny Dürbach leaves her position of governess. The Tchaikovsky family moves to Moscow.

November — The family moves to St. Petersburg. Pyotr Tchaikovsky is placed into a boarding school there.

May **1849** — The Tchaikovsky family moves to Alapayevsk where Ilya Tchaikovsky is appointed manager of the Alapayevsk and Nizhne-Nevyansk iron factory.

1/13 May 1850 — Birth of Pyotr Tchaikovsky's twin brothers Anatoly and Modest.

September — Tchaikovsky enrolls in the Imperial School of Jurisprudence in St. Petersburg.

13/25 June 1854 — Death of Tchaikovsky's mother, Aleksandra, from cholera.

1857 — Tchaikovsky makes his first attempt at conducting the school choir.

13/25 May 1859 — Tchaikovsky graduates from the Imperial School of Jurisprudence.

June — Tchaikovsky begins to work at the Ministry of Justice.

Fall — Tchaikovsky begins attending classes at the Russian Music Society.

6/18 November 1860 — Tchaikovsky's sister Aleksandra marries Lev Davydov.

July–August 1861 — Tchaikovsky travels to Europe for the first time.

1862 — Tchaikovsky enrolls at St. Petersburg Conservatory.

April 1863 — Tchaikovsky resigns from his position at the Ministry of Justice to concentrate on his study at the conservatory.

30 August/11 September 1865 — Tchaikovsky's *Characteristic Dances* are performed by Johann Strauss II and his orchestra in Pavlovsk.

30 October/9 November — Tchaikovsky's String Quartet in B-flat major is performed at the St. Petersburg Conservatory.

27 November/9 December — Tchaikovsky's Overture in F major is performed at the Mikhailovsky Palace in St. Petersburg, conducted by the author.

29 December 1865/10 January 1866 — Tchaikovsky's cantata *Ode to Joy* is performed at the St. Petersburg Conservatory graduation. Tchaikovsky graduates from the conservatory with a silver medal.

January — Tchaikovsky leaves St. Petersburg to teach music theory at the Moscow branch of the Russian Musical Society.

1/13 September — Tchaikovsky begins to teach at the newly opened Moscow Conservatory.

29 January/10 February 1867 — Tchaikovsky's *Festival Overture on the Danish National Anthem* is performed in Moscow.

3/15 February 1868 — Tchaikovsky's Symphony No. 1 is performed in Moscow, conducted by Nikolay Rubinstein.

30 January/11 February **1869** — Tchaikovsky's opera *The Voyevoda* premieres in Moscow.

15/27 February — Tchaikovsky's symphonic fantasia *Fatum* premieres in Moscow.

4/16 March **1870** — Tchaikovsky's overture-fantasia *Romeo and Juliet* (the first version) premieres in Moscow.

16/28 March **1871** — Tchaikovsky's String Quartet No. 1 premieres at all-Tchaikovsky concert in Moscow.

5/17 February **1872** — The revised version of *Romeo and Juliet* is performed in St. Petersburg.

26 January/7 February **1873** — Tchaikovsky's Symphony No. 2 premieres in Moscow.

7/19 December — Tchaikovsky's symphonic fantasia *The Tempest* is premiered in Moscow.

10/22 March **1874** — Tchaikovsky's String Quartet No. 2 premieres in Moscow.

13/25 October **1875** — Hans von Bülow gives the premiere of the Piano Concerto No. 1 in Boston.

7/19 November — Tchaikovsky's Symphony No. 3 premieres in Moscow.

16/28 January **1876** — Tchaikovsky's *Sérénade mélancolique* premieres in Moscow.

18/30 March — Tchaikovsky's String Quartet No. 3 premieres in Moscow.

4/16 November — Tchaikovsky's opera *Vakula the Smith* premieres in St. Petersburg.

5/17 November — Tchaikovsky's *Slavonic March* premieres in Moscow.

December — Tchaikovsky meets Lev Tolstoy in Moscow.

December — Tchaikovsky receives his first letter from Nadezhda von Meck.

25 February/9 March **1877** — Tchaikovsky's symphonic poem *Francesca da Rimini* premieres in Moscow.

May — Tchaikovsky begins to write the opera *Eugene Onegin*.

6/18 July — Tchaikovsky marries Antonina Milyukova in Moscow.

27 July/8 August — Tchaikovsky leaves Moscow by himself to stay with his sister's family in Kamenka.

24 September/6 October — Tchaikovsky's marriage to Antonina ends in a permanent separation.

October — Nadezhda von Meck offers Tchaikovsky a regular allowance of 6,000 rubles, which allows him to quit teaching.

18/30 December — Premiere of the *Variations on a Rococo Theme* in Moscow by Wilhelm Fitzenhagen.

10/22 February **1878** — Premiere of the Symphony No. 4.

November — Tchaikovsky resigns from the Moscow Conservatory on health grounds.

8/20 December — Tchaikovsky's *Sérénade mélancolique* and *Valse scherzo* performed in Paris.

17/29 March **1879** — Premiere of *Eugene Onegin* in Moscow.

June — Premiere of the *Liturgy of Saint John Chrysostom* in Kiev.

21 October/2 November — Premiere of the *Grand Sonata* in Moscow by Nikolay Rubinstein.

8/20 December — Premiere of the Suite No. 1 in Moscow.

9/21 January **1880** — Death of Tchaikovsky's father, Ilya.

6/18 December — Premiere of the *Italian Capriccio*.

13/25 February **1881** — Premiere of *The Maid of Orleans* in St. Petersburg.

18/30 October — Premiere of the *Serenade for String Orchestra*.

31 October/12 November — Premiere of the Piano Concerto No. 2 by Madeline Schiller in New York.

22 November/4 December — Premiere of the Violin Concerto in Vienna by Adolph Brodsky.

21 May/2 June **1882** — Russian premiere of the Piano Concerto No. 2 in Moscow by Sergey Taneyev.

7/19 June — Premiere of the *All-Night Vigil* in Moscow.

8/20 August — Premiere of *1812 Overture* at the Arts and Industry Exhibition in Moscow.

18/30 October — Premiere of the piano trio *In Memory of a Great Artist* in Moscow.

15/27 May **1883** — Premiere of the coronation cantata *Moscow* at the Kremlin in Moscow.

23 May/4 June — Premiere of the *Coronation March* at the coronation of Alexander III in Moscow.

3/15 February **1884** — Premiere of the opera *Mazeppa* in Moscow.

4/16 February — Premiere of the Suite No. 2 in Moscow.

7/19 March — Tchaikovsky is invited for an audience with Alexander III in St. Petersburg, who confers on him the Order of Saint Vladimir.

19/31 October — St. Petersburg premiere of *Eugene Onegin* at the Mariinsky Theater.

16/28 December — Premiere of the *Elegy* for string orchestra in
   Moscow.

12/24 January **1885** — Premiere of the Suite No. 3 in St. Petersburg.

22 February/6 March — Premiere of the Concert Fantasy for piano and
   orchestra in Moscow.

11/23 March **1886** — Tchaikovsky attends the premiere of *Manfred* in
   Moscow.

19/31 January — Tchaikovsky conducts the premiere of his opera *Chere-*
   vichki at the Bolshoi Theater in Moscow.

5/17 March **1887** — Tchaikovsky conducts the St. Petersburg premiere of
   the Suite No. 2.

20 October/1 November — Tchaikovsky conducts the premiere
   of his opera *The Enchantress* at the Mariinsky Theater in
   St. Petersburg.

14/26 November — Premiere of the Suite No. 4 in Moscow, conducted
   by Tchaikovsky.

12/24 December — St. Petersburg premiere of the Suite No. 4, conducted
   by Tchaikovsky.

24 December **1887**/5 January **1888** — Tchaikovsky's first European conducting tour begins with a concert at the Leipzig Gewandhaus.
   Meetings with Johannes Brahms, Edvard Grieg, and Ethel Smyth.

January — Tchaikovsky is granted a lifetime annuity of 3,000 rubles by
   Alexander III.

8/20 January — Tchaikovsky conducts at the Conventgarten in
   Hamburg.

16/28 January — Tchaikovsky meets Gustav Mahler.

27 January/8 February — Tchaikovsky conducts a Philharmonic Society
   concert in Berlin.

February — Tchaikovsky conducts two concerts in Prague, and meets
   Antonín Dvořák.

February–March — Tchaikovsky conducts three concerts in Paris,
   and meets Charles Gounod, Léo Delibes, and other French
   musicians.

8/20 March — Tchaikovsky conducts a concert at the Saint James's Hall
   in London.

5/17 November — Premiere of the Symphony No. 5 in St. Petersburg,
   conducted by Tchaikovsky.

12/24 November — Premiere of the overture-fantasia *Hamlet* in
   St. Petersburg, conducted by Tchaikovsky.

10/22 December — Moscow premiere of the Symphony No. 5, conducted by Tchaikovsky.

10/22 December — Tchaikovsky meets Anton Chekhov in St. Petersburg.

January–March 1889 — Tchaikovsky's second European concert tour, with concerts in Cologne, Frankfurt am Main, Dresden, Berlin, Geneva, Hamburg, and London.

25 November/7 December — Premiere of the *Pezzo capriccioso* in Moscow with Anatoly Brandukov, conducted by Tchaikovsky.

3/15 January 1890 — Premiere of *The Sleeping Beauty* at the Mariinsky Theater in St. Petersburg.

28 November/10 December — Premiere of *Souvenir de Florence* in St. Petersburg.

7/19 December — Premiere of *The Queen of Spades* in St. Petersburg.

9/21 February 1891 — Premiere of the incidental music to *Hamlet* in Moscow.

24 March/5 April — Tchaikovsky conducts a concert of his own works in Paris.

29 March/10 April — Death of Tchaikovsky's sister Aleksandra.

14/26 April — Tchaikovsky arrives in New York for his American tour, which also includes performances in Buffalo, Baltimore, Washington, and Philadelphia.

23 April/5 May — Tchaikovsky conducts his *Coronation March* at the inauguration of the Carnegie Hall in New York.

9/21 May — Tchaikovsky departs from America.

4/16 November — Moscow premiere of *The Queen of Spades*.

21 December 1891/2 January 1892 — Tchaikovsky conducts an all-Tchaikovsky concert in Kiev.

2/14 January — Tchaikovsky conducts an all-Tchaikovsky concert in Warsaw.

7/19 January — Tchaikovsky attends a performance of *Eugene Onegin* in Hamburg conducted by Gustav Mahler.

7/19 March — Premiere of the suite from *The Nutcracker* in St. Petersburg conducted by Tchaikovsky.

6/18 December — Premieres of *Iolanta* and *The Nutcracker* at the Mariinsky Theater in St. Petersburg.

20 December 1892/1 January 1893 — Tchaikovsky visits Fanny Dürbach in Montbéliard, Switzerland.

2/14 January — Tchaikovsky conducts an all-Tchaikovsky concert in Brussels.

20 May/1 June — Tchaikovsky conducts his Symphony No. 4 at a Royal
        Philharmonic Society concert in London.
31 May/12 June — Tchaikovsky conducts *Francesca da Rimini* at a con-
        cert in Cambridge.
1/13 June — Tchaikovsky receives an Honorary Doctorate of Music at
        Cambridge University, along with Arrigo Boito, Camille Saint-
        Saëns, Max Bruch, and Edvard Grieg.
16/28 October — Tchaikovsky conducts the premiere of the Symphony
        No. 6 in St. Petersburg.
21 October/2 November — Tchaikovsky complains of stomach pains
        and becomes seriously ill. Doctors suspect cholera.
25 October/6 November — Tchaikovsky dies.
28 October/9 November — Tchaikovsky's funeral takes place in the
        Kazan Cathedral in St. Petersburg. He is buried in Tikhvinsky
        Cemetery at the Aleksandr Nevsky Monastery.

Notes

ABBREVIATIONS

Almanac 1	*P. I. Chaikovskii: Almanakh,* 1, Comps. P. E. Vaidman, G. I. Belonivich, M., 1995
Almanac 2	*P. I. Chaikovskii: Almanakh,* 2, Comps. P. E. Vaidman, G. I. Belonivich, M., 2003
CIu	Chaikovskii P. I. perepiska s P. I. Iurgensonom. V 2-kh tomakh, red., comment. V. A. Zhdanov i N. T. Zhegina, M. 1938–1952 [Tchaikovsky P. I. correspondence with P. I. Jurgenson, ed., commt. V. A. Zhdanov i N. T. Zhegina, M. 1938–1952
CM	Chaikovskii P. I. perepiska s N. F. fon Mekk. V 4-kh tomakh, sost., red., comment. P. E. Vaidman, Cheliabinsk, 2007 [Tchaikovsky P. I. Correspondence with N. F. von Meck, comp., ed., commt. 4 volumes, Cheliabinsk, 2007]
CPSS 1–63	P. I. Chaikovskii, *Polnoe sobranie sochinenii.* T. 1–62. M., 1940–1971; T. 63. M., 1990 [P. I. Tchaikovsky Complete Collected Works. Vol. 1–62. M., 1940–1971; Vol. 63. M., 1990]
CPSS I-XVII	P. I. Chaikovskii, *Polnoe sobranie sochinenii:* Literaturnye proizvedeniia i perepiska. T. II, III, V-XVII.

	M., 1953–1981 [P. I. Tchaikovsky *Complete Collected Works: Literary Works and Correspondence*. Vol. II, III, V-XVII. M., 1953–1981]
Diaries	Dnevniki P. I. Chaikovskogo. 1873–1891. M.-Pg., 1923 [*The Diaries of P. I. Tchaikovsky, 1873–1891*. M.-Pg., 1923]
GDMC	Gosudarstvennyi dom-musei P. I. Chaikovskogo, Klin [The Tchaikovsky House-Museum], Klin
GIALO	Gosudarstvennyi istoricheskii arkhiv Leningradskoi oblasti, Sankt-Peterburg [The State Historical Archive of the Leningrad District, St. Petersburg]
GTsMMK	Gosudarestvennyi tsentral'nyi musei muzykal'noi kul'tury imeni M. I. Glinki, Moskva [The Glinka State Central Museum of Musical Culture], Moscow
IRMO	Imperatorskoe Russkoe muzykal'noe obshscestvo [The Imperial Russian Musical Society]
MO	Moskovskoe otdelenie [the Moscow branch]
RGALI	Rossiiskii gosudarstvennyi arkhiv literatury i iskusstva [The Russian State Archive of Literature and the Arts], Moscow
RGB	Rossiiskaia gosudarstvennaia biblioteka [The Russian State Library], Moscow
RGIA	Rossiiskii gosudarstvennyi istoricheskii arkhiv [The Russian State Historical Archive], St. Petersburg
RIII	Rossiiskii institut istorii iskusstv [The Russian Institute of the History of Arts], St. Petersburg
RNB	Rossiiskaia natsional'naia biblioteka, Sankt-Peterburg [The Russian National Library], St. Petersburg
SPbO	Sankt-Peterburgskoe otdelenie [The St. Petersburg branch]
TsA MVD SSSR	Tsentral'nyi arkhiv ministerstva vnutrennikh del SSSR [The Central Archive of the Ministry of Internal Affairs of the USSR in Leningrad]
TsGA UR	Tsentral'nyi gosudarstvennyi arkhiv Udmurtskoi Respubliki, Izhevsk. [The Central State Archive of the Udmurt Republic], Izhevsk
TsGIA SPb	Tsentral'nyi gosudarstvennyi istoricheskii arkhiv Sankt-Peterburga. [The Central State Historical Archive of St. Petersburg]

ZhC   Chaikovskii, M. I., *Zhizn' Petra Ilyicha Chaikovskogo:*
v 3-kh tomakh, M.-Leiptsig, 1900–1902 [Modest Tchaikovsky, *The Life of P. I. Tchaikovsky: in 3 volumes,*
M.-Leipzig, 1900–1902]

Technical Terms Used in the Russian Archives

d.   *delo* (file)
ed. khr. *edinitsa khraneniia* (unit of storage)
f.   *fond* (collection)
K. P.   *кniga postuplenii* (the accession record book)
l.   *list* (folio)
L.   *litsevaia storona lista* (the front side of a folio)
N$_o$ *nomer* (number)
ob.   *oborot lista* (the reverse side of a folio)
op.   *opis'* (inventory)

INTRODUCTION

1. However, the first scholarly book on the composer, Boris Asa-
fyev's (literary pseudonym Igor Glebov) *P. I. Chaikovskii. Ego zhizn'*
i tvorchestvo [P. I. Tchaikovsky: His Life and Work], was published in
1922, when Tchaikovsky was not considered politically correct for post-
revolutionary Russia because, from the perspective of the new ideology,
he had been a composer in an aristocratic regime.

2. That includes a copy of the imperial decree awarding Tchaikovsky the order of St. Vladimir Equal-to-the-Apostles, Fourth Degree—
the tenth highest order in the hierarchy of the Russian Imperial orders
(reprinted in Chapter 5 of this book).

3. For a general survey of Tchaikovsky's use of the national anthem
of the Russian Empire in his orchestral works, see William H. Parsons,
"Tchaikovsky, the Tsars, and the Tsarist National Anthem," in *Tchaikovsky and His Contemporaries: A Centennial Symposium,* ed. Alexan-
dar Mihailovic (Westport, Conn.: Greenwood, 1999), 227–236.

4. The Soviet ban on the Liturgy of St. John Chrysostom had an
interesting historical precedent. When Tchaikovsky's publisher, Jurgenson, issued the work, he failed to secure approval from the director of
the Imperial Chapel. As soon as the chapel director Nikolay Bakhmetev
found out about the publication, he obtained an injunction instructing
the Moscow police to halt further sales of the published score and to

confiscate all existing copies. See Vladimir Morosan, "A Stranger in a Strange Land: Tchaikovsky as a Composer of Church Music," in *Tchaikovsky and His Contemporaries: A Centennial Symposium,* 197–225.

5. See the editor's commentary in *P. I. Tchaikovsky. Perepiska s N. F. von Mekk,* in three volumes, ed. Vladimir Zhdanov and Nikolay Zhegin (Moscow: Academia, 1934, 1935, 1936).

6. A more detailed treatment of this subject at that period can be found in Herbert Weinstock, *Tchaikovsky* (New York: Alfred A. Knopf, 1943).

7. Some notable publications from that period include *Tchaikovsky: A Symposium,* ed. Gerald Abraham (London, 1945); *The Diaries of Tchaikovsky,* translated from Russian by Wladimir Lakond (New York: W. W. Norton, 1945); Catherine Bowen and Barbara von Meck, *Beloved Friend: The Story of Tchaikowsky and Nadejda von Meck* (New York: Dover, 1946); new editions of Edwin Evans, *Tchaikovsky* (New York, 1949, 1957, 1960); and John Warrack, *Tchaikovsky* (New York, 1973).

8. David Brown, *Tchaikovsky: A Biographical and Critical Study,* 4 vols. (W. W. Norton, 1979–1992).

9. See Aleksandra Orlova, "Tajna zhizni Tsajkovskogo" and "Tajna smerti Tsajkovskogo," in *Novyj Amerikanets* [Jersey City], no. 39 and no. 40, 1980, pp. 21–23; Alexandra Orlova and David Brown, "Tchaikovsky: The Last Chapter," in *Music & Letters* 62, no. 2 (1981), pp. 125–145.

10. As it has been dubbed by Alan M. Kriegsman in his article under that title, in *Washington Post,* 28 March 1982.

11. Richard Taruskin, "Pathetic Symphonist: Chaikovsky, Russia, Sexuality, and the Study of Music," in *On Russian Music* (University of California Press, 2009), 76–104.

12. Roland John Wiley, *Tchaikovsky* (Oxford University Press, Master Musicians Series, 2009), 443.

13. Alexander Poznansky, *Tchaikovsky: The Quest for the Inner Man* (New York, Omnibus, 1991).

14. *Neizvestnyi Chaikovskii,* ed. Polina Vaidman (Moscow: P. Jurgenson, 2009). In this edition, the materials previously published with alterations appear in their complete form, with nothing omitted from the originals.

15. As Simon Karlinsky once aptly remarked, "certain character traits [of Tchaikovsky] were the result of his upbringing in the family headed by his father, Ilya, a man who belonged in a sentimentalist novel

of the end of the eighteenth century rather than in the second half of the nineteenth." See "Man or Myth? The Retrieval of the True Chaikovsky," in *Freedom from Violence and Lies: Essays on Russian Poetry and Music by Simon Karlinsky,* ed. Robert P. Hughes, Richard Taruskin, and Thomas A. Koster (Academic Studies Press, 2013), 343–344 (originally published in *Times Literary Supplement,* 17 January 1992).

16. I am using the notion introduced by Dr. Murray Bowen in his theory of the family system. He suggests that individuals are to be understood not in isolation, but as part of the emotional unit that is their family. A family is a system of individuals who are interconnected and interdependent, and cannot be understood apart from the system.

17. Mary W. Cavender, *Nests of the Gentry: Family, Estate, and Local Loyalties in Provincial Russia* (University of Delaware Press, 2007), 33.

18. William Mills Todd, *The Familiar Letter as a Literary Genre in the Age of Pushkin* (Northwestern University Press, 1976).

19. Alessandra Tosi, *Waiting for Pushkin: Russian Fiction in the Reign of Alexander I, 1801–1825* (Editions Rodopi, 2006), 198–199.

20. There is an amusing parallel between the opening of I. P. Tchaikovsky's earlier letter to his future wife, "What was the meaning of those tears?" [*Chto znachat eti slyozy?*], and the opening of Liza's aria, "Why these tears?" [*Otkuda eti slyozy?*], from *The Queen of Spades,* composed by their son Pyotr to the libretto by their other son Modest almost sixty years later.

21. See Fanny Dürbach's letter to Modest Tchaikovsky dated October 1, 1894.

22. Née Sabine Casimire Amable Voïart (1798–1885).

23. *A Companion to European Romanticism,* ed. Michael Ferber (Blackwell Publishing, 2005), 501.

24. Madame Guizot, née Elisabeth Charlotte Pauline de Meulan (1773–1827).

25. François Pierre Guillaume Guizot (1787–1874).

26. Sarah Esther Horowitz, *States of Intimacy: Friendship and the Remaking of French Political Elites, 1815–1848* (ProQuest, Umi Dissertation Publishing, 2011), 41.

27. Maria Edgeworth (1768–1849).

28. Tchaikovsky's Complete Collected Works, vol. XIV B, p. 213.

29. For more information about Modest Ilyich Tchaikovsky and his twin brother, Anatoly Ilyich, see the introductory note to Chapter 3.

30. It's unclear why that handover did not take place, and the whereabouts of these documents is unknown.

31. Nevertheless, Dostoevsky's debut novel, *Poor Folk* (1844–1845), is written in the form of letters and emulates many characteristics of Sentimentalism.

32. Their correspondence has been already presented in a number of editions and is not a part of this volume.

33. *P.I. Tchaikovsky–N.F. von Meck: perepiska v 4-kh tomakh, 1876–1890* / sostavlenie, nauchno-tekstologicheskaia redaktsiia, kommentarii P. E. Vaidman (Cheliabinsk: Music Production International, 2007), vol. 1, p. 45.

34. Modest Chaikovskii, *Zhizn' Petra Il'icha Chaikovskogo: po dokumentam, khranivshimsia v archive v Klinu, v 3-kh tomakh* (Moscow: Algoritm, 1997), vol. 1, p. 407.

35. *To My Best Friend: Correspondence Between Tchaikovsky and Nadezhda von Meck,* translated by Galina von Meck, ed. Edward Garden and Nigel Gotteri (Oxford: Clarendon Press, 1993), 184, 187.

36. Valerie Purton, *Dickens and the Sentimental Tradition* (Anthem Press, 2014). On Dostoevsky and sentimentalism see, for example, Mikhail Bakhtin, *Problems of Dostoevsky's Poetics* (University of Minnesota Press, 1984). See also Joe E. Barnhart, *Dostoevsky's Polyphonic Talent* (University Press of America, 2005), 219–234 ("'Living at Double Intensity': Dialogized Consciousness, the Question of Satire, and the Ethics of Representation in Dostoevsky's *Poor Folk,*" by Stephen Souris).

1. Correspondence Between Pyotr Ilyich Tchaikovsky's Parents

1. Today known as the National Mineral Resources University, the Mining University.

2. His son, Pyotr Ilyich Tchaikovsky, also received the silver medal upon his graduation from the St. Petersburg Conservatory.

3. Today known as the Mozhaisky Military Space Academy.

4. The name of Tchaikovsky's mother was originally d'Assier. But her father, Andrey Mikhailovich, had changed it to Assier (an alternative spelling is Acier).

5. The eldest daughter of I. P. Tchaikovsky from his first marriage, Zinaida (Z. I. Tchaikovskaya, Olkhovskaya after her marriage).

6. P. I. Evreinov, son of I. P. Tchaikovsky's sister, A. P. Evreinova (née Tchaikovskaya).

7. Z. I. Tchaikovskaya.

8. He is referring to his first marriage, to M. K. Keizer.

9. St. Mitrofan of Voronezh, the first bishop of Voronezh, considered to have miracle-working power.

10. Implying that his fiancée, Aleksandra, has already assumed the role of mother to his daughter Zinaida.

11. P. I. Evreinov.

12. Andrey Mikhailovich Assier, A. A. Tchaikovskaya's father and P. I. Tchaikovsky's grandfather.

13. Apparently Zinaida Tchaikovskaya lived with her future step-mother even before her father had married A. A. Assier. Her nanny's name was Arisha, most likely one of the Tchaikovsky family's serfs.

14. Amaliya Grigorievna Assier, née Gogel, stepmother of A. A. Tchaikovskaya.

15. A song by A. A. Alyabiev on a poem by V. A. Zhukovsky.

16. A. M. Assier and his second wife, A. G. Assier, née Gogel.

17. A suburb of St. Petersburg, a popular place for summer vacations.

18. According to M. I. Tchaikovsky, A. M. Assier suffered from bouts of nervous breakdowns similar to epileptic fits.

19. The day of the angel, or name day, is dedicated to the memory of the saint a person is named for as a Christian newborn: in this case, the feast day of Ilya the Prophet, or St. Ilya's Day, celebrated on 20 July/2 August.

20. The family of P. G. Sobolevsky, who worked as a mechanic and, subsequently, a manager at the Votkinsk factory from 1817 to 1824. After 1824 he lived in St. Petersburg and was an employee of the Mining and Salt Mines Department.

21. This letter was written by A. A. Assier when she had already become I. P. Tchaikovsky's wife and was traveling from St. Petersburg to his place of work at the Votkinsk factory.

22. Ekaterina Andreevna Alekseeva (née Assier), A. A. Tchaikov-skaya's (née Assier) sister.

23. A doctor in Nizhny Novgorod.

24. A doctor in Nizhny Novgorod.

25. Katenka (Katya)—E. I. Tchaikovskaya, the first child of A. A. and I. P. Tchaikovsky, died in her infancy.

26. I. P. Tchaikovsky's acquaintance.

27. A servant of the Tchaikovsky family, most likely a serf.

28. Family of a Votkinsk factory employee.

29. Viktor Timofeevich Sherchin, an employee of the Votkinsk factory.

30. The official rank of an employee.

31. A servant of the Tchaikovsky family. She lived with the family in Votkinsk and Alapayevsk. P. I. Tchaikovsky mentions her in his letter to M. I. Tchaikovsky after he visited Fanny Dürbach in Montbéliard in the last year before he died. (CPSS, Vol. XVI-B, p. 213)

32. Aleksandr Stepanovich Alekseev.

33. A chairman of the court chamber in Nizhny Novgorod.

34. E. A. Alekseeva (née Assier), A. A. Tchaikovskaya's sister. She and her husband, Major-General A. S. Alekseev, accompanied A. A. Tchaikovskaya on her trip from St. Petersburg to the Votkinsk factory.

35. E. A. Alekseeva.

36. E. A. Alekseeva was a good musician and possessed a fine voice (contralto). She has been considered an outstanding amateur singer.

37. P. M. Stremoukhov.

38. Apparently an Italian singer residing at that time in Nizhny Novgorod.

39. The domestic or household serfs.

40. E. A. and A. S. Alekseev.

41. Approximately a kilometer.

42. Lieutenant-general I. A. Neratov, head of the Izhevsk factory.

43. S. I. Semennikova (née Kun), who was married to the chief of police, A. S. Semennikov.

44. F. E. Neratova (née Velikopolskaya), General I. A. Neratov's wife.

45. The classic English card game whist was very popular in nineteenth-century Russia.

46. Abbas-Mirza (1789–1833) was a crown prince of Persia and a military commander during the Russo-Persian Wars of 1804–1813 and 1826–1828. In 1828, he signed the Treaty of Turkmenchay, concluding the second of these wars. At the signing ceremony, Abbas-Mirza was accompanied by his illustrious entourage.

47. Vasily Egorovich Blinov, archpriest of the Annunciation Cathedral at Kamsko-Votkinsk factory, became godfather to all of Ilya Tchaikovsky's children born in Votkinsk. He taught Pyotr Tchaikovsky the Russian language and the law of God.

48. Andrey Khristianovich von Ziegel, a member of the Perm Mining Board, son of the mayor of Votkinsk.

49. I. P. Tchaikovsky's daughters.

50. Silvester Feodorovich Tuchemsky, a doctor at the Votkinsk factory. He was head of the Votkinsk hospital and became close with the Tchaikovsky family.

51. I. P. Tchaikovsky served as a member of the Perm Mining Board in 1818–1820.

52. Vasily Ipatovich Romanov, a mining engineer and the factory's manager.

53. Samuel Penn, a foreman-metallurgist.

54. Penn had two daughters, Alice and Susanna.

55. A mechanical musical instrument (Winterhalter) in the Tchaikovsky household, which made it possible for Pyotr Ilyich Tchaikovsky to hear the music of Mozart, Bellini, Rossini, and Donizetti for the first time in his childhood (*Almanch,* 1, p. 41).

56. Apparently, the stepmother of A. A. Tchaikovskaya, A. G. Assier (née Gogel).

57. Most likely, Glafira Timofeevna Rapinova, I. P. Tchaikovsky's cousin. P. I. Tchaikovsky mentions her in a humorous letter to his mother in 1851.

58. Apparently the Tchaikovskys' domestic servant. P. I. Tchaikovsky mentions her name in his letter to M. I. Tchaikovsky after visiting Montbéliard in the last year of his life. (CPSS, Vol. XVI-B, p. 213)

59. A type of horse carriage used for unstable or sandy roads.

60. Apparently, the church had been left from the previous owners of the house.

61. Nizhny Novgorod.

62. A. A. Tchaikovskaya was accompanied on her trip by her sister and brother-in-law. Apparently, I. P. Tchaikovsky wanted E. A. Alekseeva, his wife's sister, to stay with his family in Votkinsk.

63. The future emperor of Russia, Alexander II, who visited Kamsko-Votkinsk factory in 1837. I. P. Tchaikovsky was introduced to him at that time.

64. A. G. Assier (née Gogel), A. A. Tchaikovskaya's stepmother.

65. Dmitry Aleksandrovich Kavelin, a high-ranking official, at one point served as rector of St. Petersburg University. I. P. Tchaikovsky apparently met him during the Grand Duke Alexander's visit, when D. A. Kavelin was part of his retinue.

66. I. P. Tchaikovsky tried to obtain financial support from the Mining and Salt Mines Department for his daughter Zinaida's enrollment at the Catherine Institute in St. Petersburg. The Catherine Institute was under the jurisdiction of the Mining and Salt Mines Department. (TsGA UR, f. 212, op. 1, d. 4918, l. 1)

67. The Patriotic Institute in Moscow (former School for Orphan Girls) had been established for orphans whose fathers had participated in the War of 1812. A. A. Tchaikovskaya was educated there, and her teacher of Russian had been P. A. Pletnev, a friend of Alexander Pushkin.

68. Pavel Petrovich Anosov, an engineer, a graduate of the Mining Institute, worked at the Zlatoust factories. He made improvements to the steel industry and studied mineral resources of the Ural region.

69. Kolya is Nikolay Ilyich Tchaikovsky (1838–1910), the older brother of the composer. Petya refers to Pyotr Ilyich Tchaikovsky; this is the first mention of him.

70. Nadezhda Timofeevna Valtseva, I. P. Tchaikovsky's cousin, who was also P. I. Tchaikovsky's godmother and lived with the Tchaikovsky family.

71. A. S. Badaev, an engineer at the Votkinsk factory.

72. Village Toykino of Sarapul district, Vyatka province.

73. A. I. Tchaikovskaya, I. P.'s daughter (married name Davydova).

74. Ippolit Ilyich Tchaikovsky, I. P.'s son.

75. Ivan Ilyich Evreinov.

76. Pyotr Ivanovich Evreinov.

77. St. Ilya's Day (St. Ilya is known in English as the Old Testament prophet Elijah).

78. N. T. Valtseva.

79. Anastasia Vasilievna Popova, I. P. Tchaikovsky's niece.

80. A. A. Tchaikovskaya's sister, Elizaveta Andreevna Shobert, and her husband, Vasily Vasilievich Shobert.

81. V. E. Blinov.

82. V. A. Olyshev, an engineer, a graduate of the Mining Institute, worked at the Ural factories, studied the Swedish metallurgical industry, and authored articles on the puddling process at the Kamsk-Votkinsk factory. He began working at the factory in 1839.

83. A. P. Alekseev, an engineer, a manager of the naval yard. His son, Venidikt (Venichka), after his mother's death was schooled together with Tchaikovsky's children at their home.

84. Lidiya Vladimirovna Tchaikovskaya, I. P. Tchaikovsky's niece; she lost her parents at an early age and was brought up in Tchaikovsky's household.

85. S. F. Tuchemsky.

86. A. S. Semennikov.

87. This name is not written out in full, and instead uses an ellipsis at the end. Who it refers to is not known. I. P. Tchaikovsky writes about this person later, again hiding his name behind an ellipsis.

88. A fine French broadcloth.

89. Ledengsk, a town in the Totminsk district of the Vologda province known for its mineral waters and saltwater treatment.

90. Mishkino, a small factory town in Vyatka province.

91. Beryozovka, an outskirt of the Votkinsk factory town.

92. S. I. Olysheva, the engineer Olyshev's wife.

93. A servant in the Tchaikovsky family.

94. The balneological resort in Samara province known for its mineral springs, which produced the Sergiev mineral waters. A. A. Tchaikovskaya had traveled there with her son Pyotr and A. V. Popova in 1845.

95. The family of engineer A. P. Alekseev.

96. S. F. Tuchemsky.

97. An opera by Gioachino Rossini.

98. P. I. Evreinov.

99. S. I. Olysheva.

100. V. I. Romanov.

101. E. A. Shobert (née Assier), A. A. Tchaikovskaya's sister.

102. A. A. Tchaikovskaya's stepmother.

103. Vasily Vasilievich Shobert; I. P. Tchaikovsky mistakenly replaced his patronymic with "Andreevich."

104. A. S. Semennikov.

105. This rather peculiar fragment is the very first known example of Pyotr Ilyich Tchaikovsky's handwriting.

106. A. I. Romanov.

107. Usolka was a servant.

108. Aleksandr Andreevich Iossa (1810–1894)—a mining engineer from a family of mining engineers, a graduate of the Mining Institute, later a leading expert of the mining industry in Russia. From 1855, he served as the head of the Kamsk-Votkinsk district and had also founded a mining vocational school for training highly qualified technicians.

109. P. P. Anosov.

110. Artinsk factory is one of the oldest factories in the Urals.

111. V. P. Shiroshkin, an employee of the Izhevsk factory, husband of I. P. Tchaikovsky's sister, E. P. Shiroshkina (née Tchaikovskaya).

112. The family of Samuel Penn, an English engineer at the Votkinsk factory; close acquaintances with the Tchaikovsky family.

113. Apparently, a relative of the Gogel family.

114. Apparently a relative of the Gogel-Assier family.

115. This song could be considered the first musical piece written by the future composer.

116. Galevo [Galyovo] was a village near the Kama River surrounded by lush forest.

117. A postscript written by A. V. Popova, I. P. Tchaikovsky's niece.

118. A. G. Assier (née Gogel).

119. A. P. Aleekseev.

120. A. I. Romanov.

121. Daughter of A. S. Semennikov, the Votkinsk police chief.

122. A. G. Obodovsky was a well-known educator and author of numerous works. He participated in launching the first journal of pedagogy in Russia.

123. From this trip, A. A. Tchaikovskaya brought to Votkinsk Fanny Dürbach, who was apparently recommended to her by relatives of her stepmother, A. G. Assier (née Gogel).

124. The family of Aleksandr Karlovich Shatelen, a cousin of M. K. Keizer, the first wife of I. P. Tchaikovsky.

125. S. I. Olysheva.

126. V. A. Glinka, lieutenant general, chief executive director of the Ural mining factories.

127. "Undina" is a long narrative poem by Vasily Zhukovsky, based on a very popular prose novella *Undine* by Friedrich de la Motte Fouqué. This was one of the favorite books in the Tchaikovsky family. A copy of the first edition of "Undina," along with herbarium between the cover and the title page, has been preserved in Pyotr Ilyich Tchaikovsky's personal library.

128. Wife of an engineer at the Votkinsk factory, A. S. Badaev.

129. A river in the Perm province.

130. An employee at the Votkinsk factory.

131. A. Kh. Von Ziegel (1795–1863) was a senior adviser to the Ural mining industry.

132. N. I. Kriskov.

133. A public park near the Votkinsk factory, planted at the beginning of the nineteenth century by the local engineer Lev Ivanovich Otrada.

134. The engineer Olyshev's family.

135. A suburb of St. Petersburg. The train terminal of Pavlovsk, Vauxhall Pavilion, was built as a concert hall and regularly hosted musical performances.

136. Joseph Hermann of Vienna arrived in St. Petersburg in 1838 and became principal conductor and artistic director of the Pavlovsk orchestra.

137. M. A. Evreinova (née Keller), wife of P. I. Evreinov.

138. A postscript written by A. V. Popova.

139. In this letter, I. P. Tchaikovsky describes his conflict with the owners of the Alapayevsk factory, which resulted in his resignation from his job there and the relocation of the Tchaikovsky family to St. Petersburg.

140. Two clerks at the Alapayevsk factory who were exposed as dishonest by I. P. Tchaikovsky.

141. Grigory Grigorievich Moskvin, a colonel, manager of the Nevyansk factory who would replace I. P. Tchaikovsky as manager of the Alapayevsk factory.

142. Nikolinka is I. P. Tchaikovsky's elder son. The father is talking about prospects for his education.

143. Ardalion Vasilievich Ivanov, I. P. Tchaikovsky's classmate at the Saint Petersburg Mining Institute. Later, he taught Russian and Church Slavonic languages at the School of Jurisprudence.

144. The Markovs were relatives of P. A. Vakar, whose brother, M. A. Vakar, was a close friend of I. P. Tchaikovsky.

145. E. A. Shobert (née Assier).

146. Meaning the father of the family.

147. Iosif Iosifovich Berard (1800–1883), an instructor and house master at the School of Jurisprudence, including the preparatory division where P. I. Tchaikovsky began attending classes.

2. Letters by Fanny Dürbach to Pyotr Ilyich Tchaikovsky and His Brothers

1. Modest Tchaikovsky, *The Life and Letters of Peter Ilich Tchaikovsky*, ed. by Rosa Newmarch, vol. 1 (New York: Vienna House, 1973), 6.

2. GDMC, a⁴ no. 1005–1016.

3. N. I. Tchaikovsky.

4. Z. I. Olkhovskaya (née Tchaikovskaya).

5. I. I. Tchaikovsky.

6. L. V. Olkhovskaya (née Tchaikovskaya).

7. Fanny Dürbach kept Tchaikovsky's childhood journals, and it is thanks to these that we have his childhood translations and poems. They have been published in M. I. Chaikovskii, *Zhizn' Petra Ilyicha Chaikovskogo: v 3-kh tomakh*, M.-Leiptsig, 1900–1902 (ZhC), and *P. I. Chaikovskii: Almanakh*, 1, Comps. P. E. Vaidman, G. I. Belonivich, M., 1995 (*Almanac 1*).

8. Venya (Venedikt) Alekseev.

9. Nothing is known of the photograph Tchaikovsky apparently sent to her.

10. There is only one known photograph of Fanny Dürbach. It is kept in the archive of P. I. Tchaikovsky.

11. This letter, as well as other childhood letters from Tchaikovsky to Dürbach (six in total), is preserved in copies made by M. I. Tchaikovsky in 1894 when he visited Dürbach in Montbéliard.

12. The composer's father, I. P. Tchaikovsky, died in 1880.

13. Tchaikovsky's sister A. I. Davydova (née Tchaikovskaya) died in the spring of 1891. She was married to L. V. Davydov, the son of a Decembrist.

14. Frederika Dürbach.

15. A. V. Popova, who was called "Sestritsa" [little sister] within the Tchaikovsky family and who, at the time, was living with Tchaikovsky's sister A. I. Davydova, in Kamenka, Ukraine.

16. A. V. Popova.

17. Fanny is evidently replying to Tchaikovsky's letter telling her about the deceased members of his family: parents and sisters.

18. Most likely this refers to a Lutheran Church and its Sunday school.

19. L. V. Olkhovskaya (née Tchaikovsky).

20. Z. I. Olkhovskaya died in 1878.

21. A public park near Votkinsk where I. P. Tchaikovsky's family and those of his co-workers went for picnics.

22. At the beginning of this letter, the date is written 13 July, but at the end it is 19 July.

23. This refers to the illness of P. V. Tchaikovskaya (née Konshina), the wife of A. I. Tchaikovsky.

24. A. I. Tchaikovsky was appointed vice-governor of Nizhny Novgorod.

25. Lev Vasilievich Davydov, husband of Tchaikovsky's deceased sister A. I. Davydova.

26. In Vichy, Tchaikovsky had been taking the waters with his nephew Vladimir Lvovich Davydov.

27. Modest Ilyich Tchaikovsky spent a number of years teaching a young pupil named Nikolay "Kolya" Konradi to speak, read, and write, with great success, using a method recommended by the Swiss pedagogue Jacques Hugentobler.

28. Tchaikovsky visited Dürbach in Montbéliard. He wrote of this encounter: "upon her return to Montbéliard, she spent the next forty-two years living quietly and uneventfully. And her younger years, so different from the rest of her life in Montbéliard, remained completely undisturbed in her memory. At times, I have been so vividly transported to that distant past that it felt somewhat eerie but also sweet; we both were holding back tears all the time." (CPSS, Vol. XIV-B, p. 213)

29. These photographs have not been identified.

30. There is one presently known photograph of the Tchaikovsky family taken in 1848 that matches the description given here by Fanny Dürbach.

31. Fanny's cousin.

32. This photograph is unknown.

33. Tchaikovsky conducted a concert featuring some of his works in Brussels in January 1893.

34. This refers to the opera *Iolanta*.

35. Tchaikovsky stayed in Kharkov in March 1893 on the way from Kamenka in Klin.

36. Tchaikovsky conducted a concert of his own compositions in Kharkov in March 1893.

37. The identity of the thief has not been determined. In his last will (published in this edition), P. I. Tchaikovsky made the following provision: "From my goods and chattels, the gold, black enamel watch inlaid with little stars and the gold figures of Joan of Arc, Apollo, and two of the Muses, which has been stolen, in the event of its being found together with the watch chain and returned to me, I leave to my nephew Vladimir Lvovich Davydov and, in the event of his death, to my nephew Yury Lvovich."

38. Tchaikovsky's brother-in-law L. V. Davydov married E. N. Olkhovskaya in 1891, after the death of his wife A. I. Davydova, the sister of the composer.

39. E. N. Olkhovskaya was related to the composer's cousin L. V. Tchaikovskaya (Olkhovskaya after marriage) and his half-sister Z. I. Tchaikovskaya (Olkhovskaya after marriage).

40. Georgy Tchaikovsky, the illegitimate son of Tchaikovsky's niece T. L. Davydova, was adopted by N. I. Tchaikovsky. His adoption into the family was kept secret.

41. On that day Tchaikovsky conducted his Fourth Symphony in London, in a concert at the Philharmonic Society.

42. Cambridge University awarded an honorary doctorate in music to Tchaikovsky in June.

43. G. N. Tchaikovsky.

44. L. V. Olkhovskaya (née Tchaikovskaya).

45. It is clear from this phrase that Dürbach was familiar with Pushkin's works, including his famous *Exegi monumentum,* the contents of which she retells.

46. Professor Frederic Maitland, who hosted Tchaikovsky when he visited Cambridge to receive his honorary doctorate, took a photograph of him wearing his academic robes.

47. It is unlikely that Tchaikovsky ever read Fanny Dürbach's last letter to him, as he left Klin on 7/19 October 1893, and never returned there. During the night of 24–25 October/5–6 November, the composer died in St. Petersburg.

48. A. V. Popova.

49. Tchaikovsky was planning to leave for St. Petersburg, and the Dürbach sisters were aware of this.

50. This letter from Fanny Dürbach to Nikolay Ilyich Tchaikovsky is from GDMC, b[11] no. 14.

51. G. N. Tchaikovsky.

52. This refers to the death of P. I. Tchaikovsky in October 1893.

53. Fanny Dürbach met M. I. Tchaikovsky in person in Montbéliard, and gave him the composer's childhood letters to her, letters from the composer's mother A. A. Tchaikovskaya, letters from A. V. Popova, and some others. She also gave him one of P. I. Tchaikovsky's childhood poems. Now part of it is kept in RNB, another in GDMC. M. I. Tchaikovsky also made copies of Tchaikovsky's childhood notebooks, which are kept in the composer's archives in Klin.

54. Olga Sergeevna Tchaikovskaya (née Denisieva).

55. V. A. Alekseev.

56. The letters of A. A. Tchaikovskaya (née Assier) are now kept in GDMC, so Fanny must have sent or given them to P. I. Tchaikovsky's brothers.

57. V. E. Blinov, archpriest of the Annunciation Cathedral at Kamsko-Votkinsk factory, godfather of Tchaikovsky, instructed him in Russian language and religion.

58. L. V. Tchaikovskaya (née Olkhovskaya). Fanny Dürbach gave these letters to M. I. Tchaikovsky, and they are kept in GDMC.

59. A. V. Popova.

60. The letters written by Fanny Dürbach to Modest Ilyich Tchaikovsky are from GDMC, b[10] no. 2118–2129.

61. V. L. Davydov.

62. A. V. Shobert (Litke after marriage).

63. E. A. Shobert (née Assier).

64. Vladimir Andreevich Glinka, lieutenant-general, chief executive director of the Ural mining factories.

65. Nikolay Vasilievich Romanov, son of the Votkinsk engineer V. I. Romanov.

66. Maximilian Josèphe Eugène Auguste Napoléon de Beauharnais (1817–1852) inherited the title of Duke of Leuchtenber in 1839, and married Grand Duchess Maria Nikolaevna of Russia, daughter of Emperor Nicholas I. A well-educated man, he became president of the Academy of Fine Arts and director of the Saint Petersburg Mining Institute. He was a member of the academic council of the Corps of Mining Engineers. In 1845 he visited factories in the Ural Mountains, but specific information about his visit to Votkinsk has not been found.

67. Evidently, by that time neither Fanny Dürbach nor her sister, having so long ago left Russia, could themselves read or translate letters written in Russian.

68. This refers to the fact that, in later years, V. A. Alekseev did not pay sufficient respect to his godfather I. P. Tchaikovsky, who took care of him in his childhood.

69. The books listed here were ones that Fanny used in teaching the children: *L'Education Maternelle* by Amable Tastu (Paris, 1848); *Family Education* by Maria Edgeworth in French translation by Louise Belloc and Adolf Montgolfier; *Natural History* by Georges-Louis Leclerc de Buffon; as well as *Moral Tales* by Elisabeth-Charlotte-Pauline Guizot and *Celebrated Children* by August-Michel-Benoît Masson.

70. M. M. Palchikova (Loginova after marriage).

71. This refers to *Atlas de géographie sacrée,* by Achille Meissas and Auguste Michelot—who were also the authors of a number of popular scientific works.

72. The German writer Johann-Franz Ahn was the author of *A New Practical and Easy Method of Learning the French Language* [Praktischen Lehrgang zur schnellen und leichten Erlernung der französischen Sprach]. Within a short period of time the book received widespread recognition and was translated into all European languages.

73. A photo album with views of Montbéliard is preserved in the archive of P. I. Tchaikovsky.

74. *The Biography of P. I. Tchaikovsky, Composed by M. I. Tchaikovsky,* was published in three volumes between 1900 and 1902.

75. The end of this letter is lost.

76. Ivan Knorr, a writer and composer, taught music at Kharkov and later at the Frankfurt Conservatory. He was the author of a German-language biography of P. I. Tchaikovsky published in Berlin in 1900.

77. Venya (Venedikt) Alekseev.

78. The Klin house was initially bought in the name of the composer's servant A. I. Sofronov. From 1899 M. I. Tchaikovsky began to buy the house in payments, and finally succeeded in purchasing it completely by 1904.

79. I. I. Tchaikovsky's first granddaughter, M. N. Alekseeva (subsequently, Shein after marriage) was born.

80. Emperor Nicholas II.

81. Fanny Dürbach.

82. This refers to the wives of the brothers Anatoly, Nikolai, and Ippolit Tchaikovsky: P. V. Tchaikovskaya (née Konshina), O. S. Tchaikovskaya (née Denisieva), and S. P. Tchaikovskaya (née Nikonova).

83. The biography of P. I. Tchaikovsky written by M. I. Tchaikovsky was released as separate editions as well as journal publications, and later, in three volumes. Apparently, M. I. Tchaikovsky sent some editions to the Dürbach sisters. This is evident from a postcard written by Frederika Dürbach to the publisher P. I. Jurgenson:

> "Sir, I have received the eighth issue of Pyotr Ilyich Tchaikovsky biography written by his brother, Modest Ilyich Tchaikovsky. I thank you. Please convey my sincere gratitude to Monsieur Tchaikovsky and accept my greetings. Sincerely yours, F. Dürbach."

On the back of the postcard is written "M. Jurgenson" and the Moscow address of P. I. Jurgenson's publishing company and store (GDMC, b^{10} no. 2131).

3. LETTERS BY PYOTR ILYICH TCHAIKOVSKY

1. Nikolay Ilyich Tchaikovsky (1838–1910), the older brother of P. I. Tchaikovsky, an engineer, a graduate of the Mining Institute; Ippolit Ilyich Tchaikovsky (1843–1927), a younger brother of P. I. Tchaikovsky, an officer of the Russian Imperial Navy; and Aleksandra Ilyinichna Davydova, née Tchaikovskaya (1841–1891), a younger sister of P. I. Tchaikovsky.

2. CPSS, Vol. V, pp. 73–75.

3. See, for example, P. I. Tchaikovsky's letter of 3 February 1871 to Anatoly describing his friendly meeting with a high official from the Ministry of Jurisprudence and their conversation about what would be best for Anatoly's career. CPSS, Vol. V, p. 251.

4. P. I. Tchaikovsky's letter of 13/25 February 1878 published in this book.

5. In 1882 Anatoly Tchaikovsky married Praskoviya Vladimirovna Konshina (1864–1956), the daughter of a prominent industrialist and the niece (on her mother's side) of Pavel Tretyakov, a famous Russian art collector.

6. CPSS, XIII (1971), pp. 306–308.

7. Lawrence and Elisabeth Hanson, *Tchaikovsky: A New Study of the Man and His Music* (London: Cassell, 1965), 246–247.

8. CPSS, V (1959), p. 154.

9. CPSS, VII (1962), p. 53.

10. Performances in Kiev, Moscow, and Prague followed, with premieres in Vienna (1902) and New York City (1910), both conducted by Gustav Mahler.

11. This work, originally titled *Zhizn Petra Il'icha Chaikovskovo*, was published in Moscow from 1900 to 1902.

12. Modest Ilyich had the same sexual orientation as Pyotr Ilyich. And while they openly talked about homosexuality in their personal letters, it remained a taboo subject outside a close circle of like-minded friends.

13. Letter no. 1. GDMC, a^{17} no. 16. K. P. no. 19587. From an unidentified collection dated 1938. Tchaikovsky's letter to his mother is a

postscript added to a letter written by the composer's father to his wife on 21 September 1851 from St. Petersburg. The letter is printed in this edition as a part of Tchaikovsky's parents' correspondence. It was first published in CPSS, Vol. V, p. 38 from the copy made by M. I. Tchaikovsky, who incorrectly read the text of the original. Now, it is being published from the original document for the first time. In his letter to his wife, I. P. Tchaikovsky goes into great detail describing the progress of his negotiations regarding his new place of service and the working conditions there. At the end of the letter, he writes: "Petya has been with me since I first arrived, good old Berrard released him until my departure." This referred to I. I. Berrard, the headmaster of the preparatory level of the School of Jurisprudence, where Tchaikovsky was studying at the time.

14. CPSS, Vol. V, p. 179. Manuscript in RNB, f. 834, ed. khr. 36, l. 17–18ob.

15. *Fifty Russian Folk Songs* for piano, four hands, published in 1869 by P. Jurgenson.

16. Tchaikovsky was teaching music at the Moscow Conservatory.

17. The stage name of Tchaikovsky's friend Konstantin Nikolaevich Delazari (De Lazari, 1838–1903). He was an opera and dramatic actor, and author of memoirs about the composer.

18. V. I. Bibikov, a Moscow acquaintance of Tchaikovsky's.

19. Prince Pavel Ivanovich Gruzinsky and Pyotr Petrovich Okoneshnikov belonged to the circle of Moscow homosexuals. Tchaikovsky did not like either of them.

20. Barbara and Carlotta Marchisio, sisters and Italian singers. They performed in the Italian Opera in St. Petersburg.

21. Désirée Artôt (Marguerite-Joséphine-Désirée Artôt de Padilla, 1835–1907), a Belgian soprano with an Italian opera company touring in Moscow in 1868–1870 and 1875–1876. She was Tchaikovsky's fiancée for a short time in 1868, but their engagement ended, and in 1869 she married the Spanish baritone Mariano Padilla y Ramos. Tchaikovsky dedicated his Romance for Piano, op. 5, and Six Romances, op. 65, to her.

22. Aleksandra Grigorievna Menshikova (1840–1902), singer, actress at the Bolshoi Theater in Moscow from 1860–1871. First performer of the part of Maria Vlasievna in Tchaikovsky's opera *The Voyevoda*. He dedicated to her the song "Do Not Believe, My Friend," op. 6, no. 1.

23. *Undine.*

24. Stepan Aleksandrovich Gedeonov (1816–1878), director of the Imperial Theaters, 1867–1875. See Tchaikovsky's letter to him dated 12

October 1869 in CPSS, Vol. V, pp. 177–178. It refers to the opera *Undine,* which Tchaikovsky submitted to the Imperial Theaters, but for a long time received no reply. In the end, a production of *Undine* did not take place. The composer destroyed the score of the opera, but later he used its music in other compositions, such as the ballet *Swan Lake,* the incidental music for A. N. Ostrovsky's spring tale *The Snow Maiden,* and others.

25. Dmitry Nikolaevich Petrovsky (1847–1913), friend of M. I. Tchaikovsky from the School of Jurisprudence.

26. Servant of N. G. Rubinstein at the apartment (in an old conservatory building on Vozdvizhenka) where the composer was living at the time.

27. Vladimir Stepanovich Shilovsky (Count Vasiliev-Shilovsky, 1852–1893), a close friend of Tchaikovsky's, his student in music theory. Their relationship was grounded not only in the study of music but also in intimate closeness (Shilovsky belonged to the homosexual community). Also, Shilovsky habitually lent money to the composer. Tchaikovsky dedicated to him two pieces for piano, op. 10 and, presumably, Symphony No. 3.

28. Konstantin Ivanovich Ryumin, trustee of V. S. Shilovsky.

29. Letter no. 2. GDMC, b[10] no. 6490. K. P. no. 19760. From an unidentified collection dated 1938. At the time of the museum's foundation, the letter was kept in M. I. Tchaikovsky's personal collection. Later it was also kept in his personal collection, as it was written on the back of a letter from I. P. Tchaikovsky to M. I. Tchaikovsky. The verification of the date of P. I. Tchaikovsky's letter is attributed to the date indicated by I. P. Tchaikovsky in his letter, since the composer's letter is written on the back of his father's letter.

30. Vladimir Stepanovich Adamov was a schoolmate of Tchaikovsky's at the School of Jurisprudence. He became a statesman, a chamberlain, and the director of a department of the Ministry of Justice.

31. Kreitern, an official in Simbirsk, was M. I. Tchaikovsky's supervisor.

32. The Kartsevs (or the Kartsovs) were the family of Aleksandra Petrovna Kartsov (née Tchaikovskaya), a cousin of the Tchaikovsky brothers.

33. Aleksey Alekseevich Valuev, a schoolmate of M. I. Tchaikovsky at the School of Jurisprudence.

34. CPSS, Vol. V, p. 316. The manuscript in GDMC, a[3] no. 2140.

35. Music for A. N. Ostrovsky's spring fairy tale *Snegurochka* [The Snow Maiden].

36. Tchaikovsky jokingly referred to his two servants, Mikhail and Aleksey Sofronov, who lived with him, as well as his dog, Bishka, as his "extended family."

37. CPSS, Vol. VI, p. 44. The manuscript in RNB, f. 834, khr. 25, l. 1–10b. The copy GDMC, a^{11} no. 540. Aleksey Ivanovich Sofronov (1859–1925) was P. I. Tchaikovsky's servant from 1874 to 1893. He was a native of the Klin district.

38. Nizy, a village in the Sumsk district in Kharkov province, was the location of N. D. Kondratiev's estate.

39. CPSS, Vol. VI, pp. 52–53. The manuscript in RNB, f. 834, ed. khr. 25, l. 3–40b. The copy GDMC, a^{11-b} no. 541.

40. N. L. Bochechkarov.

41. M. I. Sofronov, brother of A. I. Sofronov, was Tchaikovsky's first servant.

42. A. I. Sofronov stayed with his relatives in the village of Teliktino, Klin district, Moscow province.

43. Olga Nikolaevna Sofronova was M. I. Sofronov's wife.

44. CPSS, Vol. VI, pp. 75–76. GDMC, a^3 no. 1367.

45. Nikolay Dimitrievich Kondratiev (1832–1887), one of the composer's most intimate friends. He dedicated to him the piece for piano *Evening Dreams,* op. 19, no. 1.

46. Mikhail Ivanovich Bulatov, Tchaikovsky's classmate at the School of Jurisprudence.

47. Tchaikovsky is referring to the failed marriages of some of his homosexual acquaintances.

48. A. I. Davydova.

49. Aleksandra Arkadievna Davydova (1849–1902) was a writer, publisher of the magazine *God's World,* contributor to the magazine *Northern Herald,* and wife of the director of the St. Petersburg Conservatory, cellist K. Yu. Davydov.

50. Kolya Konradi, Modest Tchaikovsky's deaf-mute pupil.

51. Mme. Kondratieva was Alina Ivanovna Konradi, Kolya's mother, and Fofa (Sonya) was Sofiya Aleksandrovna Yershova, his governess.

52. CPSS, Vol. VI, p. 109. GDMC, a^3 no. 1106. The letter was written on stationery with the monogram "E. K." [Eduard Kotek].

53. A. I. Tchaikovsky's letter is unknown.

54. Tchaikovsky's opera *Vakula the Smith* had its premiere in November, and he considered it a "solemn failure." In his letter to S. I. Taneyev from 2 December 1876, he confessed: "I won't conceal from

you that I'm seriously shaken and confused. The main thing is that I cannot blame either the quality of the performance or the production. Everything has been done assiduously, competently, and even sumptuously." (CPSS, Vol. VI, p. 89)

55. Aleksandra Yakovlevna Glama-Meshcherskaya (real name Barysheva) (1859–1942) was a theater actress and pedagogue; she graduated from the drama department of the Moscow Conservatory (a graduate of I. V. Samarin's acting course). In 1878 she debuted in the Alexandrinsky Theater in Petersburg, and later worked in other metropolitan and provincial theaters. For a brief period, she was A. I. Tchaikovsky's love interest.

56. In CPSS, this phrase (beginning with "alas") is omitted and marked as "[a few indiscernible words]." In the original manuscript, an unidentified individual blacked out this phrase. At the end (above the word "I"), the word "but" was apparently added later.

57. Back in 1875, Camille Saint-Saëns advised Tchaikovsky to give a recital with Édouard Colonne's orchestra. Later, via S. I. Taneyev, Tchaikovsky inquired as to the logistics of such a recital. Saint-Saëns confirmed that this required certain financing. Tchaikovsky was unable to acquire the necessary funding and the recital did not occur.

58. CPSS, Vol. VI, p. 153. GDMC, a³ no. 1476.

59. Tchaikovsky married Antonina Ivanovna Milyukova (1848–1917). Immediately after the wedding, the couple traveled to St. Petersburg.

60. Most likely this refers to an evening of musical entertainment in the "Livadia" gardens, on Krestovsky Island in Petersburg, on 7 July.

61. Tchaikovsky and his wife stayed at the estate in Karasovo, Klin district, Moscow province, owned by the composer's mother-in-law, Olga Nikanorovna Milyukova (1821–1881), from 17 to 19 July.

62. A. I. Davydova, in Kamenka.

63. Parents of Kolya Konradi.

64. S. A. Yershova.

65. CPSS, Vol. VI, pp. 153–154. GDMC, a³ no. 1111. This letter was written three days after the wedding. In the record book of the church of St. George on Vspolie, there is an entry dated 6 July 1877 regarding the marriage of P. I. Tchaikovsky and A. I. Milyukova (TsIAM, f. 203, op. 756, no. 16), noting that the guarantors representing the groom's side were the free artist Osip Osipovich Kotek and court counselor Anatoly Ilyich Tchaikovsky. The guarantors representing the bride's side were the Honorable justice of the peace Pyotr Petrovich Mikhailov and

nobleman Nikolay Aristakhov Makhalov. The service was performed by the dean of the Church of St. George, archpriest Dimitri Vasiliev Razumovskii.

66. Iosif Kotek (1855–1885), a violinist and a student of Tchaikovsky's at the Moscow Conservatory; he was one of Tchaikovsky's love interests for a time, and they remained friends until Kotek's death from tuberculosis.

67. Herman Laroche (1845–1904), a leading music critic, professor of music theory and history at the Moscow and St. Petersburg conservatories, and a close friend of Tchaikovsky's. By this time, Laroche had begun to abuse alcohol.

68. Nikolay Fyodorovich Litke (1839–1887), the director of the Baltic Railroad System and the husband of Amaliya Vasilievna Litke (neé Shobert, 1841–1912), the composer's cousin.

69. Konstantin Nikolaevich Delazari.

70. The date of the proposed departure (without his wife) to Kamenka.

71. CPSS, Vol. VI, p. 155. The location of the original is unknown. It is reproduced from M. I. Tchaikovsky's typed copy. GDMC, b¹ no. 105.

72. Sofiya Grigorievna Rubinstein (1841–1919), a voice teacher and the sister of A. G. and N. G. Rubinstein.

73. Sofiya Aleksandrovna Malozemova (1846–1908), a pianist and professor at the St. Petersburg Conservatory; she studied there at the same time as Tchaikovsky.

74. Mikhail Mikhailovich Ivanov (1849–1927), a music critic and composer, a music theory student of Tchaikovsky's at the Moscow Conservatory; he worked for the newspaper *Novoe Vremya*.

75. This paragraph and the following one were omitted by M. I. Tchaikovsky in his typed copy. There is no other source for this text. This letter is absent from the handwritten copies made with A. I. Tchaikovsky's participation.

76. This refers to a trip to the Karasovo estate in the Klin district of Moscow province, which belonged to the composer's mother-in-law, O. N. Milyukova.

77. CPSS, Vol. VI, 188. The manuscript in RNB, f. 834, ed. khr. 25, l. 10–110b. The copy GDMC, a¹¹⁻ᵇ no. 544.

78. This refers to the apartment on Bolshaya Nikitskaya street in Moscow (not far from the conservatory), which was rented and furnished for them by the composer's wife, Antonina Ivanovna Tchaikovskaya. After a brief stay in this apartment (September 1877), Tchaikov-

sky left his wife for good, which put the status of the apartment and its furnishings in question. A. I. Tchaikovskaya left for Kamenka that October, while A. I. Sofronov stayed to watch over the apartment. Most of the news Sofronov received regarding his master came from a Moscow friend of the composer, Nikolai Lvovich Bochechkarov.

79. This refers to the score of Tchaikovsky's Fourth Symphony.

80. As written in CPSS. In the original (as in the majority of the letters to A. I. Sofronov at the time) is the signature "P. Tch.," which was crossed out by an unidentified individual.

81. CPSS, Vol. VI, p. 206. The manuscript is in RNB, f. 834, ed. khr. 25, l. 6–7. The copy in GDMC, a$^{11\text{-b}}$ no. 545.

82. N. L. Bochechkarov.

83. This is clearly a slip of the pen by Tchaikovsky: it should be November.

84. CPSS, Vol. VI, p. 297. GDMC, a^3 no. 1122, 1123.

85. Aleksey Sofronov, Tchaikovsky's servant .

86. N. L. Bochechkarov.

87. The instrumentation of the first part of Symphony No. 4.

88. I. I. Kotek's letters from 4/16, 5/17, and 6/18 December describe his treatment for an old case of syphilis, which led to throat problems. In one of the letters, Kotek signed: "Your faithful Mos'ka" (GDMC, a^4 no. 1847–1849).

89. Pablo de Sarasate (1844–1908), a Spanish violinist and composer.

90. *A Sportsman's Sketches,* by I. S. Turgenev, and *World Geography Textbook,* by P. N. Belokha.

91. A restaurant in Venice.

92. The book in question has not been identified. The composer's personal library in GDMC does not contain such a book on Napoleon.

93. CPSS, Vol. VI, p. 300. GDMC, a^3 no. 1125.

94. In the original manuscript of the score of the first part of Symphony No. 4, there is an authorial note: "Venice, 23/11 Dec[ember] 1877." GTsMMK, f. 88, ed. khr. 58.

95. Lido is a strip of seashore between the lagoons and the sea near Venice. It is a resort vacation destination.

96. See CPSS, Vol. VI, pp. 299–300 (the telegram regarding the composer's departure for San Remo).

97. M. I. Tchaikovsky's telegram is unknown.

98. A. I. Konradi. M. I. Tchaikovsky, and Kolya Konradi were able to leave Russia for Italy to visit Tchaikovsky only after Kolya's mother, A. I. Konradi, successfully gave birth.

99. Tchaikovsky left Venice on 16/28 December 1877.

100. Tchaikovsky began the opera *Eugene Onegin* in May 1877 and completed it in January 1878.

101. A novel by William Thackeray.

102. I. I. Kotek's letters from 10/22 and 12/24 December 1877. In the first of these letters, he wrote about M. I. Tchaikovsky's visit: "I am terribly glad that Modya is on his way to see you; your recovery will surely continue, for it had stopped for a while. You see what it means to write a clever letter, with flattery and a touch of . . . baseness; it worked!" (GDMC, a⁴ no. 1851). This refers to the composer's unknown letter to G. K. Konradi, Kolya's father, regarding a furlough request for M. I. Tchaikovsky.

103. A. I. Tchaikovsky's letter from 4 December 1877, in which he wrote about the Davydov family's attitude toward Pyotr Tchaikovsky's marriage and breakup with his wife: "[. . .] It is difficult for me to relay a million of these small feelings that convinced me that you would do well here, that only here you will be able to recover and lift yourself from this ill suspicion that no matter what you do for the people who love you as they love you here, they will never stop loving you or think that you've done something bad or dishonest. It is hard to describe how the people here perceive the entire story of your marriage; each views it in his own way. Apparently, it was explained to Vera and Anna [the nieces] in one way, to Aleksandra Ivanovna in another, and to Eustace in yet another. But it is clear that not once did any of them think you had done something wrong. Sasha even presented the whole tale in such a way that no one even considers it anything out of the ordinary. I certainly do not wish to convince you to come here immediately, as I know you are presently wary and no matter what one says will still feel the awkwardness of your position. My goal is to convince you to come in the summer, however, not exactly here but to Verbovka" (GDMC, a⁴ no. 4739).

104. It was actually the end of January 1872 when Tchaikovsky traveled through San Remo previously, while he was returning to Russia from Nice, via Genoa, Venice, and Vienna.

105. Emperor Alexander II's wife, Maria Aleksandrovna (1824–1880).

106. Olga Nikolaevna, the second daughter of Emperor Nicholas I, was a pupil of P. A. Pletnev and V. A. Zhukovski. In 1846 she married the Crown Prince of Württemberg, the future King Karl I. She became well known for her charity work, particularly during the Franco-

Prussian War of 1870. Her palace in Stuttgart was converted into a workshop, which drew many female volunteers of all classes. The queen would greet trains carrying injured soldiers, and take care of their housing. She was dubbed "a virtuoso of charity."

107. Letter No. 3. GDMC, a^3 no. 2044. K. P. no. 19444. From an unidentified collection dated 1938. Apparently, it was kept in M. I. Tchaikovsky's personal collection at the time of the museum's foundation. The beginning of the letter is missing. The date of this letter is based on Tchaikovsky's account of symptoms that were familiar to him, described in a letter to N. F. von Meck dated 30 March/11 April 1878, Clarens (CPSS, Vol. VI, p. 208).

108. CPSS, Vol. VII, pp. 57–58. The manuscript in GDMC, a^3 no. 2183.

109. At his publisher P. I. Jurgenson's request, Tchaikovsky translated the text of five of M. I. Glinka's arias from Italian into Russian.

110. CPSS, Vol. VII, p. 32. GDMC, a^3 no. 1139.

111. Bordighera is a seaside town with beautiful villas and palm tree groves located near San Remo.

112. Apparently this is referring to A. I. Tchaikovsky's letter from 25 December 1877 regarding, mainly, the composer's finances—his debts and their repayment. It also says, "Poor Petrusha, I regret to bankrupt you. This is just a brief note because I'm in a hurry. I kiss you, my precious, my darling, joy and happiness." (GDMC, a^4 no. 4744.) This same topic merited another letter, from 23 December 1877, where Anatoly reported on the expenditures of the sum he had received from his brother upon departure for Russia: "The rest of the money I spent on myself: on railroad fares, a hotel in Moscow, lunches and dinners, tips to servants in Kamenka and etc. I know, it's a lot of money, but what could be done. I didn't spent it on f[. . .], on theaters, neither in Kiev nor in Moscow. The cabbies in Moscow were costly—I hardly travelled anywhere on foot." (ibid., no. 4743)

113. Symphony No. 4 was dedicated to N. F. von Meck, who in her letter from 31 December 1877 expressed her wish to contribute to its publication. She wrote to Tchaikovsky: "I am thrilled that *our* Symphony is finished and I am enclosing, without delay, the money transfer for its publication. Pyotr Ilyich, perhaps you may decide to publish it abroad; but, in any case, you should do as you find most convenient. I would like very much to promote your works abroad; I would like to show the best that we have to the entire world." (CM Vol. 1, p. 150)

114. A photograph of N. F. von Meck's children was preserved in Tchaikovsky's personal photo archive in GDMC.

115. After graduating from the conservatory in 1876, I. I. Kotek began to serve as a musician in residence at the home of N. F. von Meck. Tchaikovsky and N. F. von Meck's correspondence began thanks to his mediation.

116. Tchaikovsky's letter from 4 January 1878, where the composer's brother confessed: "Isn't it strange—I could never imagine that writing letters could be a pleasure. Before, writing a love letter, or a letter to you—in short, any letter—had been a torture for me. Now, every time I write to you I feel happy, free from everything else. I've been in a terrible melancholy lately: nothing gives me joy, I do everything with anguish and disgust. But, please don't take it to heart; I'm often in such a mood, and when you read this letter, I will probably already be cheerful and in good spirits, as I should be. Presently, I'm simply in love with you, just like a girl. I stare at your portraits, reread your letters, sometimes cry a little bit, dream about us living together. Swear to God, I would have moved to Moscow right away, but for our father." (GDMC, a⁴ no. 4745)

117. Apparently this refers to one of the daughters (Iulia) of the Tchaikovsky brothers' cousin, Aleksandra Petrovna Kartsova (neé Tchaikovskaya; 1838–1899).

118. In the same letter from 4 January 1878, A. I. Tchaikovsky provides the details of negotiations with a singer, A. V. Panayeva, regarding her participation in the conservatory's staging of scenes from *Eugene Onegin*: "I've met with her and her sister, Dyagileva; as it turned out, she would agree to anything for a chance to sing a part in your opera (that means to enroll in the Moscow Conservatory). I began scheming to obtain an invitation for her. You never know, maybe something will come of this." (GDMC, a⁴ no. 4748)

119. Rusyns are an ethno-linguistic group descended from the indigenous population of the eastern Carpathian Mountains.

120. E. M. Tchaikovskaya (née Lipport), the third wife of the composer's father, I. P. Tchaikovsky.

121. CPSS, Vol. VII, pp. 113–118. GDMC, a³ no. 1153.

122. The family of the director of the St. Petersburg Conservatory, Karl Yul'evich Davydov.

123. In his letter from 5–6 February 1878, A. I. Tchaikovsky writes to P. I. Tchaikovsky: ". . . after the concert (where Panaeva was one of the performers), I saw Nikolai Derviz (a singer) who dragged me to

Palkin's restaurant where we found ourselves in the company of husband and wife Makovsky, Gorbunov and Svirsky. Makovsky is a painter and his wife is a very pretty and nice woman, though, in my eyes, her main merit is that she is Panaeva's friend. [. . .] Petrusha, my dear, should I open my heart to you? I'm head over heels in love as never before in my life. I have been in love before but it was not even close. Everything else became appalling to me; just yesterday I thought that it is only a whim, only an emerging feeling—but no, it seems that I will not get rid of this love any time soon." (GDMC, a⁴ no. 4750)

124. K. P. Palkin was a restaurant owner in St. Petersburg.

125. *Rêverie interrompue,* op. 40, no. 12.

126. Palazzo Pitti in Florence is famous for its gallery of paintings from the Medici collection; it includes works by Raphael, Titian, Tintoretto, Caravaggio, Rubens, Goya, as well as other renowned European masters.

127. This diary was not preserved.

128. Karl (Konstantin) Karlovich Albrecht (1836–1893) was a cellist, pedagogue, and inspector of the Moscow Conservatory, and one of the organizers of the Russian Choir Society. The letter has been published: CPSS, Vol. VII, pp. 118–119. The location of the original is unknown. This publication is based on a copy made by an unidentified individual for M. I. Tchaikovsky (GDMC, b¹ no. 133). A handwritten copy of the manuscript, made by M. I. Tchaikovsky and placed by him into a chronological selection of Tchaikovsky's letters for 1878, was also preserved, though the copy was made with omissions and cuts (GDMC, b¹ no. 106).

129. Wilhelm (Vasily Fyodorovich) Fitzenhagen (1848–1890) was a cellist and a professor at the Moscow Conservatory. Tchaikovsky dedicated his *Variations on a Rococo Theme* for the cello and orchestra, op. 33, to him. Fitzenhagen gave the first performance of the *Variations.*

130. F. E. C. Leuckart, a German music publishing company in Breslau and Leipzig. It belonged to Constantin Sander. Tchaikovsky gave the publication rights to his *Variations on a Rococo Theme,* as well as *Valse-Scherzo* for the violin and orchestra, op. 34, to this company.

131. P. I. Jurgenson.

132. The poster was not preserved.

133. CPSS, Vol. VII, pp. 128–129. GDMC, a³ no. 1153.

134. This is a reference to Tchaikovsky's own song И больно и сладко [I bol'no i sladko]/"Both Painfully and Sweetly" (Bittersweet), op. 6, no. 3.

135. Cascino is a forest between the Arno River and the railroad in Florence.

136. The embankment of the Arno River in Florence.

137. This is referring to the Florentine street singer, Vittorio.

138. The Pantheon church in Florence, where many great Florentines are buried.

139. A church on the southern outskirts of Florence, which contains preserved mosaics and sculptures of Luca della Robbia.

140. S. V. Shumsky was an actor at the Maly Theater in Moscow.

141. CPSS, Vol. VII, pp. 133–135. GDMC, a³ no. 1154.

142. This refers to Vittorio.

143. An Italian folk song (which shares its title with a female given name, the name of a plant, and the Commedia dell'Arte character Pimpinella). Tchaikovsky made an arrangement of this tune (using his own translation of the text). The song entered the cycle of six *Romances,* op. 38, and was dedicated to A. I. Tchaikovsky under the title "Pimpinella: Florentine Song" (no. 6).

144. Teatro della Pergola is a historic opera house in Florence.

145. Copies of these songs were not preserved in the Tchaikovsky archive. The composer, however, used their melodies, in part, in *Children's Album* ("Italian Song," "The Organ-Grinder Sings") and in *Rêverie interrompue* (op. 40, no. 12).

146. Photographs of Vittorio were preserved in the P. I. Tchaikovsky and M. I. Tchaikovsky archive in GDMC. The composer sent one of these photographs to A. I. Tchaikovsky, who on 7 March 1878 wrote: "Today, I have received Vittorio's portrait and was awfully glad. What an intelligent face! I can't call him pretty; he is rather enthralling. I'll never forget these two minutes of pleasure that he gave me. [. . .] It has always been arduous for me to return to places where I experienced the most powerful moments of my life. By and large, I don't like my past. [. . .] I console myself with a thought that your attitude toward the past is different—I know that you love to reminisce." (GDMC, a⁴ no. 4753)

147. A. I. Davydova; her letter is unknown.

148. The National Museum of Bargello in Florence houses the National Library, archive, and painting gallery.

149. The royalties for five performances of the opera *Vakula the Smith* at the Mariinsky Theater in St. Petersburg (from 10 October 1877 through 8 February 1878).

150. CPSS, Vol. VII, pp. 262–267. GDMC, a³ no. 1490. Brailov, Ukraine (in Kamenets-Podolsk province), was the location of Nadezhda

von Meck's estate, where Tchaikovsky stayed at her invitation in her absence.

151. Grankino was the summer residence Modest Tchaikovsky shared with the Konradi family at their estate.

152. Letter to A. I. Davydova, 18 May 1878 (CPSS, Vol. VII, pp. 259–260).

153. One of *Three Pieces* for violin and piano, op. 42.

154. This phrase is a quote from *Diary of a Madman* by Nikolay Gogol. It is uttered by the story's protagonist whenever he mentions the object of his affections. In correspondence with his brother Modest, Tchaikovsky more than once used this phrase as a kind of code while describing his own erotic experiences. Astapka was Evstafy Rodionovich Krivenko, a servant in the Davydovs' house in Kamenka.

155. M. I. Tchaikovsky's letter is unknown.

156. Staff captain Lev Pavlovich Kolreif was a relative of the Konradi family, and one of Tchaikovsky's creditors.

157. N. G. Rubinstein. Tchaikovsky lived in his various apartments beginning in January 1866. Only in September 1871 did he rent his own apartment.

158. Sugar factory in Brailov, owned by N. F. von Meck.

159. CPSS, Vol. VII, pp. 412–413. GDMC, a³ no. 1183.

160. In her letter from 20 September 1878, von Meck emphatically supported Tchaikovsky's intention of leaving his post at the Moscow Conservatory.

161. The director of the St. Petersburg Conservatory, K. Yu. Davydov, had offered Tchaikovsky the option of teaching theory classes at the institution. A. I. Tchaikovsky detailed the specifics for his brother in a letter from 26–27 September 1878 after having met with Davydov: "I don't know whether or not he told you that the suggested engagement is necessary at first, in his opinion, only as a formality. That you—again in his opinion, which, he has no doubts, is shared by all members of the Musical Society—should simply receive a pension from the Musical Society, sufficient for your well-being, without any teaching obligations at the Conservatory. And to force you to earn your living by teaching the harmony classes would be an unthinkable sin." (GDMC, a³ no. 4763)

162. Sergey Ivanovich Taneyev (1856–1915), Russian pianist, composer, and music theorist who studied composition with Tchaikovsky at the Moscow Conservatory. The two enjoyed a friendly professional and personal relationship.

163. Tchaikovsky is referring to a room in furnished apartments where Anatoly had moved in one floor below. In his next letter to Anatoly from 2 October 1878 he returns to this topic: "Go downstairs to the furnished apartments and check whether or not they have a comfortable room available. As a last resort, I shall stay with you." (CPSS, Vol. VII, p. 418)

164. Two of O. N. Milyukova's letters to Tchaikovsky were preserved. In the first letter, from 24 July 1878, she writes: "Upon meeting you, I became sincerely fond of you and now I feel hurt to learn of your quick departure and separation from your wife. I swear to God I still don't know what is Antonina's guilt towards you that you punish her so severely and apparently hate her so strongly. I wanted to be helpful but you don't wish to accept my involvement; you want to settle everything in the least expensive way. That is why I take a liberty—though you forbade me to write you—and make a suggestion, for I have spoken to Antonina and came to the conclusion that my plan is simpler, less expensive and faster. Antonina had fallen in love with you deeply and sincerely; she loved you more that anything in the world. Now her life is shattered and joyless; she is not going to marry someone else; and so, wouldn't it be better to separate peacefully without an expensive and scandalous divorce? You will return her passport, which she can then renew without bothering you. Instead of monthly alimony payments, give her a lump sum, thus sparing yourself and her constant confrontations. She will leave Moscow and move to Petersburg and she will give you her word to never bother you with anything and not even mention you. And you, Pyotr Ilyich, also, I hope, will take steps to assure that your friends and relatives won't spread any gossip about Antonina, which could hurt the reputation of a young woman. You can take my sincere and honest word that Antonina will faithfully comply with everything and once she has decided to take this step, neither her nor her relatives will bother you; trust me. You are a man of genius, you cherish your good name; please trust me; we will not stain it and we'll be faithful to our word as is to be expected from an honest noble family. I remain respectfully yours, Olga Milyukova" (GDMC, a4 no. 2997).

In the second letter, which concerns Tchaikovsky's invitation to the wedding of Antonina's younger stepsister, Maria Ivanovna Milyukova, the composer's mother-in-law reminds him: "You were kind to Masha and you wished her happiness. Your wish has been granted; she will be married for love to a Georgian Prince who adores her. God has rewarded Masha for her kindness, for her love and respect towards her mother. She respects and loves you and she wants you to take the role of father and, together with me, give her your blessing for the marriage. Could it be possible that you won't comply with her wish? Prove that you haven't stopped caring for us. Please come; you will give us inexpressible pleasure. With sincere devotion, Olga Milyukova" (September 1878; GDMC, a⁴ no. 2996).

165. Tchaikovsky's letter is unknown.

166. It is plausible that in some letters, written during the first days in his job at the conservatory, Tchaikovsky could have been overdramatizing his state of mind. This, in turn, brought feelings of anxiety to the composer's close friends and family. A. I. Tchaikovsky expressed this when he wrote on 29 September 1878: "I am terribly worried [. . .] there is still no letter from you. Could it be that you got sick, or went on the booze? Laroche says that you don't do anything and spend entire days walking all alone in the parks. And what is more, it's clear from your letters that you feel miserable. Could it be that the vile creature stirred up some trouble? [. . .] I'm so worried now; when everything settles down, when you leave your job at the Conservatory, then I'll be calm again." (GDMC, a⁴ no. 4769)

167. CPSS, Vol. VII, pp. 511–512. GDMC, a³ no. 1517.

168. This refers to sketches of the first three parts of the *First Suite*, op. 43, which Tchaikovsky forgot in St. Petersburg—without them he could not begin his orchestration of the score. He asked his brother Anatoly to send them to him in Florence.

169. Letter from A. I. Tchaikovsky on 26 November 1878. GDMC, a⁴ no. 4763.

170. This refers to the "Petersburg Jurgenson," Osip Ivanovich (1829–1910), owner of a music shop, brother of P. I. Jurgenson.

171. Tchaikovsky stayed in San Remo, Italy, with his brother Modest, Kolya Konradi, and A. I. Sofronov from December 1877 to January 1878.

172. The composer's servant was diagnosed with syphilis.

173. Tchaikovsky fully preserves the original spelling and punctuation.

174. This refers to Bordigera.

175. CPSS, Vol. VII, pp. 27–28. GDMC, a³ no. 1528.

176. In the opera *The Maid of Orleans*.

177. Marie Sauvion, a maid at the guesthouse in Clarens.

178. These letters and promissory notes were not preserved.

179. CPSS, Vol. VIII, pp. 34–35. GDMC, a³ no. 1210.

180. A. I. Tchaikovsky's letters from 4 and 5 January 1879. Among several details of his life in St. Petersburg, he noted, for example: "The New Year we celebrated at Kolya's [Nikolay Ilyich Tchaikovsky]; he gave a dance party [. . .] then, I went to Savina's [an actress]. Please don't suspect a renewed infatuation with her; oh no, I began visiting her because of her persistent invitations and also because she gets theater tickets for me. [. . .] Savina will never, not for a moment, arouse any desire in me anymore. I would probably screw her not without pleasure, yet she wants not just that but to see me whining at her side as before. [. . .] (4 January 1879; GDMC, a⁴ no. 4782.)

181. This refers to celebration of the New Year at N. I. Tchaikovsky's house (he was living in Petersburg at the time), which, in addition to A. I. Tchaikovsky, was attended by the Davydovs and their daughters, Tatyana and Vera.

182. O. S. Tchaikovskaya, wife of N. I. Tchaikovsky.

183. Georgy Pavlovich Kartsov (1861–1931), the son of A. P. Kartsova, nephew of Tchaikovsky, subsequently the husband of A. V. Panaeva, was a Guardsman. In his letter A. I. Tchaikovsky also mentioned his brother, Mikhail Pavlovich Kartsov (1859–1909), who also later served in the military.

184. Joseph Ernest Renan (1821–1892), French philosopher and religious historian.

185. Avgust Antonovich Gerke (1841–1902), lawyer, member of the directorate of the Russian Musical Society (RMS), and friend of Tchaikovsky.

186. Anna Petrovna Merkling (née Tchaikovskaya, 1830–1911), cousin of Tchaikovsky and his childhood friend; he dedicated to her a minuet for piano, op. 51, no. 3.

187. This refers to the opera *The Maid of Orleans*.

188. CPSS, Vol. VIII, pp. 55–56. The manuscript in GDMC, a³ no. 2230.

189. P. I. Jurgenson had a common-law wife, N. N. Pechkovskaya, who gave birth to a daughter, Elena, on 12 January 1879. He informed Tchaikovsky of this in the above-mentioned letter: "Your friend had *a* daughter born today. It brings both joy and sadness . . ." (Clu. I, p. 74).

190. P. I. Jurgenson resented the attacks on N. G. Rubinstein in the newspapers: "How is it possible that people pigwash a person so inso-

lently and so unanimously; and not just him but everything around him. And no one says a word in his defense! Lord! If I was able write well I would give a harsh reply without resorting to cursing. Alas, my abilities are limited by the weakness of my education and undisciplined mind." (CIu. I, p. 74)

191. Vladimir Vasilievich Stasov (1824–1906), a critic and art historian.

192. Aleksey Sergeevich Suvorin (1834–1912), a journalist, publisher, and owner of the Petersburg newspaper *Novoe Vremya*.

193. A letter from Tchaikovsky to V. V. Stasov, from 18/30 January 1879. CPSS, Vol. VII, pp. 48–51.

194. St. Croix is a city in Switzerland. P. I. Jurgenson suggested that Tchaikovsky visit this city ("the birthplace of all music boxes," in his expression) and establish professional connections with local mechanical musical automata masters. He offered to cover the cost of this trip.

195. CPSS, Vol. VII, pp. 112–114. GDMC, a³ no. 1220.

196. For more information on the incident in the letters to M. I. Tchaikovsky, see letters from 13/25 February 1879, 17 February/1 March 1879, and 26 February/10 March 1879. GDMC, a³ no. 1537, 1539, 1541.

197. N. F. von Meck, at the end of 1878, conveyed her plans to visit Paris from January to February 1879, and suggested that Tchaikovsky join her in February. He agreed, and during his stay in Paris (6–28 February 1879) she paid for his hotel room (which she had chosen for him), saying that she considered him her guest.

198. A. I. Tchaikovsky rented an apartment in St. Petersburg with his friend V. A. Zhedrinsky.

199. *The First Orchestral Suite*, op. 43.

200. Furnished rooms in St. Petersburg.

201. In a letter dated 5 February 1879, A. I. Davydova reported the details of her family's visit to St. Petersburg, including Vera's bout of measles.

202. Pyotr Emilievich Genke (1862–1908), lawyer, cousin of Tchaikovsky, son of Lidiya Petrovna Genke (née Tchaikovskaya; 1838–1901). This refers to P. E. Genke's letter from 7 February 1879.

203. Tchaikovsky's telegram is unknown.

204. Yury Lvovich Davydov (1876–1965), nephew of Tchaikovsky, later the main archivist at GDMC.

205. The journal *The Russian Herald* had begun publication of F. M. Dostoevsky's novel *The Brothers Karamazov* in its first issue, in

January 1879. The final installment was published in April 1880, in issue number 4.

206. A. I. Tchaikovsky did not share the general impressions of his brother. In his letter of 25 February 1879 he wrote: "I've read *The Brothers Karamazov*; the episode with Zosima and the peasant woman who lost her children is touching indeed, but the rest of the novel is awfully bad, in my opinion. Would it be possible to believe the probability of cursing in Zosima's presence? Although, we can talk about all that when we see each other again." (GDMC, a^3 no. 4795)

207. A restaurant in Paris.

208. CPSS, Vol. VII, p. 126. GDMC, a^3 no. 1221.

209. Jules Étienne Pasdeloup (1819–1887), French conductor, orchestra founder (1861) and leader of "Popular Concerts" in Paris.

210. The soloists who performed the *Symphonie Fantastique* by Hector Berlioz (1830) were the son and daughter of famous singer Pauline Viardot (née García; 1821–1910): violinist, conductor, and musicologist Paul Viardot (1857–1914) and singer Marianne Viardot (Duvernoy after marriage; 1854–1891).

211. Tchaikovsky was working on the opera *The Maid of Orleans*.

212. Tchaikovsky answered the question posed by N. F. von Meck in her letter of 19 February 1879 thusly: "My whole life I have been a martyr to my obligatory contacts with people. By nature I am an unsociable person. Every new acquaintance, every contact with a stranger has been always the source of acute moral suffering. It is hard to say what is the nature of this suffering. Perhaps it is my shyness developed into mania, perhaps it is my complete absence of need for human interaction, or perhaps it is a false fear to present myself not as I am, perhaps it is my inability to not say what I really think (and any first encounter could not be possible without this skill). In short, I don't know what it is. I can only say that while—because of my position—I was unable to avoid such interactions, I had regular contacts with people, pretended to enjoy myself, played out of necessity this or that role (which is absolutely impossible to avoid when living in society)—and suffered terribly all the time. [. . .] The company of another person is only enjoyable when there is a history of long-standing interaction and shared interests (especially among family members); then one can remain himself in this person's presence. Unless this is the case, the company of any people is a burden that I cannot endure due to the nature of my personality. That is the reason, my dear friend, why I have not called upon Turgenev or anyone else." (19–20 February/3–4 March 1879; CPSS, Vol. VIII, pp. 121–122)

213. Tchaikovsky gave consultations in composition to V. A. Pakhulsky, who was residing in Paris with N. F. von Meck in the capacity of her secretary.

214. CPSS, Vol. VIII, pp. 118–119. GDMC, a³ no. 1539.

215. The "young girl" is actually a young boy; Tchaikovsky customarily used female names to disguise the gender of his homosexual partners. This one is called "Louise" at the end of the letter.

216. Script of the opera *The Maid of Orleans.*

217. A comedy by Émile Augier and Julien Sandeau, *Le Gendre de Monsieur Poirier* [Monsieur Poirier's Son-in-Law]. Tchaikovsky saw it at the Comédie-Française on 12 February.

218. CPSS, Vol. VIII, p. 129. GDMC, a³ no. 1540.

219. M. I. Tchaikovsky worked on the story "The Drone."

220. *First Suite,* op. 43.

221. The symphonic fantasy *The Tempest,* op. 18, was performed at the Châtelet Theater under the direction of Édouard Colonne, 25 February/9 March 1879.

222. *Le Grand Casimir,* an operetta by Charles Lecocq (1879), was being performed at the Théâtre des Variétés, used for vaudeville and, later, operetta performances.

223. CPSS, Vol. VII, pp. 144–145. GDMC, a³ no. 1223.

224. Tchaikovsky's telegram is unknown.

225. N. I. Tchaikovsky.

226. The telegram was not preserved, but P. I. Jurgenson duplicated its content in a letter on 26 February/2 March 1879. In his answer Tchaikovsky confessed: "My desire to hear *Onegin* is prevailing over my predilection for hiding and thus I resolutely decided to be in Moscow on the 17th, but only incognito; that is no one but a very close conservatory circle would know about it. I hope that Karlusha (Albrekht) would be so kind and find a way to hide me so I could enjoy listening to my own creation while being invisible." (CPSS, Vol. VII, p. 140.) Tchaikovsky's plan did not work. The composer attended the dress rehearsal of the opera on 16 March 1879 and its premiere at the Maly theater, performed by students of the Moscow Conservatory on 17 March. He was repeatedly called to the stage, presented with a wreath, and after the end of the performance, a celebratory dinner was held in the "Hermitage" restaurant, where in addition to the "conservatory circle" and family members, there were many honorable guests, including A. G. Rubinstein.

227. A newspaper clipping that was sent with this letter was not preserved. At the Paris concert on 25 February/9 March 1879 led by

Édouard Juda Colonne, the symphonic fantasy *The Tempest* was performed, along with dances from the opera *Étienne Marcel* by Camille Saint-Saëns.

228. *The Maid of Orleans* and *Eugene Onegin*.

229. This all refers to the same "girl" that Pyotr described in his letters to M. I. Tchaikovsky during this period. Undoubtedly, his brother Anatoly also understood this disguised reference to a gay male perfectly.

230. *The Confessions* by Jean-Jacques Rousseau. In a letter to N. F. von Meck on 4/16 March 1879, Tchaikovsky wrote: "The allure of this book is based on the fact that the reader cannot decide what is more astonishing, the attractive or repulsive traits of Rousseau's personality. This man, while possessing excellent ethical qualities, sometimes performed acts which induce a hatred and loathing toward him. The most appalling of his deeds is that he placed five of his children, whom he conceived with a fine woman whom he loved, into an orphanage as *enfants trouvés* and was able to live on for dozens of years, apparently not in the least disturbed by his actions and making no attempts to learn their fate. Something in this act makes me feel so insulted and indignant that I spend hours thinking about it and trying to reconcile such a phenomenal heartlessness with undeniable proof of a kind and loving soul as revealed on other occasions during his life. [. . .] I would like to know how Rousseau's contemporaries saw him and by comparing his autobiography with reflections of other people, to find a key to understanding this extraordinary person, who very much intrigues me, since some of his weaknesses are strikingly similar to mine. Obviously this similarity lies not in our intellects, of which his is grand, though paradoxical, but something I don't and can't claim to possess." (CPSS, Vol. VII, pp. 147–148)

231. CPSS, Vol. VIII, p. 335. The original in GDMC, a^3 no. 2261.

232. Part of *Suite No. 1*, op. 43.

233. In the final draft, the "Andante" became the third part of the suite as the "Intermezzo." In the first edition of the score, the "Miniature March" was attached as an additional piece. In the following editions, it is listed as the fourth part of the *Suite*.

234. CPSS, Vol. IX, pp. 71–72. GDMC, a^3 no. 1581.

235. The Berlin Zoological Garden.

236. The Kaiser-Friedrich-Museum in Berlin (renamed the Bode Museum in 1956), home to collections of Byzantine art, Persian art, European paintings, and sculptures.

237. The Borghese Place in Rome.

238. Richard Wagner's opera *The Flying Dutchman* in the Berlin State Opera.

239. Benjamin Bilse (1816–1902), German conductor, founder of the popular orchestral concerts in Berlin.

240. CPSS, Vol. IX, p. 119. The manuscript in GDMC a³ no. 2295.

241. Yury Messer was a proofreader at the Jurgenson publishing house. He also taught at the Moscow Conservatory.

242. This refers to the transcription of the opera *The Maid of Orleans* for piano and vocals.

243. A. I. Tchaikovsky.

244. CPSS, Vol. IX, p. 131. The original in GDMC, a³ no. 2297.

245. Initially, Tchaikovsky intended *Italian Capriccio* to be called *Italian Fantasia*.

246. CPSS, Vol. IX, pp. 229–230. GDMC, a³ no. 1603.

247. Château de Fleur, a restaurant and garden in Kiev.

248. Evgeny Dmitrievich Kondratiev, brother of N. D. Kondratiev.

249. Sergey Ivanovich Donaurov (1838–1897), official at the Ministry of Foreign Affairs, composer and author of many popular romances; he translated some of Tchaikovsky's romances into French. He was a member of the homosexual community.

250. This refers to N. I. Tchaikovsky and his Ukolovo estate in Kursk province, where Anatoly stayed at the time.

251. Because of work, A. I. Tchaikovsky moved from St. Petersburg to Moscow to become deputy prosecutor of the District Court.

252. Ekaterina Ivanovna Sinelnikova, daughter of wealthy landowners, common-law wife of G. A. Laroche.

253. The name of a farmstead at the estate of N. F. von Meck, where Tchaikovsky lived in July 1880, in Brailov, Ukraine.

254. The nickname for the governess P. O. Kostetskaya.

255. CPSS, Vol. IX, p. 231. GDMC, a³ no. 1604.

256. Maria Fominichna Eastwood, an Englishwoman, governess of the Davydovs' younger children.

257. Flegont Konstantinovich Biesterfeld, teacher of the Davydovs' sons.

258. Tchaikovsky comically distorts the Latin medical names of these diseases: dysentery with bloody diarrhea, gastric fever, constant migraine, and also "some sort of" fever (the common cold).

259. This refers to the amateur performance at the Davydovs' home of the comedy *Tasty Morsel* by V. Aleksandrov (alias V. A. Krylov).

260. D. L. Davydov.

261. Vera Vasilievna Butakova (née Davydova; 1848–1923), sister of L. V. Davydov, wife of Vice-admiral I. I. Butakov. In the late 1860s she was in love with Tchaikovsky, but the composer did not return her feelings and rejected plans to get married. He dedicated to her *Memories from Haapsalu* (three pieces for piano, op. 2) and the romance *Go to Sleep,* op. 57, no. 4.

262. Aleksandra Ivanovna Davydova (née Potapova; 1802–1895), wife of the Decembrist V. L. Davydov, mother of L. V. Davydov.

263. Elizaveta Vasilievna Davydova (1823–1904), older sister of L. V. Davydov.

264. The Second Piano Concerto, op. 44, and *Italian Capriccio,* op. 45.

265. This refers to Evstafy Krivenko, a servant in Kamenka.

266. CPSS, Vol. IX, pp. 323–324. GDMC, a³ no. 1608.

267. The comedy by M. I. Tchaikovsky, *The Benefactor* (1874), which the author signed with the pseudonym Govorov.

268. Maria Gavrilovna Savina (1854–1916), dramatic actress in the St. Petersburg Aleksandrinsky Theater, wife of Ivan Aleksandrovich Vsevolozhsky (1835–1909), director of the Moscow and St. Petersburg Imperial Theaters (from 1881 to 1899). The comedy *The Benefactor* was performed in the Aleksandrinsky Theater as a benefit for M. G. Savina on 9 February 1881.

269. The opera *Eugene Onegin* was rehearsed to be performed in Moscow's Bolshoi Theater (it was premiered on 11 January 1881).

270. Vladimir Petrovich Begichev (1828–1891), dramatist, inspector of the repertoire at the Moscow Imperial Theaters, and from 1864 to 1881 the managing director of these theaters; a close acquaintance of Tchaikovsky.

271. Letter no. 4. GDMC, a³ no. 3314. K. P. no. 24459. Received 28 March 1966 as a gift from the Klin Museum of Ethnography.

272. A. I. Davydova.

273. N. A. Pleskaya, a friend of A. I. Davydova. Tchaikovsky dedicated his *Nata-Waltz* to her.

274. A village in the Klin district, the birthplace of Sofronov.

275. E. R. Krivenko, a footman in Kamenka.

276. L. V. Davydov's lackey.

277. L. V. Davydov, the husband of Tchaikovsky's sister Aleksandra.

278. CPSS, Vol. X, pp. 177–178. GDMC, a³ no. 1641.

279. L. V. Davydov.

280. Tatyana Lvovicha Davydova ("Tanya"), daughter of Tchaikovsky's sister Aleksandra, suffered from headaches, became accustomed

to morphine as a painkiller (it was frequently used in the family), and gradually became an addict.

281. This refers to A. I. Davydova's stay in Karlsbad for treatment.

282. CPSS, Vol. XI, p. 95. GDMC, a³ no. 1659.

283. The composer attended the wedding of A. I. Tchaikovsky and P. V. Konshina, which took place on 4 April 1882 in Moscow.

284. Praskoviya Vladimirovna Konshina (1860–1956), the bride of A. I. Tchaikovsky and niece of the Tretyakov brothers.

285. Her father was Vladimir Dmitrievich Konshin (1824–1915), a well-known Moscow manufacturer and philanthropist; he was married to the sister of the Tretyakov brothers. Her brother was Vladimir Vladimirovich Konshin, a merchant.

286. This refers to the winter spent in Italy, paid for by the composer.

287. CPSS, Vol. XI, pp. 95–96. GDMC, a³ no. 1660.

288. CPSS, Vol. XI, p. 218. The manuscript in GDMC, a³ no. 2391.

289. In his letter from 11 September 1882, Jurgenson complained to his friend: "You cannot imagine how difficult it is for me to wrestle with the usual predicaments, without energetic assistants or even one energetic assistant. I keep on my staff almost seventy people and I don't have a single fellow-fighter, a single efficient—a truly efficient—person among them. I have only somewhat gifted associates, while I pay them very handsomely. [. . .] And what is more, the worst damage is done by ineffectual work and time lost in vain. If the publishing of a music piece takes seven months (and most likely the eighth month will pass as well), then how many lifespans are needed to publish dozens, hundreds of pieces? Willy-nilly we have to publish shit to fill the gap. [. . .] Meanwhile, sales are not bad, most of all the sale of trash, which grows like mushrooms. While your Trio is being proofread, I bought about 300 music pieces together with engraving plates from various publishers for 1000 rubles. There is no music in all 300 pieces; it's mainly shit, but in a good household even shit can be used for profit. One has to be a carthorse to haul all this music singlehandedly—it even scares me sometimes. I am biting off more than I can chew. I almost wish the police would forbid me to continue publishing . . . It's like a disease and a bad one." (CIu. I, pp. 257–258)

290. Six Pieces for the Piano, op. 51.

291. On 20 September 1882, Jurgenson replied to Tchaikovsky: "My dearest, I lost my innocence a long time ago and it is too late to mourn it now. Using the word 'shit,' I refer to many things that have market value, bring money, and move business forward. Let's say that shit is 'precious

material for a household,' however it's still shit. If I didn't publish all that garbage, my business wouldn't be so large. Where could I get six million pages of musical gems?" (CIu. I, pp. 260–261).

292. Proofreading of the trio *In Memory of a Great Artist* (In memory of N. G. Rubinstein), op. 50.

293. The opera *Mazeppa*.

294. CPSS, Vol. XI, pp. 291–292. GDMC, a³ no. 1686.

295. Orchestration of the first act of the opera *Mazeppa*.

296. A concert of sacred music took place on 13 December 1882.

297. *The Overture on a Russian Theme* by S. I. Taneyev was performed in the RMS concert on 11 December 1882.

298. Their niece Tatyana ("Tanya") Davydova had become pregnant out of wedlock, and she left Kamenka to hide the fact from her family.

299. Aleksey Vasilievich Golitsyn was a prince (1832–1901), diplomat, the state counselor, and a close acquaintance of Tchaikovsky's. He was a member of the homosexual community.

300. The name of a Moscow inn, a favorite meeting spot for Moscow homosexuals.

301. CPSS, Vol. XII, pp. 133–134. GDMC, a³ no. 1698.

302. Apparently, Tchaikovsky is talking about their pregnant niece Tatyana Davydova. Pyotr and Modest were the only members of the family who knew about her pregnancy out of wedlock, and they brought her to Paris.

303. It was apparently the Roman Catholic Easter.

304. E. M. Molas, former governess of Kolya Konradi, summoned from Russia by M. I. Tchaikovsky to assist T. L. Davydova. She subsequently remained with her.

305. E. M. Molas, T. L. Davydova, and her maid Sasha.

306. Tchaikovsky had already written to M. I. Tchaikovsky on 18/30 April about these episodes: "Then, I went to the Champs Elysées and wandered around Café Chantant. This was rather amusing for it's a place of a certain kind. There are Okoneshnikovs, Rivol[i]s, Vasilys Ignatieviches, and Rabuses at every step. It is remarkable how this type of people is the same everywhere despite being of different nationalities. Though, to tell the truth, all this does little to distract me; in general, the evenings become the worst time of day—I don't know how to kill time, all the more so since the theaters don't attract me, and even make me feel disgusted." (CPSS, Vol. XII, pp. 129. GDMC, a³ no. 1696.) The people mentioned in the letter were all homosexual acquaintances of

Tchaikovsky's, and he used their names here in a humorous and generic sense. Leonid Karlovich Rabus was a singer, a graduate of the Moscow Conservatory, studying there from 1870 to 1874.

307. Tchaikovsky worked on a transcription for the vocals and piano of the second act of the opera *Mazeppa*.

308. A few days later, on 26 April, Tanya Davydova gave birth to a son, George-Leon (Georgy), who was later adopted by Nikolay Ilyich Tchaikovsky, the older brother of Pyotr Ilyich.

309. Letter no. 7. GDMC, a³ no. 489. K. P. no. 42. Received in June 1923 from B. P. Jurgenson together with his suitcase and eleven additional letters from P. I. Tchaikovsky to Sofiya Ivanovna Jurgenson (1840–1911), the wife of Tchaikovsky's publisher and friend P. I. Jurgenson. The date of the letter is based on its content, which addresses the preparation of the score for the opera *Cherevichki,* and also by S. I. Jurgenson's letter to Tchaikovsky from 13/25 June 1885—in which she writes that she received his letter as well as Pchelnikov's receipt. The letter was written on stationery with a reprinted line of music from Olga's aria in the opera *Eugene Onegin* along with the following text: "Ya ne sposobna k grusti tomnoi . . ." [I am incapable of melancholy . . .].

310. Pavel Ivanovich Pchelnikov, the manager of the Office of Moscow Imperial Theaters.

311. Tchaikovsky's opera *Cherevichki* was being prepared for production at the Bolshoi Theater in Moscow.

312. Nikolai Leontievich Langer, a copyist at the Jurgenson Publishing House.

313. P. I. Jurgenson.

314. This is in reference to the Moscow Directorate of the Imperial Theaters.

315. By this time S. I. Taneyev had left for the Caucasus.

316. Boris Petrovich Jurgenson, son of P. I. and S. I. Jurgenson.

317. Letter no. 8. GDMC, a³ no. 3346. K. P. no. 26158. Received 14 January 1986 from G. F. Krasheninnikov. Zinaida Germanovna Laroche (married name Krasheninnikova, 1869–1959) was a teacher of foreign languages and a translator. She was the daughter of Tchaikovsky's friend the critic and professor G. A. Laroche. Tchaikovsky wrote the note on the envelope in which he sent his photograph to Z. G. Laroche.

318. Letter no. 12. Copy in GDMC, copied a¹¹⁶ no. 3360. K. P. no. 25757/1. Received in 1981 from RGALI. It was found in the administrative correspondence of RGALI in 1967 and was sent to GDMC,

together with the written opinion of the lawyer I. V. Slepak (1936). Along with this copy of Tchaikovsky's letter was a copy of the envelope with the handwritten address: "City of Tambov. Dlinnaia Street, Karl Eduardovich Veber c/o Voskresensky." The location of the original document remains unknown. In 1936 the letter was in the private collection of Karl Eduardovich Veber's son, who had emigrated from Russia and was then living in Shanghai (China). Tchaikovsky's letter was an answer to a letter from Veber (1834–1913, a pianist and pedagogue), from 26 December 1886 (GDMC, a⁴ no. 399), thanking Tchaikovsky for his support (apparently regarding a position at the Moscow Conservatory) and asking for his opinion about the libretto *The Last Day of Pompeii* by A. D. Gravert, whose nephew, a student of Tchaikovsky's and a famous folklorist, V. P. Prokunin, had passed it on to the composer. For publication purposes, the letter is dated 29 January, since it was on this day that the composer returned to Maidanovo and wrote a series of letters (see *Diaries*, p. 125).

319. Letter no. 13. GDMC, a³ no. 3327. K. P. no. 25139. Received on 28 July 1973 as a gift from V. V. Visotskaya. The beginning of the letter was not preserved. Anna Yakovlevna Aleksandrova-Levinson (1856–1930) was a pianist, pedagogue, and mother of the composer A. N. Aleksandrov. The letter is dated on the basis of its content: namely, the information about Tchaikovsky's staying in Borzhomi and the illness of N. D. Kondratiev.

320. P. V. Tchaikovskaya (née Konshina), wife of A. I. Tchaikovsky, the younger brother of the composer.

321. Nikolay Dmitrievich Kondratiev, friend of Tchaikovsky. The composer often stayed at Kondratiev's estate (Sumy, a province of Kharkov). Tchaikovsky's piece for piano *Evening Dreams*, op. 19, no. 1, is dedicated to him. Later Tchaikovsky made a special trip to Aachen to see the dying Kondratiev and spent many days at his bedside.

322. Letter no. 16. GDMC, a³ no. 3320, K. P. no. 24655. Received on 6 January 1968 from V. V. Kotek. A letter to Viacheslav Osipovich (Iosifovich) Kotek, the brother of Iosif Iosifovich—a student and friend of Tchaikovsky's. Part of the page is torn off, and only some phrases and words can be made out. The content of the letter has been reconstructed from a letter written by B. V. Koreivo in reply to Tchaikovsky's request. Koreivo's letter was written on a letterhead that reads: "The book and music stores of Boleslav Koreivo, commissioner of the IRMO in Kiev, Kreschatik no. 35; in Odessa, Deribasovskaya across from the City

Garden" (See GDMC, a⁴ no. 1783). P. I. Tchaikovsky financially supported his late friend's entire family: his parents, his brothers Vyacheslav and Justin, and his sisters Evgeniya (married name Zhukovskaya) and Yulia (married name Chistyakova), who thereby were able to receive an education.

323. Letter No. 17. A telegram draft, handwritten by Tchaikovsky. GDMC, a³ no. 2985. K. P. no. 22907//650. Received on 11 March 1950 from RIII in St. Petersburg. Sergey Mikhailovich Tretyakov (1834–1892) was a member of the directorate of the Moscow branch (MO) of the Imperial Russian Musical Society (IRMO). The date of this document is tentative. In early January 1890, A. G. Rubinstein and P. I. Tchaikovsky gave a series of fundraising concerts to build the Moscow Conservatory concert hall named after N. G. Rubinstein, the conservatory's founder (the hall is currently known as the Bolshoi Hall of the Moscow Conservatory). S. M. Tretyakov, a close friend of N. G. Rubinstein's, was at his side when the younger Rubinstein died in Paris.

324. CPSS, Vol. XV-B, p. 81. GDMC, a³ no. 1930.

325. Tchaikovsky was referring to the libretto of the opera *The Queen of Spades,* which he was working on at the time. M. I. Tchaikovsky compiled the libretto, which was sent in individual installments to Florence.

326. Herman's aria (from the Italian *brindisi,* or toast) "What Is Our Life?" in the last, seventh tableau of the opera.

327. M. I. Tchaikovsky explained, in his letter on 7 March 1890, that it should be read not as *rouget,* but *routé.* (*Routé* meant that the punter wanted to double his bet and play the same card he had just won on.) GDMC, a⁴ no. 5523.

328. The book of saints with the church calendar. In the same letter, Modest Ilyich reported that the poem was written by Konstantin Ryleev, but its contents were not suitable for the gamblers' song, apart from the first stanza. The opera also uses Alexander Pushkin's text from his epigraph to *The Queen of Spades.*

329. On 9 March 1890 M. I. Tchaikovsky sent his brother several couplets for the "Hail to You for This, O Catherine!" chorus based on the poem by G. R. Derzhavin. GDMC, a⁴ no. 5524.

330. In a letter of 23 February 1890 M. I. Tchaikovsky wrote to his brother: "I was pretty uncertain about the chorus words—perhaps you need to make changes. In my opinion, it's up to you whether to include women in the chorus. It would be more historically accurate not to have

them but I don't see a reason not to put some girls among the gamblers. It's acceptable to take such a liberty for the benefit of better musical sound." GDMC, a⁴ no. 5516.

331. In a letter of 6/18 March 1890 (CPSS, Vol. XV-B, pp. 93–94), Tchaikovsky thanked N. G. Konradi for sending him money.

332. N. F. Litrov, servant of M. I. Tchaikovsky, accompanied the composer to Florence in the spring of 1890.

333. Letter no. 21. GDMC, a³ no. 3331, K. P. no. 25927. Received on 16 February 1983 from Urmanova-Bakurkina together with original letters from Tchaikovsky to E. F. Napravnik. Among these letters, there is an envelope with the inscription: "To His Excellency Eduard Frantsevich Napravnik." On this same envelope, there is a note handwritten by Napravnik that reads: "Contains P. I. Tchaikovsky's note about soprano Markova. 25/X 1891." Enclosed were two short letters from I. A. Vsevolozhsky to E. F. Napravnik. One of them is a clarification of Tchaikovsky's note to I. A. Vsevolozhsky; the other is a letter written on letterhead from the directorate of the Imperial Theaters. (See GDMC, x² no. 30.) Ivan Aleksandrovich Vsevolozhsky (1835–1909), an eminent figure in Russian theater, was the director of the Imperial Theaters in Russia from 1881 to 1898.

334. Apparently, the singer Aleksandra Mikhailovna Markova received both letters of recommendation in April 1891 in Paris, where Tchaikovsky was at the time. Judging by Napravnik's note on the envelope, Markova passed along Tchaikovsky's recommendations only in October of that year. In April of the following year, in Moscow, Aleksandra Markova again addressed Tchaikovsky. Her letter has been preserved (GDMC, a⁴ no. 2380). In April 1892, Markova had a successful debut at the Bolshoi Theater in Moscow, and in September was accepted as a member of its troupe.

335. Letter no. 22. Generously lent for its first publication by M. A. Zilberquit from his personal collection. Pavel Leontievich Peterssen (1831–1895), a pianist, a teacher at the St. Petersburg Conservatory, and a member of the directorate of the St. Petersburg branch (SPbO) of the Imperial Russian Musical Society (IRMO), was also a general manager of the Becker Piano Company. In August 1891, Peterssen, on behalf of the directorate of the RMS, invited Tchaikovsky to conduct concerts in Petersburg. In their correspondence they discussed the details of the concert program, for which Tchaikovsky had planned to perform Beethoven's Fourth Symphony as well as some of his own compositions—including the recently completed symphonic ballad *The*

Voyevoda. The concert, however, was postponed a number of times and eventually took place on 7 March 1892. The concert, with Tchaikovsky conducting, featured the fantasy-overture *Romeo and Juliet* and the suite from the ballet *The Nutcracker* (for the first time). Tchaikovsky's letter is a response to P. L. Peterssen's letter from 24 September 1891 (GDMC, a⁴ no. 3336). Peterssen was suggesting possible dates for the concert (November, December 1891) and was passing along L. S. Auer's offer to conduct the music piece featuring the soloist in order to spare Tchaikovsky "unnecessary effort and rehearsals."

336. Letter no. 23. GDMC, a³ no. 3352, K. P. no. 26591. Received from V. V. Ellerber via P. E. Vaidman on 15 May 1990. On the back there is a note from M. I. Tchaikovsky: "I have received the two hundred rubles from Osip Ivanovich Jurgenson. M. Tchaikovsky 14 January 1892."

337. Letter no. 24. RGB, f. 417, from A. N. Chernogubov's collection, no. 85. Konstantin Stepanovich Shilovsky (1849–1893), a friend of P. I. Tchaikovsky's, was an artist, a poet, and a musician. From 1888 to 1893 he worked as an actor at the Maly Theater in Moscow. The document is dated on the basis of his letter to Tchaikovsky from 25 April 1892; the composer wrote him this note in response. Shilovsky's letter was published in *Tchaikovsky on the Moscow Stage* (Moscow-Leningrad, 1940), 310. The owner of the collection, A. N. Chernogubov, marked in pencil the authenticity of the letter: "To K. S. Shilovsky."

4. Musical Souvenirs

1. The "Anastasia Waltz" was composed in August 1854 in Oranienbaum. It was dedicated as a gift to Tchaikovsky's governess in Alapayevsk, Anastasia Petrovna Petrova, who prepared him for his entrance exam to the School of Jurisprudence. After the family's move to Petersburg in 1852, A. P. Petrova stayed in touch with the Tchaikovskys. Later she was invited to tutor the youngest sons, the twins Anatoly and Modest. The "Anastasia Waltz" is the earliest of the preserved compositions of Pyotr Tchaikovsky. The manuscript was kept by A. P. Petrova, who later gave it to her pupil N. V. Alfyerova; after the death of the latter, her mother, P. A. Alfyerova, made it available for publication in 1913. The present location of this manuscript is unknown. This composition was not included in the CPSS. Instead, it is known due to publication of the manuscript facsimile in the newspaper *Den'*, 21 October 1913, no. 285 in the article by N. Zaitsev, "P. I. Tchaikovsky's Youthful Composition."

The title page is inscribed by Tchaikovsky: "Anastasie-valse composée et dédiée a mademoiselle Anastasie Petroff par Pierre Tschaikowsky Elève de l'école Imperiale des Droits. Le 15 Aout, le jour de son depart d'Oranienbaum pour S. Pétersburg" ["The Anastasia Waltz" composed and dedicated to mademoiselle Anastasia Petrova from Pyotr Tchaikovsky, a student of the Imperial School of Jurisprudence, 15th of August, the day of his departure from Oranienbaum to St. Petersburg]. An oval piece of paper glued to the same page has an additional inscription: "Expromtum [sic] Anastasie-valse par Pierre Tschaikowsky" [An improvised composition. "The Anastasia Waltz" by Pyotr Tschaikowsky]. The last page reads: "Le fine couronne l'oeuvre (Proverbe francaise)" ['The ending crowns the work' (as per the French proverb)].

A native of Petersburg, A. P. Petrova grew up in a foster home. She received a well-rounded education at the Nikolaevsky Institute, from which she graduated with excellent grades in 1849. The Tchaikovsky house was her first workplace. Later, she served for twenty-five years at the Smolny Institute, where she met her pupil N. V. Alfyerova.

2. GDMC, op. no. 1, l. 61. K. P. 24465. The document was received from Ya. I. Rabinovich in 1966. Prior to that, it was kept in the collection of L. I. Rabinovich. This manuscript was preserved in an album, in which V. V. Davydova (married name Butakova) collected the first editions of Tchaikovsky's early works. These works included a cycle of piano pieces dedicated to her: "Souvenir de Hapsal," op. 2 (with an inscription from the author), as well as two manuscripts given to her by the composer as a gift. One of them is "Mazurka," published in this edition, and the other is a piano transcription of the Entr'acte and dances from the opera *The Voyevoda,* which was apparently specially prepared by Tchaikovsky for her. The sheet music for the "Mazurka" is inscribed by Tchaikovsky: "[for] V. V. Davydova. June 15, 1867, Hapsal." It is not established whether this date refers to the day the piano version of the "Mazurka" was composed, or the day when it was given to V. V. Davydova. It is known, however, that in June of 1867, Tchaikovsky was indeed vacationing in Hapsal, Estonia, with the Davydov family. This piano version of the "Mazurka" has been adapted by Tchaikovsky from his music for the stage production of A. N. Ostrovky's *The False Dmitry and Vasily Shuisky* at the Maly Theater. The same production featured the Polonaise from Mikhail Glinka's opera *A Life for the Tsar.* Later the "Mazurka" was reworked into the "Salon Mazurka," op. 9, no. 2, for the piano. The "Mazurka" was performed, for the first time, from the manuscript by Mikhail Pletnev in April 1986 at the Tchaikovsky House-

Museum in Klin. It was played especially for Vladimir Horowitz, who visited the Tchaikovsky House-Museum that day.

3. RGALI, f. 1949, an album belonging to Maria Alekseevna Golovina, with three entries written by Tchaikovsky between 1875 and 1876. The album also contains a poem by I. V. Samarin (1877); some music drafts by A. G. Rubinstein (date unknown); a drawing of E. F. Napravnik (the artist is unknown), and others. Golovina was an acquaintance of Tchaikovsky, and their contacts were marked by a humorous tone, particularly in their letters to each other. She died early from consumption.

4. The origin of this little song, known to every Russian, is unclear. Though, according to one urban legend, the ditty refers not to a bird called *chizhik* (known in English as a siskin) but to the students of the Imperial School of Jurisprudence, which Tchaikovsky attended. The future lawyers wore a uniform in colors resembling those of the *chizhik* and were regular customers at the neighboring taproom on the Fontanka River Embankment.

5. GDMC, a^3 no. 267. K. P. no. 20052. The document was received from V. A. Litke on 6 May 1939. This is a musical letter sent from Tchaikovsky to his cousin's son Aleksandr Nikolaevich Litke (1879–1918), written in response to Litke's letter of 13 July 1891 to the composer. In this letter, Litke jokingly wrote: "Here I am again in Petersburg and again honestly like an idiot sit in the evening at the Zoo Garden and listen to the same songs, carry on the same conversations [. . .] and drink the same nasty beer. I recall with pleasure, dear uncle Petya, the two days from last week we spent together. [. . .] The previous day, I was pleasantly surprised, when I received two letters at the office, one of them from Bobik [a family nickname for V. L. Davydov]. Bobik's letter was so nice and endearing that I immediately replied with a very long epistle. Please allow us to receive letters from Bob! Yes! We have earned his respect! I don't know!—others don't receive letters from him." (GDMC, a^4 no. 2145)

6. GDMC, a^1 no. 119. A musical letter written by Tchaikovsky for V. L. Davydov (circa 1893, date conjectured from the composer's correspondences). Thus, on 11 February 1893, when the composer was in full swing working on his Symphony No. 6 (dedicated to his nephew), Tchaikovsky wrote: "You could have at least spat on the stationery and sent that in an envelope! The complete and utter disregard! Well, let God be your judge. But I would have liked to receive at least a few words from you." (CPSS, Vol. XVII, pp. 42–43)

5. KEY DOCUMENTS

1. A copy in GDMC, a^{12} no. 249, K. P. no. 23644. Received on 12 November 1956 from the restoration workshops of TsA MVD SSSR in Leningrad. The original is in RGIA, f. 1405, op. 63, d. 3356, l. 10. The information on the certificate is taken from records kept at the parish register of the Cathedral of Annunciation of the Kama-Votkinsk factory (TsGA UR f. 409, op. 1, d. 148, l. 71 ob.–72) as requested by Tchaikovsky's parents in 1846—six years after his birth—for their personal records.

2. A copy in GDMC, a^{12} no. 187 K. P. no. 23532. Received in 1952 from GIALO. The original is in TsGIA SPb, f. 355, d. 3390, l. 1. The registration number, date, and Tchaikovsky's age, "10 years and 4 months on August 1st 1850," are recorded on the application.

3. A copy in GDMC, a^{12} no. 188 K. P. no. 23532. Received in 1952 from GIALO. The original (in I. P. Tchaikovsky's handwriting) is in TsGIA SPb, f. 355, d. 3390, l. 5.

4. GDMC, a^{12} no. 4/4. K. P. no. 19742. Received together with the IRMO file from the Leningrad Conservatory in 1938.

5. GDMC, a^{12} no. 4/2. K. P. no. 19742. Received together with the IRMO file from the Leningrad Conservatory in 1938. The application is in P. I. Tchaikovsky's handwriting, and in his words regarding his desire to study "particularly music theory," meaning that he wanted to study composition. This is because at the time, in the European and the Russian system of music education, there were no classes focused specifically on composition (they were introduced into the music curriculum at Russian conservatories much later).

6. A copy in GDMC, a^{12} no. 195, K.P. no. 23532. Received in 1952 from GIALO. The original is in TsGIA SPb, f. 361, d. 3, l. 28. The reproduced fragments are related specifically to Tchaikovsky.

7. A copy in GDMC, a^{12} no. 194, K. P. no. 23532. Received in 1952 from GIALO. The original is in TsGIA SPb, f. 361, d. 3, l. 32. Inscribed above the students' last names are abbreviations of their specializations. Above Tchaikovsky's name, it reads: "t[heory]." The conservatory's charter was imperially approved on 17 October 1861. The charter established certain rights for professional musicians, along with the title of Liberal Artist, to be bestowed on every graduate who completed the entire course of study at the conservatory. This title, in part, absolved its bearers of taxation and conscription, which was a significant victory for professional musicians in Russia. A. G. Rubinstein, founder of the first

Russian conservatory in St. Petersburg, championed the fight for these
privileges.

8. The GDMC, e[1] no. 49. K. P. no. 19742. Received together with the
IRMO file from the Leningrad Conservatory in 1938. P. I. Tchaikovsky
received his conservatory degree in 1870 (though he graduated in 1865).
The delay was a result of a directive "regarding degrees, certificates,
and medals issued by the conservatory" that was introduced in January
1866, a year after Tchaikovsky's graduation (from the *History of the
Leningrad Conservatory* [Leningrad, 1964], pp. 36–37). In this document, there is an article about academic medals: "Graduating students
of the conservatory who excel in their professional results and abilities
will be awarded with gold and silver medals." The decision was then
made to award silver medals to Tchaikovsky and Kross, members of the
conservatory's first graduating class (A. I. Puzyrevsky and L. A. Sak-
ketti, *On the Fifty-Year Anniversary of the St. Petersburg Conservatory*
[St. Petersburg, 1912], p. 25).

9. A copy in GDMC, a[12] no. 230. K. P. no. 23565. The original is
in RGALI, f. 658, op. 2, no. 27. This is the first agreement between P. I.
Tchaikovsky and the IRMO upon his arrival in Moscow after graduation from the Petersburg Conservatory. The text of the document contains edits, made in pencil, for the 1869 agreement. The 1872 and 1875
agreements were also preserved. None of the main points of the contract
changed during Tchaikovsky's time working at the Moscow Conservatory, although his salary did grow from his starting figure in 1866 of
seventy-five rubles in silver annually for every hour of class. In the 1875
contract, Tchaikovsky's position changed.

10. A copy in GDMC, a[12] no. 5. K. P. no. 20234. Received on
25 March 1940 from GIALO. The original is in TsGIA SPb, f. 408,
d. 234, l. 9.

11. A copy in GDMC, a[116] no. 1680a. K. P. no. 23641. Received on
12 November 1956 from the restoration workshops of TsA MVD SSSR
in Leningrad. The original is kept in TsGIA SPb, f. 408, op. 3, d. 383,
l. 1. The document is a typewritten form, where P. I. Tchaikovsky
wrote—by hand—his name, title, membership fee, and other personal
information. A. I. Tchaikovsky's address is also written in pencil.

12. A copy in GDMC, a[116] no. 1680b. K. P. no. 23641. Received on
12 November 1956 from the restoration workshops of TsA MVD SSSR
in Leningrad. The original is kept in TsGIA SPb, f. 408, op. 3, d. 383,
l. 2. The document is a typewritten form, where P. I. Tchaikovsky wrote,
by hand, his name, the date, the loan amount, and payment due date.

13. Crossed out by Tchaikovsky: "a monthly payment of."

14. A copy in GDMC, a[116] no. 1680v. K. P. no. 23641. Received on 12 November 1956 from the restoration workshops of TsA MVD SSSR. The original is kept in TsGIA SPb, f. 408, op. 3, d. 383, l. 4. The document is a typewritten form, where P. I. Tchaikovsky wrote by hand his name, the date, the loan amount, and payment due date.

15. Crossed out by Tchaikovsky: "a monthly payment of."

16. The GDMC, a[12] no. 15. The Order of Saint Vladimir was established on 22 September 1782. Prior to 1845, recipients of the Order of Saint Vladimir of any degree received hereditary nobility. After 1845, hereditary nobility was given only to those who were already cavaliers of the Order of Saint Anne, first degree, or other hierarchically preceding orders. Some of Tchaikovsky's ancestors were also recipients of this order. Tchaikovsky's father, I. P. Tchaikovsky, was awarded the Order of Saint Vladimir, third degree, in 1861.

17. A copy in GDMC, a[12] no. 212. K. P. no. 23560. The original is in TsGIA SPb f. 408, op. 1, d. 269, l. 5. The document about the MO of the IRMO form has the number 984 and the date of 10 February 1885.

18. A copy in GDMC, a[12] no. 19. K. P. no. 20074. Received in 1939. Black ink, pencil. The original is in RGIA, f. 468 (Office of H.I.M. [His Imperial Majesty]), d. 434. l. 1–10b. The document contains various notes made by officials.

19. A copy in GDMC, a[12] no. 213. K. P. no. 23560. The original is in TsGIA SPb, f. 408, op. 1, d. 269, l. 69–690b. The document on the MO of the IRMO form has the number 1246 and the date of 22 February 1888.

20. GDMC, a[12] no. 18. The document is two sheets sewn together: reports from the local police office regarding places of residence from 1890 to 1893 (Kiev, Warsaw, Moscow, St. Petersburg).

21. GDMC, e[1] no. 28/2. K. P. no. 27663/2. The document was kept in P. I. Tchaikovsky's personal collection. The tribute is signed by A. G. Rubinstein, A. A. Gerke, and others. It is dated based on a notice in the newspaper *Moskovskie Vedomosti* [Moscow News] from 6 December 1890.

22. GDMC, e[1] no. 24. K.P. no. 27633/5. The document was kept in P. I. Tchaikovsky's personal collection. More than fifty people signed the tribute, including Anatoly Lyadov, Leopold Auer, and others. It is dated based on a notice in the newspaper *Moskovskie Vedomosti* from 6 December 1890.

23. GDMC, e[1] no. 27/2. K. P. no. 27633/2. The document was kept in P. I. Tchaikovsky's personal collection. More than a hundred conserva-

tory students, including A. T. Grechaninov, signed the tribute. It is dated based on a notice in *Moskovskie Vedomosti* from 6 December 1890.

24. GDMC, a^{12} no. 31/2 K. P. no. 2047. 2 l. Typed. Received in March 1926 from the widow of A. I. Sofronov. GDMC Archive has also preserved two typed copies of the will. One of them, more likely than not, belonged to V. L. Davydov, and the other was received in May 1930 from S. D. Razumovsky. There is also a handwritten copy made by A. A. Gerke. The will written in 1891 and published in this edition was not the first of its kind. Four years earlier, on 30 August 1887, the composer wrote in his diary: "[. . .] I went for a walk in the field. The weather is gray and autumnal, though not entirely unpleasant. At home. I've written in my diary, to cover many missed days. Went for a walk. Played Schumann's *Genoveva*. After dinner, I played some more. *I wrote my will*." (*Diary*, p. 175)

25. GDMC, a^{12} no. 32. K. P. no. 19792. Purchased from M. Sofronova on 20 July 1938. 2 l. Black ink. P. I. Tchaikovsky's handwriting. This is a draft of the power of attorney (the main document was handwritten by a notary).

26. GDMC, a^{12} no. 40/79. 1 l. Pencil (the telegram was handwritten by the telegraphist). At the time of the museum's founding, this document was in M. I. Tchaikovsky's personal collection.

27. GDMC, a^{12} no. 40/80. 1 l. Pencil. At the time of the museum's founding, this document was in M. I. Tchaikovsky's personal collection.

28. GDMC, a^{12} no. 40/27. 1 l. Pencil. At the time of the museum's founding, this document was in M. I. Tchaikovsky's personal collection. Maria Nikolaevna Ermolova was a celebrated Russian actress. Her husband, Nikolay Petrovich Shubinsky, was a famous Moscow lawyer and attorney.

29. GDMC, a^{12} no. 34. K. P. no. 20131. From an unrecorded collection in 1939. 1 l. Typed. On the back of the document, it reads: "Urgent response [. . .] for immediate delivery to His Excellency Anatoly Ilyich Tchaikovsky, who is traveling to Petersburg this evening."

30. Yuly Ivanovich Blok (Jules Block, 1858–1934), a successful businessman and amateur pianist. His family business "Jules Blok" flourished in Russia under his leadership. He introduced Russian society to many novel and state-of-the art technological achievements, contributed to the implementation of American and British factory equipment, introduced bicycles into everyday Russian life, as well as typewriters and the famous Thomas Edison phonograph. Blok was a friend of P. I. Tchaikovsky's. He recorded the composer's voice on the phonograph and

assembled a collection of recordings of the most important artists and personalities in Russian culture of his time. It can be heard at https://www.youtube.com/watch?v=7DEEdFLjUiw.

31. GDMC, a^{12} no. 34. K. P. no. 20131. From an unrecorded collection in 1939. 9 l. Black ink. The petition is signed by almost two hundred students and professors of the Moscow Conservatory. Among them were S. I. Taneyev, I. V. Grzhimaly, P. A. Pabst, E. A. Lavrovskaya, A. B. Goldenweiser, K. N. Igumnov, the Gnesin sisters, A. A. Brandukov, A. F. Gedike, N. K. Medtner, and others.

32. GDMC, a^{12} no. 40/28. 1 l. Pencil. At the time of the museum's founding, this document was in M. I. Tchaikovsky's personal collection.

33. GDMC, a^{12} no. 36/31. K. P. no. 19741. 2 l. Typed. Received together with the IRMO file from the Leningrad Conservatory in 1938. The document was composed by a clerk in the commerce division of His Imperial Majesty's office at the Ministry of the Imperial Court, and was based on a letter from a North American envoy to the Ministry of Foreign Affairs (GDMC, a^{12} no. 36/32. K. P. no. 19741).

34. This is referring to a sculpture of P. I. Tchaikovsky created by V. A. Beklemishev (1861–1919) for the St. Petersburg Conservatory, which is where it was unveiled in 1898. Apparently there was some confusion about the two conservatories, largely because at the time, in 1895, the construction of the new Moscow Conservatory building was frequently discussed in the press. The statue of P. I. Tchaikovsky was not envisaged for the Moscow Conservatory, as is evidenced in Beklemishev's letter, in which he sent photographs of his sculpture—including one to be forwarded to the United States. In the new building, both in the Grand [*Bolshoi*] and Small [*Maly*] Halls of the Moscow Conservatory, bas-reliefs of the conservatory's founder N. G. Rubinstein were installed. The Tchaikovsky monument in front of the Moscow Conservatory building was unveiled in 1954 (the sculptors were V. I. Mukhina, N. G. Zelenskaya, and Z. G. Ivanova; the architects were A. A. Zavarzin and D. B. Savitsky). The decision to erect a monument to Tchaikovsky was made in 1940 to mark the hundred-year anniversary of the composer's birth.

Index